D0989587

THE UPPER
MOHAWK COUNTRY

THE
UPPER MOHAWK COUNTRY

An Illustrated History of Greater Utica

By David Maldwyn Ellis
Picture research by Douglas M. Preston
Partners in Progress
by Anne P. (Happy) Marsh and Gwynn V. Jones

Sponsored by The Oneida Historical Society

Windsor Publications, Inc., Woodland Hills, California

Preceding pages
The original course of the Mohawk River ran within yards of Bagg's
Square and Main Street as shown in this romantic engraving from 1878.
The old New York Central depot and Bagg's Hotel can be seen beneath
the rainbow. Courtesy, Oneida Historical Society.

Windsor Publications
History Books Division

Publisher: John M. Phillips
Editorial Director: Lissa Sanders
Administrative Coordinator: Katherine Cooper
Senior Picture Editor: Teri Davis Greenberg
Senior Corporate History Editor: Karen Story
Production Manager: James Burke
Art Director: Alexander D'Anca
Art Production Manager: Dee Cooper
Composition Manager: E. Beryl Myers

Staff for The Upper Mohawk Country
Editor: Phyllis Rifkin
Picture Editor: Jana Wernor
Editorial Assistants: Phyllis Gray, Mary Mohr, Susan Block , Susan Wells
Compositors: Barbara Neiman, Shannon Mellies
Proofreaders: Jeff Leckrone, Doris Malkin
Designer: John Fish
Layout: Melinda Wade
Production Artists: Shannon Strull, Beth Bowman, Ellen Hazeltine, Janet Bailey

Library of Congress Cataloging in Publication Data

Ellis, David Maldwyn.
   The upper Mohawk country.

   "Partners in progress, profiles of Greater Utica's
leading businesses, by Anne P. (Happy) Marsh and Gwynn V.
Jones": p. 160
   Bibliography: p. 216
   Includes index.
1   1. Utica Region (N.Y.)—History. I. Oneida Historical
Society at Utica. II. Title.
F129.U8E44   1982   974.7'63   82-50182
ISBN 0-89781-054-6

©1982 by Windsor Publications. All rights reserved.
Published 1982
Printed in the United States of America
First Edition

TABLE OF CONTENTS

PREFACE

Change—constant, sweeping, uprooting—has marked the history of the Upper Mohawk Country and its people. New modes of transportation, patterns of trade, and innovations in manufacturing have buffeted Uticans and their neighbors. Waves of newcomers have swirled through the Mohawk gateway, altering the population composition and depositing representatives of many races, creeds, and nationalities.

An endless procession of people—Iroquois braves, redcoated soldiers, frontier families, boatmen, immigrants, tourists—have passed through or settled down in this area. After the Revolution the wilderness became almost overnight an outpost of New England, reproducing framed houses, churches, village squares, and industries, and most important of all, Yankee values: individual enterprise, community feeling, democratic institutions, and schools on every level.

The tiny settlement surrounding Old Fort Schuyler (Utica after 1798) included English, Scots, Irish, Germans, Dutch, and Welsh, the latter group numerous enough to found two churches. In the 1840s thousands of Irish, Germans, and smaller numbers of English and Welsh swarmed into the canal city, where they and their children soon formed a majority of the population. Late in the century Italians, Poles, Lebanese, Jews from eastern Europe, and other groups came to work in the textile mills and on construction projects. After World War II hundreds of blacks, Puerto Ricans, and some Asians added more variety to living patterns and culture.

Indians, French, British, and Americans schemed and fought for control of this strategic ground, the only gap through the Appalachian mountain barrier. In 1777 Mohawk Valley militiamen halted St. Leger's invading army at Fort Stanwix and helped force the surrender of General Burgoyne at Saratoga, thus guaranteeing American independence. The Revolutionary War, by destroying Iroquois power, opened up millions of acres to tens of thousands of land-hungry New Englanders. A cluster of stores and taverns sprang up around Old Fort Schuyler, where pioneers could secure supplies before plunging into the surrounding wilderness.

Utica in short order became a major turnpike center, a canal port, a railroad city, and a factory town. As early as 1810 New Englanders had discovered that nearby streams—Sauquoit and Oriskany—would turn waterwheels. In Whitestown, New Hartford, and Oriskany gristmills, sawmills, and woodworking shops sprung up. More significant, Yankee newcomers founded textile mills, the nucleus of the largest textile manufacture west of New England for more than a century. Utica's shift toward manufacturing in the late 1840s spurred another boom and

In the decade following the close of the American Revolution, the site of Utica was the gateway to the "western district of New York" and thousands of settlers forded the Mohawk River near Old Fort Schuyler. Egbert N. Clark rendered this and dozens of other scenes of local history in oil, watercolor, and pencil around the time of Utica's centennial in 1932. Courtesy, Children's Museum, Utica.

carried its products, Utica sheets and Utica Bodyguard, to store shelves in every part of the nation.

The Finney revival, the most important religious quickening of the century, erupted in Oneida County. Evangelists and their converts formed societies and journals to combat Demon Run, undermine slavery, promote education, and improve the rights of women. Professor Mary Ryan has called Oneida County in the early 19th century the "cradle of the middle class," a distinction that other cities might also claim. Utica, however, was the nursery for several figures who won high places in state and national politics. Governor Horatio Seymour ran for President on the Democratic ticket in 1868, losing to Ulysses S. Grant who, ironically, relied heavily on Senator Roscoe Conkling, Seymour's brother-in-law.

Uticans entered the 20th century with confidence because the knit goods industry was attaining new heights of prosperity. Italian, Polish, and other immigrants sought jobs in the mills even though wages provided a meager living. Defense spending in both World War I and World War II brought prosperity but the weakness of the textile industry became increasingly evident. Political and business leaders after World War II showed resourcefulness in attracting new business such as the General Electric plant in New Hartford and Chicago Pneumatic Tool east of the city. The booming 1950s sustained another upsurge in population, employment, and business. Over 30,000 new jobs in machine tools, metalworking, and services more than offset the loss of 12,000 jobs in textiles. The two decades after 1960, however, saw an economic slowdown characteristic of many older cities of the Northeast.

Greater Utica, however, made dramatic gains as a cultural and educational community after 1945. The varied programs of the Munson-Williams-Proctor Institute, housed in a splendid new palace, stimulated a widespread interest in the arts. Educational institutions as well as a series of parks and open spaces ring the city. To the west on Burrstone Road lies Utica College; to the east, Mohawk Valley Community College, like Utica College, provides education for adults as much as for undergraduates. Ten miles to the south is Hamilton College, a coeducational institution. To the north bulldozers have begun to dig the foundations for the College of Technology in North Utica. All these institutions conserve the learning of the past but they also serve as powerhouses of change.

Utica has not escaped the "urban crisis": population loss, a declining tax base, aging residential sections, tensions between center city and the suburbs, and the shift of people and business to the outskirts. Slowly the city government and business leaders have revitalized downtown with new government and banking buildings, housing developments, and hotel accommodations.

Have the citizens of the Upper Mohawk region created the good society? The *Places Rated Almanac* in early 1982 ranked the Utica-Rome area as the 25th best out of 277 metropolitan areas in the nation. The area scored high in recreation and educational opportunities, very low in crime, and well above average in health. This survey of our history shows that tens of thousands of immigrants have secured a comfortable livelihood and have given their children a good start in life. More than a few from almost every nationality, race, or religious group have achieved wealth and an honored position. They have shown a remarkable ability to adapt to change.

I wish to acknowledge my indebtedness to historians of Utica, especially Moses Bagg, T. Wood Clarke, and the Honorable John J. Walsh. They collected an amazing amount of information about the city and have presented interesting accounts of its development. Oneida County has been fortunate in its historians, starting with Pomroy Jones' *Annals and Recollections of Oneida County,* perhaps the best early county history in the Empire State. The Bicentennial *History of Oneida County* provided a most valuable survey of many aspects of local history.

Douglas Preston has read the entire manuscript, protected me from several errors, and made intelligent suggestions. I owe a large debt to Dr. Virgil Crisafulli for reading with care the last two chapters and making many valuable suggestions. I wish to thank Dr. Alan Peabody for his assistance on the contemporary religious scene.

The Hamilton College Library as usual provided much backup assistance. I am grateful to Ralph Stenstrom, librarian, and Joan Wolek and Frank Lorenz for many courtesies. Douglas Finch, director of the Audio-Visual department, has kindly supplied pictures to this project. Helen Dirtadian, librarian of the Utica Public Library, has always given her assistance most graciously.

I wish to thank Phyllis Rifkin of Windsor Publications, Inc., for her diligence and intelligence in editing this manuscript.

Facing page
This map was printed in 1836, four years after Utica's incorporation as a city. In addition to the Erie Canal, it shows two new routes of travel completed in 1836, the Chenango Canal, and the Utica & Schenectady Railroad. According to the legend, churches outnumbered inns by 16 to 10. (OHS)

INTRODUCTION

This is your 150th anniversary, city of Utica. May you happily enjoy many more. Your name, drawn from a hat in 1798, was a beginning. But your charter in 1832 established the city that grew, and changed, and grew again, and is still changing. Little did the first mayor, Joseph Kirkland, know that he would face the crisis of a cholera epidemic, but he stayed at his post when others fled. Since then, you have been a place of passing through, of staying, of accomplishing. It is all here, in text and pictures.

The Oneida Historical Society at Utica is delighted to offer this commemorative volume, which we hope will appeal to citizens of the Upper Mohawk Country who wish a balanced survey of our history and good reading, grounded in scholarship. Anniversaries are useful devices, forcing us to look back on our origins and to examine our development. The Historical Society has already been at hand for two of them. In 1882 it celebrated with the members of the Half-Century Club, publishing the speeches and letters in the society's transactions. It played a leading role in the centennial in 1932.

When Windsor Publications, Inc., proposed to the society's trustees an illustrated history of Greater Utica, they readily agreed to sponsor this project. Windsor approached business firms and institutions, seeking their support and their own stories. The half a hundred supporters are a fine cross section of the business and institutional life of our community.

We were fortunate in securing the services of David Maldwyn Ellis and Douglas Preston, Director of the Oneida Historical Society. Ellis, P.V. Rogers Professor Emeritus of American History at Hamilton College, has published several books on New York State topics, the most recent being *New York: State and City* (1979). Preston has written a history of firefighters of Utica and has intimate knowledge of photographic sources within the holdings of our society and in private hands. We are grateful to many Uticans who have generously lent pictures and given advice to the authors of this enterprise.

The gateway to the West and the thoroughfare for the nation's travel and trade, the Upper Mohawk underwent constant adjustment. Each generation of newcomers sought to express its concept of what was fitting and beautiful, not only in wood and stone, but also in prose, song, cutlery, insurance policies and, yes, underwear. The authors have captured the texture of life as the tiny settlement around Old Fort Schuyler evolved into a commercial center, a factory city, and a diverse, modern community. This impressive collection of facts and pictures will enrich one's sense of the past and assist in measuring change.

Martha K. Shepard
President, 1978-1981
The Oneida Historical Society

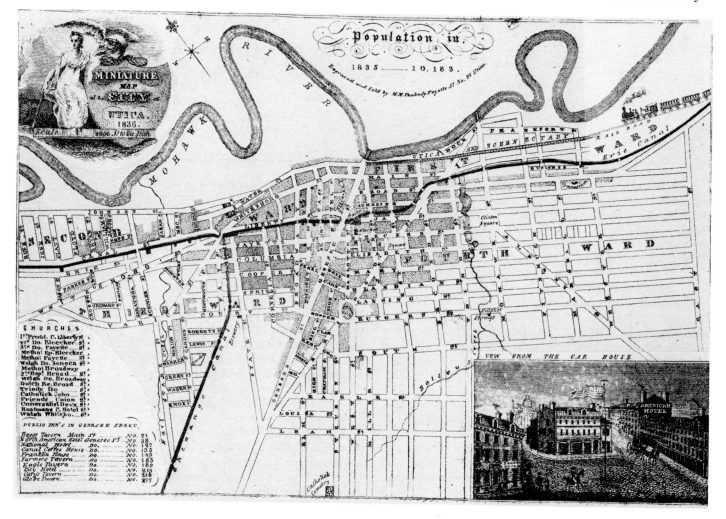

CHAPTER ONE

THE
PATHWAY
OF
EMPIRE

The site of Utica, called Unundadages or "around the hill" by the Iroquois Indians, lay in the buffer zone between the Mohawk villages located east of Little Falls and the Oneida villages dotting the region south of Oneida Lake. Braves from both tribes fished and hunted in this zone and all the Iroquoian tribes used the ford where a horseshoe bend brought the Mohawk River close to the place where North Genesee Street crosses the railroad tracks today.

War parties, but more often red and white traders, crossed the Mohawk here before following trails to the north, south, and west. Dutch traders from Albany rowed or poled their boats past the ford to the Carrying Place (Rome) where they carried their goods to Wood Creek, a winding stream emptying in Oneida Lake. Some followed the Oswego River to its mouth on Lake Ontario where the British built a fort at Oswego in 1726. Others ascended the Seneca River to trade with the Onondagas, Cayugas, and Senecas.

The Iroquois Confederacy of the Five Nations dominated not only central and western New York for centuries after these Native Americans arrived around the year 1300 but also exerted its power over much of

northeastern North America. The 2,000 or more warriors belonging to the Mohawk, Oneida, Onondaga, Cayuga, and Seneca tribes held the balance of power between France and Britain for more than a century after the English took New Netherland in 1664.

Officials in London, Paris, New York, and other centers recognized the strategic importance of the Upper Mohawk Valley. Not only did the Mohawk permit the passage of expeditions with cannon but the tiny Palatine German settlements along its course also provided foodstuffs, horses, and even manpower for such expeditions. Whoever controlled the Carrying Place could dominate a vital trade route, threaten both the Iroquois Confederacy and the frontier settlements, and challenge enemies for military control of the Mohawk-Hudson waterway.

Among those casting greedy eyes at the Mohawk Valley land were officials and the landed grandees in the Hudson Valley, believing that in time the area would become valuable. Colonial governors used the power of their office to recoup family fortunes and to reward favored cronies. Except for an occasional defense contract, land grants provided the easiest way of accomplishing these ends. In

mary, Squah of the oneida tribe. utica 7 br 1807.

Above
Mary, Squah of the Oneida Tribe *was painted by the Baroness Hyde de Neuville, a visitor from France, during her stay in Utica in 1807. Courtesy, The New-York Historical Society, New York City.*

1705 five friends of the grafting and frivolous Governor Edward Cornbury secured the Oriskany Patent, a tract of 32,000 acres near the Carrying Place and extending two miles from the Mohawk on each side. The owners made no attempt to settle this exposed area through which war parties, French raiders, and British soldiers passed.

Governor William Cosby, whose quarrelsome nature was exceeded only by his greed, arrived in New York in 1732 and arranged for a grant of 32,000 acres, three miles on each side of the Mohawk and extending eastward 11 miles from the Sauquoit Creek. Today it covers roughly the area from Yorkville to Frankfort and from the Parkway in Utica to Smith Hill on the north above Cosby Manor Road. The scheming Cosby used dummy entrymen in order to get around the rule forbidding a governor awarding land to himself. The grant passed to his friends and relatives who six days later deeded him their shares. The terms required the owner to pay two shillings and six pence for each 100 acres as an annual quitrent to the crown. Like most landowners Cosby and his heirs ignored this clause.

The struggle between France and Great Britain for the valuable Mohawk Valley lasted for over a century and reached its climax in the French and Indian War, 1754-1763. At first the French won many victories, partly because of British bungling and partly because of Iroquois neutrality. The Indians accused the English of stealing their lands and refusing to guarantee them protection from French raiders. It took all the cunning and charm of Sir William Johnson to swing the Iroquois Confederacy to the British side.

By 1758 the spirited leadership of William Pitt, the new prime minister of England, began to produce results even as far away as the New York frontier. He sent James Abercrombie to the region, who authorized the construction

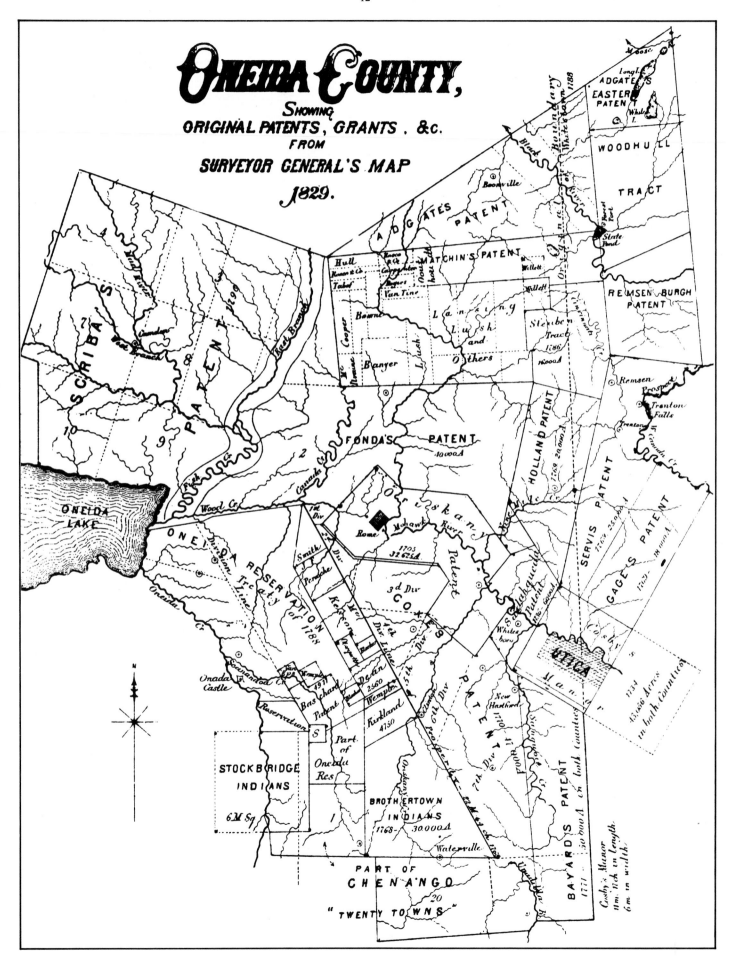

of a string of forts and blockhouses west of Albany. Following Abercrombie's orders, General John Stanwix built at the Carrying Place one of the strongest fortifications in North America. To protect the river crossing at Unundadages, Colonel Peter Schuyler of New Jersey erected Fort Schuyler with its main blockhouse near present-day Main Street. Mud walls bolstered with upright logs some 15 feet high stretched down to the river. The soldiers cleared away trees outside the fort in order to prevent Indians from shooting down on the defenders. There is no record of an Indian attack.

In 1758 Lieutenant Colonel John Bradstreet led 3,000 militiamen up the Mohawk, down the Oswego, and across Lake Ontario where he captured Fort Frontenac (Kingston). The next year General John Prideaux and Sir William Johnson led a larger force which managed to take Fort Niagara. In 1760 Fort Schuyler witnessed the largest military procession in its history. Major General Jeffrey Amherst commanded 4,000 British regulars, about 6,000 provincial soldiers, and 600 Indians. Tough rivermen poled hundreds of bateaux laden with supplies while regiments of redcoats and bands of militia straggled over the tortuous trails. Amherst's forces swept north to Oswego and then on to the heart of Montreal. The fall of New France made the Mohawk Valley forts useless in the eyes of the British. Soon underbrush covered the deserted forts and their log walls rotted.

After the French and Indian War, speculators renewed their interest in backcountry land and a few settlers began to move west to the upper reaches of the Mohawk. John George Weaver, Christian Reall (or Reel), Marcus Demoth, and George G. Weaver were making small clearings in the Deerfield area as early as 1773.

The sheriff of Albany County seized Cosby Manor in 1772 because of nonpayment of quitrents, a form of taxation continuing the old feudal dues on land. The buyers included Philip Schuyler, wealthy Albany landowner who later became commander of American forces opposing Burgoyne; Rutger Bleecker, another Albany landowner; John Bradstreet, retired general; and John Morin Scott, a Manhattan lawyer who led the "liberty boys" against the Stamp Tax and later served in the Continental Congress.

The Sadequahada Patent, a tract of about 6,000 acres lying between Oriskany Patent and Cosby Manor, passed into the hands of Frederick Morris and friends in 1736. When the Revolution broke out, it was owned by Hugh Wallace, a leading Tory. The new state government confiscated this tract and sold it to a group of "patriot" speculators led by Hugh White.

When Chief Pontiac and his allies attacked the western forts in 1763, the British government placed a temporary ban on white settlement west of the Appalachians. This prohibition had no practical effect in New York. Sir

William Johnson, superintendent of Indian Affairs, called a meeting of what had by then become the Six Nations, their allies, and dependent tribes at Fort Stanwix in 1768. The task of feeding more than 3,000 Indians for over six weeks took all of Sir William's skill and resources, not to mention 20 boatloads of presents. The treaty of Fort Stanwix drew a line of property from Wood Creek (Fort Stanwix) southward to the headwaters of the west branch of the Unadilla River and thence to the Susquehanna. The Oneidas charged that this treaty cheated them of some of their land.

Once the treaty was signed, speculators rushed in to gobble up vacant land to the east of the line. Hiding behind the name of Peter Servis, Sir William acquired a tract lying to the west of West Canada Creek. Lord Holland of England secured a tract surrounding the present village of Holland Patent. Thomas Gage, British commander, took most of the area later included in the town of Deerfield.

Facing page
Cosby Manor extended east from the mouth of the Sauquoit Creek well into modern Herkimer County. Most local property owners can trace their deeds back to these 18th-century land grants. (OHS)

Above
William Cosby (1685-1736) was a pleasant-looking but corrupt and unpopular royal governor. For exposing some of Cosby's wrongdoings, journalist Peter Zenger was brought to trial in what came to be a celebrated early American test of freedom of the press. Courtesy, The New-York Historical Society.

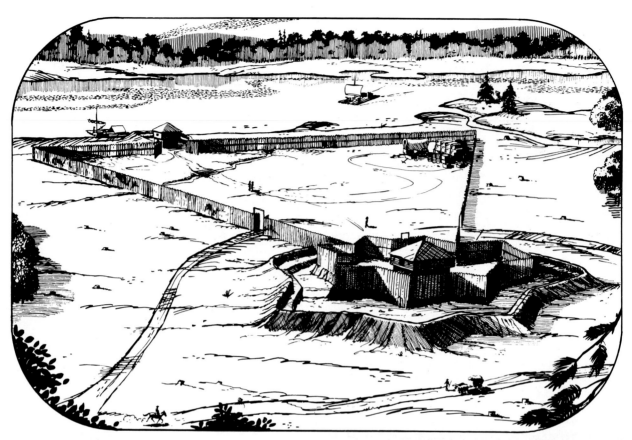

To the FREEHOLDERS and IN-HABITANTS of the COUNTY of TRYON.

TRYON-COUNTY, May 22 1775.

FRIENDS and FELLOW-COUNTRYMEN,

IT is now obvious to every Man of the least Judgment, that the British Ministry are fully resolved, to inforce the late cruel oppressive and unconstitutional Acts of Parliament---to deprive us of our constitutional Rights and Liberties --to lay Taxes on our Estates without our Consent by our legal Representatives---and to trample upon the sacred Rights of Englishmen and the Constitution. At such a Time then, it is our duty, our bounden duty, to stand forth in the Common Cause of Freedom, and even at the Hazard of our Lives, preserve our devoted Country from Misery and Ruin. Rouse therefore my dear Countrymen, sleep no longer in a State of Supineness and Inattention---Behold Rapine and Murder, Blood and Slaughter, have already entered into the Bowels of a neighbouring Province ---Men and Women inhumanly slaughtered---Behold our brave and virtuous Countrymen the Bostonians, actually struggling bleeding and even sacrificing their Lives in defence of American Liberty. Let us then no longer remain quiet Spectators of our Country's Ruin, but shew ourselves equal to them in Resolution and Courage---Let us meet, consult, elect Officers, form ourselves into Companies, appear in the broad Face of Day, protecting each other in military Exercises. This is recommended by a Committee of New-York, and was advertised in the Public News Papers. All the Colonies are in Arms in Defence of their Liberties. Let us then follow the same glorious Example. We have now no Mercy to expect from England, she has long since determined upon the final Ruin of America, she has publickly declared us Traitors and Rebels, and will offer no Terms of Mercy till we, like Slaves, humbly prostrate at her Feet. We must now therefore meanly submit to the most abject State of Slavery, or nobly fight ourselves into Freedom. Necessity urges us to Battle, we cannot escape it. Come on then my dear Countrymen, prepare yourselves with Diligence, since, the Hour of danger is so near at Hand, let us oppose our Enemies in their diabolical Designs and proceedings, and ward of, if possible, a lasting Night of Misery and Ruin. No Time is now to be lost---Every Hour's delay is big with danger. Wait but a few days longer, and you will find your Lands ravaged, your Houses plundered and in Flames, your Wives and Children inhumanly butchered; and the whole Country laid waste by Fire and Sword. Open your Eyes therefore, my dear Countrymen. Be no longer amused by those who hold Offices under the Crown, whose Interest it is to deceive you---who will attempt to lead you astray and at Length plunge you headlong, into slavery---Let me conjure you then, in the name of Heaven, to summon up all your Courage, to consult, to act, to resolve to bleed, and even die, in your Country's Cause. By your Firmness and Resolution in this important CRISIS, you will save your Country from total Ruin, and preserve to yourselves and Posterity all the glorious Blessings of Freedom.

A TRYON-COUNTY FREEHOLDER.

Facing page

Top
Old Fort Schuyler stood at the former juncture of Ballou Creek and the Mohawk River (near Main Street and Third Avenue today). This sketch is based upon a British military plan.   From Utica: A City Worth Saving.

Bottom left
Colonel Peter Schuyler (1710-1762), native of New Jersey, was commander of the British forces at Oswego during the French and Indian War and namesake of Old Fort Schuyler on the site of Utica. (OHS)

Bottom right
Sir William Johnson (1715-1774), trader, diplomat, and Indian agent for the Crown, is shown as he appeared during the French and Indian War. (OHS)

Above
Published only a month after the battles at Lexington and Concord, this notice urged Mohawk Valley residents to organize armed resistance against England and "to resolve to bleed, and even die" for the cause of freedom. (OHS)

The clash between the redcoats and militiamen at Lexington in 1775 caused tempers to rise among New Yorkers, who had already engaged in many demonstrations over the controversial Stamp and Tea acts. When the British government closed the port of Boston, a group of colonists met in the first Continental Congress in Philadelphia and authorized a boycott of British imports. In May 1775 a group of citizens organized a Committee of Correspondence in Fonda, just west of Johnson Hall. Although Sir William Johnson died in 1774, his son and nephew upheld the cause of King George III. The Mohawk Valley teetered toward civil war.

Debate, argument, and protest turned into military plans and skirmishes between "patriots" and Tories. When the patriot expedition led by Benedict Arnold and Richard Montgomery of New York failed to capture Quebec in the winter of 1775-1776, Philip Schuyler ordered the reconstruction of Fort Stanwix to hold off the expected counterattack.

Both sides realized the Mohawk Valley was more than a military highway. The lowlands produced wheat and its pastures fed horses and livestock, all useful for soldiers and civilians. The Tories enlisted most of the aristocratic families, notably the heirs of Sir William. Some Johnson tenants, Scottish Highlanders, remained loyal, as did the Mohawks. An Anglican clergyman served the two Mohawk villages, containing about 400 men, women, and children. Joseph Brant, whose sister Molly presided at Johnson Hall, was secretary to Sir Guy Johnson, who followed his uncle as superintendent of Indian Affairs. A man of exceptional talent and education, Brant believed that the Mohawks had a better chance of survival under the king than under the rule of land-hungry colonists.

A majority of inhabitants of the Mohawk Valley,

Above
Joseph Brant (Thayendanegea) lived from 1742-1807. Chief of the Mohawks, ally to the British, brother-in-law of Sir William Johnson, and a terror to frontier patriots, Brant fought at Oriskany to protect his homeland from the rush of settlement he knew would follow if England lost control of America. (OHS)

largely those of Dutch and German stock, leaned toward the patriot cause. Most of the Germans lived in two pockets: Palatine Bridge and German Flatts (later Herkimer). The Herchheimers (or Herkimers) were the leading family; their stockaded stone mansion stood a short distance to the east of the village of Herkimer.

Both patriots and British agents tried to win over the Iroquois. General Schuyler called a conference at German Flatts in July 1776 where 1,200 Indians drank "incredible" amounts of rum and agreed to stay neutral. Joseph Brant, however, kept urging the Mohawks to take up the hatchet. The Oneidas, who numbered about 1,500 people, gave him a

Top
Samuel Kirkland (1741-1808) was an interpreter, government agent, and the father of Hamilton College. Courtesy, Hamilton College Library.

Above
Colonel Peter Gansevoort (1749-1812), hero of Fort Stanwix. This circa 1794 painting by Gilbert Stuart is one of many treasures of local history found in the collections of the Munson-Williams-Proctor Institute.

chilly reception, following the advice given to their chiefs by Samuel Kirkland, a beloved missionary and ardent patriot.

General John Burgoyne drew up a plan in 1777 for his government to capture New York province. It called for an army to strike south from Montreal to Albany, where it would be joined by a smaller expedition moving eastward from Oswego along the Mohawk Valley. General William Howe, the commander in chief of British forces, was to send a force north from New York City.

Burgoyne pulled every string among his powerful friends in the clubs of London and at the royal court to secure command of the main force, an army of over 7,000 regulars. His persistence paid off; he won the prize and sailed to Quebec. News of British activity led General Schuyler to strengthen Fort Stanwix. In May 1777 Colonel Peter Gansevoort of Albany arrived and energetically worked on its reconstruction. Soon Marinus Willett entered with another unit. The men worked hard; while half stood guard, the other half built roads, felled trees, hauled logs, and placed sod on the walls.

Meanwhile Barry St. Leger, handpicked by Burgoyne, was collecting a motley force: 400 regulars, including 100 Germans dressed in forest green. His Indian allies, varying in number from day to day, totaled somewhere around 700. Another 400 Tories led by John and Walter Butler joined the expedition. St. Leger was elated when in July the Senecas and several other Iroquois tribes decided to ally with the campaign. John Butler's rum and Brant's rhetoric had undone the work of Hiawatha and Digawidah in forming the Great Peace among the Iroquois two centuries earlier.

St. Leger arrived before Fort Stanwix on August 3, 1777, but Gansevoort rejected his demand for surrender. When he heard that Nicholas Herkimer was leading a relief expedition of Tryon County militia, St. Leger sent Brant to ambush Herkimer.

What schoolchild has not thrilled to read in *Drums Along the Mohawk* how General Herkimer, while smoking his black pipe, fought off Brant's Indians in the Oriskany ravine. The Americans finally retreated, taking some 50 of their wounded. The patriots had lost close to 500 men, killed, wounded, or taken prisoner; British losses were considerably smaller. The patriots carried Herkimer on a crude litter to the protection of Fort Schuyler. There the wounded were carried on boats down to German Flatts. When a doctor unfortunately botched the job of amputating Herkimer's leg, the general died a few days later.

Meanwhile the Iroquois had slipped away from St. Leger, who in turn had to give up the siege of Fort Stanwix. In fact his retreat became a rout. The battle for the Upper Mohawk, combined with the American victory at Bennington, deprived Burgoyne of supplies and swelled the number of militiamen under General Horatio Gates. In October Burgoyne surrendered at Saratoga, a victory that guaranteed American independence.

Indian and Tory raiders continued to swoop down on the Mohawk until 1781, leaving it a barren landscape of blackened homesteads. Settlers on the Upper Mohawk seldom thought in geopolitical terms. Rather they regarded the struggle as one for the defense of their homesteads. Little did they realize that peace would soon turn the region into a granary and boom country.

CHAPTER TWO

THE HEROIC AGE OF PIONEERING
1784-1817

No state had suffered greater losses in population and property during the Revolutionary War than New York. British armies invaded the state from the north, west, and south, accounting for one-third of all the skirmishes fought in the war. The blackened ruins of cabins and the underbrush growing up in abandoned clearings spoke eloquently of war's ravages on the Mohawk frontier.

Postwar New York made an amazing recovery. A flood of newcomers, especially from New England, poured into New York, which soon assumed its proud title of Empire State. By 1820 it led all other states in foreign and domestic commerce, transportation, banking, manufacturing, and agriculture. Fifty years after the treaty of Fort Stanwix, more than half of the state's population lived in the area west of Rome. No section made more spectacular gains than the Upper Mohawk, the gateway to the west. Oneida County's population rose from 1,891 in the first census of 1790 to 20,839 only a decade later. This total more than doubled in the next 15 years.

Several factors account for this heady growth: the destruction of the Iroquois Confederacy, the demands by England and France for wheat and ship stores, and the availability of millions of acres that the states of New York and Massachusetts rushed to sell to land-hungry speculators. But the key to New York's expansion lay in its excellent transportation from the seaboard to the interior. The Hudson River became an artery of commerce, with hundreds of landings and dozens of ports providing cheap transportation to overseas markets. The Mohawk Valley, the only "water-level route" through the Appalachian mountain barrier, became a channel to the interior and a funnel for frontier goods seeking a market.

Hundreds of thousands of New Englanders left their exhausted fields, stony hillsides, and prying neighbors to take up fertile lands in New York. Early pioneers such as Hugh White, who settled three miles west of Old Fort Schuyler, sent back specimens of potatoes and corn to convince his friends in Middletown, Connecticut, how bountiful the Oneida frontier could be. Landowners posted handbills and printed advertisements offering tracts at tempting prices and on generous terms. When Dr. Timothy Dwight, president of Yale, praised Whitesboro and New Hartford for "the sprightliness, thrift, and beauty of New England," he convinced skeptical Yankees that a bright

Above
In this deed dated July 22, 1790, Jedediah Sanger received 234 acres of land from George Washington and George Clinton, the first governor of the State of New York. Today this land constitutes much of the Village of New Hartford. (OHS)

future awaited migrants to central New York. Almost 90 percent of the pioneers of Whitestown hailed from Connecticut and Massachusetts.

A mania for land speculation swept both state and nation after the Revolution. Wealthy citizens of New York, Boston, and Albany invested large sums in wild lands that sold for about one dollar an acre in Oneida County between 1788 and 1791. Both capitalists and frontiersmen expected to make as much money in increased land values as in the sale of wheat. Uncleared land in the Servis Patent, just north of Utica, was bringing $10 an acre in 1806, a tenfold jump in less than two decades. No wonder that speculators

from England, Holland, and Germany joined the rush to secure land in Oneida County. Even Governor George Clinton and President George Washington joined in a land speculation within the present towns of Kirkland and New Hartford.

Hugh White purchased the Sadequahada Patent, jointly with Zephaniah Platt, a Dutchess County notable; Ezra L'Hommedieu, prominent patriot; and Melancton Smith, a leading follower of Governor Clinton. They agreed to meet on the tract in the summer of 1784 and divide it after a survey. When the patentees drew lots, White won the lush intervale along the river. Later White bought out Smith's holdings and acquired about 1,500 acres, more than enough for his 10 children. He built his homestead near the eastern side of what became the village green of Whitesboro. Whitestown in 1788 included over half the state and its eastern boundary passed through the ford at Old Fort Schuyler.

George Clarke, Jr., held some 10,000 acres in the Oriskany Patent, which straddled the Mohawk River around the Carrying Place. He offered to lease farms, as did General William Floyd, a signer of the Declaration of

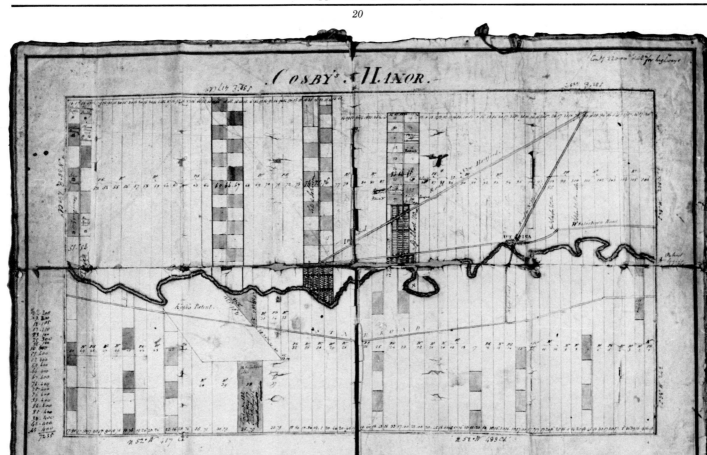

Independence, who moved in 1803 from Long Island to his tract north of the Mohawk River. Floyd gave out leases in perpetuity similar to those on Van Rensselaer Manor, the tract surrounding Albany. In 1786 the State of New York offered to Baron Von Steuben 16,000 acres for his services to the Continental Army. Von Steuben's tract lay some five miles north of the river in a hilly region. His effort to attract tenants met with little success because settlers preferred the better soils in Paris and Clinton south of the Mohawk, which they could buy outright. The old soldier died in 1794 and his tract passed to Benjamin Walker, his Revolutionary aide. Walker, who represented several other landowners, became a leading figure in Utica society.

In 1792 the Dutch banking houses who formed the Holland Land Company sent their agent Gerrit Boon to America to buy land. Boon bought the Servis Patent, which contained some 30,000 acres stretching from Old Fort Schuyler to beyond Remsen. In 1816 the Dutch bankers sold their remaining holdings in Oneida County to Abraham Varick of Utica and Adam Mappa of Barneveld (Trenton).

Cosby Manor also witnessed renewed activity. In 1786 John C. Bleecker of Albany surveyed that portion of the tract that lay within Oneida County and divided it into 106 lots, each extending three miles to the north or three miles to the south of the Mohawk. The narrow width (about 1,000 feet) of these lots later complicated the laying out of streets in Utica. Bleecker distributed the lots to General Philip Schuyler, the heirs of General Bradstreet and John Morin Scott, and himself. Schuyler set to work to develop his holdings and leased over 60 farms, principally in 1790 and 1792. Several of the six Schuyler heirs intended to move to

Top
John Bleecker, son of Rutger Bleecker, surveyed Cosby's Manor in 1786 and laid it out into 106 lots, each about 1,100 feet by three miles. Many of the older streets in downtown Utica and Corn Hill follow the original dividing lines of these great lots. (OHS)

Above
Used by pioneer trader John Post, this stove has been blamed for the fire that destroyed his store in 1804. (OHS)

Above
Moses Bagg, Sr.'s tavern appears as it may have looked circa 1795. It was moved to the south side of Main Street in 1812 to make way for a new brick Bagg's Hotel. Courtesy, Savings Bank of Utica.

the Upper Mohawk but only one, the wife of Major James Cochrane, established permanent residence.

The Bleeckers drew up elaborate plans providing that each of four children in the family was to erect a homestead on Rutger Street, with farmland running south to Steele Hill (now Roscoe Conkling Park). Three heirs refused to move to Utica because of the proximity of the proposed Erie Canal. Mary Bleecker, the wife of Morris S. Miller, established a "seat" in Rutger Park, which extended south to South Street and east as far as Dudley. Her son, Rutger Miller, erected a mansion at the top of John Street. Because the Bleeckers were reluctant at first to sell land outright, settlers avoided the area.

The Bradstreet estate also retarded village growth and caused difficulties for the villagers. Mrs. Martha Codd, the daughter of a stepson of General Bradstreet, arrived a little after 1800. Contentious and shrewish, she divorced her ne'er-do-well husband and resumed her maiden name. For years she sued many citizens who had bought property from other Bradstreet heirs. Although she never won her claims, her lawsuits disturbed many citizens and enriched several lawyers.

Old Fort Schuyler lagged behind the settlements at Whitesboro, New Hartford, Clinton, and Lynchville (Rome) because the marshy ground and land policies of landowners discouraged newcomers. In 1786 only three families of boatmen lived near the ford, but the tremendous growth of central and western New York soon created a thriving center there.

Major John Bellinger, who had fought with General Herkimer at Oriskany, built a frame house in 1788 on what became Whitesboro Street. A sturdy follower of George Clinton, Bellinger challenged the Federalist leanings of Utica's merchants and landowners, and his tavern, the New England House, became a center of roughhewn "democracy." In 1789 Peter Smith bought the log cabin of Widow Damuth and began to trade with the Oneidas. For several years he and John Jacob Astor had a partnership in fur trading. In 1806 Smith moved to Peterboro to supervise the sale of his land. John Post, who had arrived in 1790, challenged Smith in the Indian trade. Post's business flourished to the point that he employed a small fleet of boats on the Mohawk and constructed a warehouse on its bank. Like most early settlers Post offered lodging and food to travelers, but one disgruntled Frenchman called his tavern the "dirtiest" in the nation. Post's son-in-law, who worked in the store, bought too heavily and extended credit too freely. When a fire swept through the store and warehouse in 1804, Post went bankrupt.

Moses Bagg of Westfield, Massachusetts, came in 1794 and opened an inn on the corner of John and Main streets, a business that his son took over in 1805. Moses Bagg, Jr.,

prospered, and in 1812 built the central section of the famous hostelry that was to endure for a century. General Lafayette found accommodations there, as did prominent politicians Henry Clay, Abraham Lincoln, Grover Cleveland, and Theodore Roosevelt, and British authors Thomas Moore and Charles Dickens.

Gerrit Boon needed a place where he could entertain potential purchasers of Dutch land north of Old Fort Schuyler, and in 1797 he decided to build a hotel, a three-story structure on Whitesboro Street with a frame stable, shed, and smokehouse. The ballroom on the top floor became the center of social life and the first Masonic lodge (1805) held its meetings there. Boon widened Whitesboro Street so that stagecoaches with their six horses might turn around more easily; the street, which he cut through to Genesee, received the name Hotel. But neither their lands nor their hotel brought much profit to the Dutch.

Nearly all the early settlers were traders or mechanics, the latter term covering most kinds of craftsmen. The small trading center attracted a much more cosmopolitan population than either Whitesboro, New Hartford, or Clinton, outposts of New England. The Reverend John Taylor in 1802 called Utica a "mixed mass of discordant materials. Here may be found people of ten or twelve different nations, and almost all religions and sects, but the greatest part are of no religion." Among the English were Benjamin Walker and William Inman, father of the painter Henry Inman. Dr. Alexander Coventry was the leader of the small Scottish contingent. John C. Devereux from Ireland began a famous Catholic family. There were also Dutch, such as the James Kip and the John Post families. Second only to New Englanders in numbers were the Welsh, who in 1801 formed a Baptist Church with 22 members and the next year a Congregational Church with 14 members. "Poor but industrious," as one observer described them, the Welsh maintained close ties with their kinfolk in the Steuben-Remsen area.

Bryan Johnson, formerly of England, came to America

and settled in Old Fort Schuyler in 1797. He opened a store on the corner of Whitesboro and Division streets and soon attracted many customers by paying high prices for farm produce. Johnson's store enjoyed so much success that Jeremiah Van Rensselaer of the firm of Kane and Van Rensselaer in Canajoharie moved to Utica. In 1801 Bryan Johnson sent for his wife and son, Alexander, who helped to build his father's fortune. Young Johnson was to become Utica's leading banker, the author of many books on philosophy and economic theory, and a father of the science of linguistics.

The citizens of Old Fort Schuyler met in Bagg's Tavern in 1798 to organize a village government and to choose a proper name. Since that generation of Americans regarded the classics as the mark of learning and gentility, Erastus Clark put the name Utica (the port of ancient Carthage), into the hat and this name won the draw. The village of Utica lay partly in the town of Whitestown and spilled over into German Flatts. In 1798 Oneida County was set off from Herkimer County with an area much larger than its present one. When the legislature created Oneida County, it moved the eastern boundary of the town of Whitestown to the present line dividing Oneida from Herkimer County.

The tiny settlement on the Upper Mohawk depended entirely upon its agricultural hinterland for its livelihood. Its merchants sought to attract the wheat, potash, and other products of frontier families. It became the jumping-off point for westering emigrants who were heading for the

Above
Baroness Hyde de Neuville's View of Utica from the hotel, September 1807 *looks up Hotel Street toward Genesee Street. Hotel Street was built as a shortcut to the Holland Land Company Hotel for travelers coming from the west. Whitesboro Street was widened at this point to allow stagecoaches to turn around in front of the hotel. From the I.N. Phelps Stokes Collection. Courtesy, The New York Public Library.*

Top
Alexander Bryan Johnson (1786-1867) was a philosopher, economist, author, and linguist. (OHS)

Above
Talcott Camp (1762-1832) is believed to have served as the first "village president" or mayor of Utica in 1798, although a fire in 1848 destroyed the earliest village records. Merchant and land speculator, he was inspired to come to the Upper Mohawk country when he saw two barrels of silver coins sent to New York City by William G. Tracy of Whitesboro. (OHS)

Finger Lakes, the Genesee Valley, or beyond.

Like others who settled in America's wilderness, the main task of the pioneers was to clear the forest and bring the land under cultivation. From dawn to dusk and in all seasons they spent most of their time felling trees, burning brush, manufacturing potash, and building fences, sheds, and cabins. Thousands overcame the toil and dangers of farm-making but many others lost their health and their modest resources. Travelers often commented on the sallow faces of the women who endured privation and isolation in these heroic years of pioneering. Some gave up the struggle and straggled back to their home communities; others moved to village centers where stores and shops needed help. Many kept moving west in a search, often fruitless, for fortune. Readers of Moses Bagg's *The Pioneers of Utica* will find the capsule biographies of scores of individuals who tried their luck in Utica but later moved to other centers. The Oneida frontier was truly a gateway society that was constantly in flux.

Twentieth-century Americans celebrate the ability of frontier families to supply most of their own needs. Because pioneers lacked cash and credit, they exchanged labor by working together at barn raisings and logging bees. Most pioneers sought desperately to escape a life of self-sufficiency because it necessarily meant drudgery and a low standard of living. Many searched for a cash crop in order to pay for the kettles, salt, sugar, guns, axes, and tools they needed. In central New York they found potash and wheat the best crops.

Utica merchants sent wheat down the Mohawk in boats but others used wagons. Christian Schultz in 1807 reported that farmers:

> still continue to transport their produce by land in preference to water, as each has his team, which will carry one hundred bushels. They generally go to town once or twice a year, to dispose of their crops, see their friends, and look for great bargains at auction; and when ready to return, can take back a load as cheap as the boatman. . . .

Heavily built wagons, drawn by three or four span of horses, carried to market beneath their canvas tops wheat, flour, cheese, potash, and whisky. Loaded wagons averaged about 15 to 20 miles a day. But land transport remained expensive because of turnpike tolls and the cost of maintaining horses and drivers. These heavy costs proved the driving force behind the agitation for the Erie Canal.

Transportation improvements are a common and persistent theme throughout this period. All members of the frontier communities—landowners, farmers, merchants—demanded public aid to cheapen the cost of transport. In 1792 the legislature responded to western demands by two measures. First of all, it earmarked funds for special roads. One road from Albany was to reach Old Fort Schuyler where the Genesee Road was to strike west through the forest to Geneva and Canandaigua. These so-called roads were scarcely more than traces through the forest, with stumps and roots obstructing passage.

The legislature also took steps to improve navigation on the Mohawk River. At Little Falls, rapids and cataracts forced boatmen to seek the assistance of Palatine farmers to bypass these obstructions. Because of low water and rifts,

the size of boats was limited to less than two tons burden. The legislature authorized the Western Inland Lock Navigation Company to build a small canal around Little Falls, to clear out the Upper Mohawk channel, and to construct a ditch across the portage of Fort Stanwix. These improvements permitted boats of 16 tons capacity to navigate the river, and several men with long poles pushed these broad scows, often 60 feet in length, against the current. River traffic rose sharply and as a result Lynchville (later Rome), grew and indeed surpassed Utica until 1820. Farmers and merchants, however, continued to complain of the high cost of tolls and the delays in the locks.

The "spirit of turnpiking" swept through the state after 1795 when businessmen learned of the successful toll roads in England and Pennsylvania, which private associations had organized. The first turnpike, the Albany and Schenectady, begun in 1797, completed a hard-surfaced road by 1805. From Schenectady the Mohawk Turnpike and Bridge Company constructed a toll road to Utica. The Seneca Road Company, incorporated in 1799, took over the battered Genesee Road for its right of way to Canandaigua. This road today is Genesee Street in Utica, Syracuse, and Rochester. The Mohawk route had to beat off the challenge of the Great Western Turnpike or Cherry Valley system of turnpikes that U.S. Route 20 follows today.

Jason Parker of Utica was a giant in the stagecoach era. After clearing trees on two farms had impaired his health, Parker began to carry the mail pouch from Canajoharie to Whitesboro. By 1794 the volume of mail had

Top
Durham boats, propelled by poles (plus the aid of a sail when the wind was right), were the common freight vessels on the Mohawk River in the days before the Erie Canal. They were about 50 feet long, carried four to 10 tons, and traveled, at best, 25 miles per day. (OHS)

Above
Canal packets were more comfortable, but for the traveler who wanted speed in 1832, the stagecoach filled the bill. Pioneer stage operator Jason Parker published this schedule the year Utica became a city, just four years before the first railroad came to town. Courtesy, Buffalo & Erie County Historical Society.

Village Directory.

20

COPORATION OFFICERS.

Annual Village Meeting, 1st Tuesday in May.

RUDOLPH SNYDER,
GURDON BURCHARD,
AUGUSTUS HICKCOX,   } Trustees.
EZRA S. COZIER,
WILLIAM GERE,

RUDOLPH SNYDER, *President.*
JOHN H. OSTROM, *Clerk.*

POST-OFFICE REGULATIONS, &c.

Mails Arrive.		*Mails Depart.*
Eastern,	8 o'clock, every day,	3 o'clock, A. M.
Western,	do. Mondays excepted,	do. Sundays excepted.
Northern,	do. Tuesdays and Saturdays.	do. Wednesdays and Fri.
Southern,	6 o'c. P. M. Tuesdays,	5 o'c. A. M. Wednesdays.
Rome,	do do. M. T. and W.	8 do. do. Mon. W. and Fri.
Clinton,	11 o'c. A. M. Tues. and Fri.	2 do. P. M. Tues. and Fridays.
Cooperstown do do. do.	Tuesdays,	2 do. do. Tuesdays.
Hampton,	do. do. do. do.	1 do. do. do.

☞ Letters intended for next day's mail, must be handed into the Post-Office before 8 o'clock——if received after that hour they will lie over one mail.

Rates of Postage.

On Single Letters.

For any distance not exceeding 30 miles,	6 cents.
Over 30, and not over 80 miles,	10
Over 80, and not over 150 miles,	12 1-2
Over 150, and not over 400 miles,	18 3-4
Over 400 miles,	25

Double Letters, or those composed of two pieces of paper, double those rates.

Triple Letters, or those composed of three pieces of paper, triple those rates.

Packets, or letters composed of four or more pieces of paper one or more articles, and weighing one ounce avoirdu-

Village Directory. 21

pois, quadruple those rates, and in that proportion for all greater weight.

Newspapers.

Each paper carried not over 100 miles,	1 cent.
Over 100 miles,	1 1-2

But if carried to any place within the state where printed, whatever be the distance, the rate is only one cent.

Magazines and Pamphlets are rated by the sheet.

Carried not over 50 miles	1 cent.
Over 50 and not over 100 miles	1 1-2
Over 100 miles	2

Every four folio pages, eight quarto pages, and 16 octavo or lesser pages, are to be considered a sheet ; also the surplus pages beyond even four, &c. Journals of the state legislatures are to be charged with pamphlet postage, altho' not stitched or half bound.

☞ Letters going out of the United States, must be paid for when lodged in the Post-Office.

MEMBERS OF THE UTICA FIRE COMPANY.

John Camp,	John E. Evertsen,
Moses Bagg,	George Macomber,
Shubael Storrs,	Benjamin Paine,
Ira Merrell,	W. H. Wolcott,
Enos Brown,	Killian Winne,
Jesse Newell,	E. B. Shearman,
James Hooker,	Asahel Seward,
Lewis Macomber,	Samuel Stocking,
Walter Fleming,	Harry Camp,
Joseph S. Porter,	Jas. Van Rensselear,
John C. Hoyt,	Wm. P. Shearman,
Carles M. Lee,	Thomas Walker.
Judah Williams,	

Enos Brown, *Foreman.*
E. B. Shearman, *Assistant Foreman.*
Thomas Walker, *Clerk.*
George Macomber,
Jesse Newell,
Lewis Macomber,   } *Ladder-Men.*
Judah Williams,
Samuel Stocking,

Time of Meeting, the last Saturday of each month.

increased to such an extent that Parker shifted from horseback to a wagon. The wagon in turn became a stage, operating twice a week between Schenectady and Utica. In 1802 he took over the weekly stagecoach service from Utica to Geneva and won exclusive rights to this route.

Stagecoaching became one of the largest businesses and perhaps the most complicated form of enterprise in early Utica. In 1830 the village had eight daily lines running east and west while another four lines ran north and south. The business employed hundreds of agents, runners, drivers, and clerks as well as innkeepers, blacksmiths, and hay dealers. Hollywood has immortalized the "knights of the road" in the Rocky Mountain states. If one uses a bit of imagination, one can recapture the dramatic days of stagecoaching in the Upper Mohawk region. The driver blew his bugle as his galloping team swept down upon Bagg's Square. Stableboys rushed out to lead horses to the barn and to bring out fresh animals. Meanwhile the driver, the envy of small boys, took off his greatcoat and strode into the barroom, where he regaled the locals with stories and the latest gossip.

Utica was second only to Albany as a staging center and derived much of its livelihood from servicing this industry. In 1810 the village had approximately 1,600 residents. One is tempted to dismiss such a small village as insignificant but actually it performed many vital functions. Here one could go to court, buy land, hire a lawyer or surveyor, visit a doctor, buy two newspapers, or attend church in at least four different denominations. Those with money could secure first-class accommodations at Bagg's Hotel. Those with scanty funds could find lodging and drink in a score of groggeries and inns. Dozens of stores offered the usual necessities but also books, silks, and other luxuries. The first village directory of 1817 shows that 17 percent of the men called themselves "merchants." The largest dealers dealt in agricultural commodities such as wheat, flour, and hides. Artisans, who made and sold tools, chairs, barrels, shoes, nails, and the like, comprised almost half of male workers over the age of 15.

The manufacture of glass attracted the interest of several capitalists in Utica: Watts Sherman, a merchant; Abraham Varick, land agent; John Steward, Jr., a rich lawyer; Alexander Bryan Johnson, son of a wealthy merchant; and Richard Sanger, the leading landowner of

Above
The first Utica directory was published in 1817. It listed 2,861 inhabitants (1,496 males and 1,365 females) with their addresses and occupations. Note how expensive the postal rates were for that time. The fire department roster (at right) was a "who's who" of prominent citizens. (OHS)

MUSICAL INSTRUMENTS.

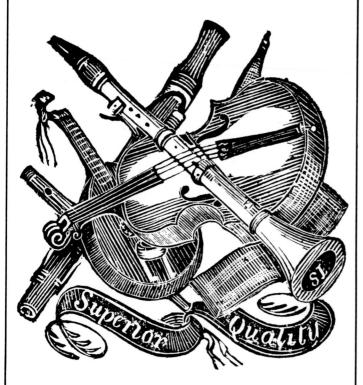

WILLIAM WHITELEY,

29 GENESEE-STREET, UP STAIRS, UTICA.

Musical Instrument Maker and Music Seller,

Keeps for sale Bassoons, Clarionets, Flageolets, Flutes, Bugles, SERPENTS, Fifes, and almost every other article of Musical Merchandize, forming in the whole, a more choice collection than is often found in market. ☞ His long experience in the business enables him to say with confidence that he can furnish INSTRUMENTS to buyers, wholesale or retail, on as good terms as can be afforded by any other manufacturer or seller.

☞ *Instruments repaired in the neatest manner.*
$3.

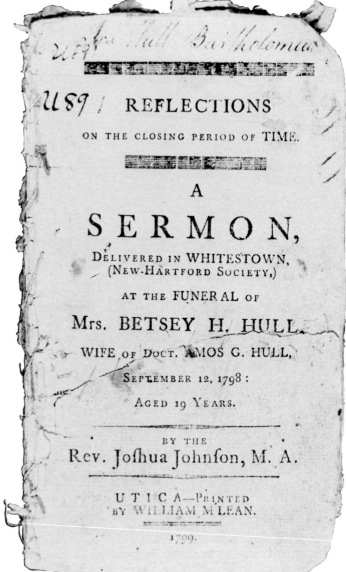

New Hartford, who organized the Oneida Glass Factory Company in 1809 with a capitalization of $100,000. This firm built a plant at Verona to make cylinder glass, but after some years of success it lost money and in 1836 failed.

Johnson, a young man of 20, took an active role, visiting the plant several times a month. In 1810 Peter Bours, another young merchant, inveigled his father-in-law, Benjamin Walker to back a new venture, the Utica Glass Factory Company, whose capitalization was $250,000. This firm constructed its plant on a road a few miles north of Utica but foundered in 1820.

Craftsmen worked many kinds of metals—silver and gold, tin and copper, iron and brass—into articles needed

Above
William Whiteley made musical instruments in Utica between 1810 and 1853 and placed this full-page advertisement in the 1832 city directory. His flutes and clarinets are highly prized by collectors and museums. (OHS)

Above
This funeral sermon, printed in 1799, is the earliest known Utica imprint. William McLean and William Williams were among those who established printing as an important local industry. The tradition is carried on to this day by such firms as Utica Typesetting Company, Brodock Press, and Dodge-Graphic Press. (OHS)

by settlers and the prospering farmers and merchants. Nine blacksmiths found plenty of work before 1800. James Delvin formed a partnership with John D. Gray to manufacture copper and tinware. Silversmiths made Utica a leading center and sold their wares, especially spoons, to residents. Wells M. Gaylord settled in Utica in 1810 and began making looking glasses.

Woodworking trades flourished because the demand for chairs, agricultural tools, bureaus, cabinets, wagons, barrels, and the like seemed limitless. William Whiteley even made fine woodwind instruments and organs. Earthenware pottery appeared on the local scene, but the great age of Utica pottery was to come in mid-century. Other craftsmen did crude and fine painting, especially of signs. Jesse Newell, a painter, formed a partnership with George Macomber that later grew into an important business.

Utica became a major publishing center for upstate New York and William Williams was the major figure in this business. A native of Framingham, Massachusetts, his parents settled in frontier New Hartford. In 1800 young Williams, a stripling of 13 years, moved to Utica where he served an apprenticeship under Asahel Seward, his brother-in-law. By 1807 he had become a partner in the firm known as Seward and Williams. Williams set the type, operated the hand press, learned how to manufacture paper from rags, and used sheepskins for binding books. Thurlow Weed related how Williams tested his ability to set type and "domiciled" him in his own household. Williams learned how to make engraved woodcuts that were so well done that banks employed him to make their bank notes.

An imposing figure of exemplary character, Williams tried with success to meet the needs of upstate villagers and farmers. He became superintendent of the Sunday School of the First Presbyterian Church in 1816 and his publications ran heavily to devotional literature. He published *Musica Sacra,* edited by Thomas Hastings, choirmaster of Trinity Church, who wrote *Rock of Ages* and many other popular hymns. He even published Handel's *Hallelujah Chorus,* a piece that every generation in the world has enjoyed.

During the same period Yankees had observed that nearby streams—the Sauquoit and the Oriskany—would turn waterwheels. In Whitestown, Oriskany, and Paris they built sawmills and gristmills. More important they established textile mills, the nucleus for the largest textile center west of New England for more than a century. The Embargo Act, which would seriously affect commerce and business, threatened hostilities with England, and the War of 1812 stimulated Dr. Seth Capron and Benjamin Walcott, both from Rhode Island, to establish mills. The Sauquoit Creek, which falls more than 1,000 feet in only 17 miles, provided the best sites. In 1809 capitalists from Utica and Albany banded together to organize the Oneida Manufacturing Society. Encouraged by handsome profits, the directors soon built a woolen factory at Oriskany. By 1817 a dozen cotton and woolen factories had sprung up along the Sauquoit and Oriskany creeks.

The first mills were small enterprises, which adopted the Rhode Island system of employing the entire family. The *Utica Patriot* in 1813 advertised:

> A few sober and industrious families of at least five children each, over the age of eight years, are wanted at the Cotton Factory in Whitestown. Recommendations as to moral character will be expected.

The textile boom collapsed in 1815 when peace brought a large influx of cheap English textiles. Oneida County manufacturers petitioned Congress for a protective tariff to save their investment of $600,000. Several firms fell into bankruptcy; the stronger ones survived.

Above
The second cotton spinning and weaving mill of the Oneida Manufacturing Society was built in 1828 to replace the original 1809 mill which had burned. The company houses were probably built at the same time; some of them were replaced between 1874 and 1888 by brick houses which still stand on Mill Place in New York Mills. This mill was torn down after the present Lower Mill was completed in 1880. Courtesy, Architectural Archive, Munson-Williams-Proctor Institute.

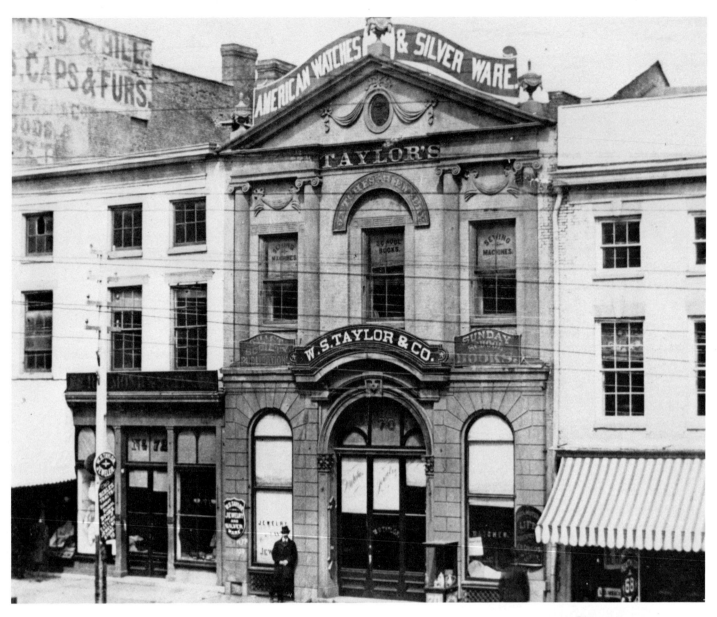

Prior to 1810 most money in circulation was silver coinage of Spanish origin. To get around the currency shortage, neighbors exchanged labor and storekeepers extended credit, which farmers often paid in kind. Paper money became available when state banks and occasionally even villages such as Utica in 1815 issued notes. But shopkeepers did not like to accept bank notes because some banks did not redeem them in hard currency.

The thriving turnpike center required paper money and credit to facilitate trade but it also needed a safe place to deposit surplus funds. The Manhattan Bank of New York in 1809 sent Montgomery Hunt to organize a branch of that institution. Hunt set up his office in a brick structure on Hotel Street just south of Whitesboro Street. This bank prospered until 1818 when financial difficulties closed its doors.

In February 1811 a newspaper call for another bank brought out a group of influential men, many of whom had served on the board of the Manhattan branch. The next year the Bank of Utica received its charter, appointed James S. Kip its president, and hired Hunt as cashier. Hunt's family lived in the bank building and Montgomery's

Top
The Ontario Branch Bank opened in 1815 in this handsome federal-style edifice on the site of today's Commercial Travelers Insurance building. The bank failed in the Panic of 1857, and in 1861, W.S. Taylor took it over for a jewelry store, shown here in 1874. Courtesy, Utica Public Library.

Above
This stout iron box served as the first vault of the original Bank of Utica. Before the invention of dynamite, such a chest was practically impregnable to anyone who did not have the key. (OHS)

Above
The New Hartford Presbyterian Church was organized in 1791 as the
First Religious Society of Whitestown, and construction of the
meetinghouse began in 1792. It had already undergone extensive
remodelling, including the installation of Victorian stained-glass
windows, when this picture was taken circa 1890. Courtesy, Architectural
Archive, Munson-Williams-Proctor Institute.

son Ward later served on the State Court of Appeals and on the United States Supreme Court. The Bank of Utica prospered a great deal from the War of 1812 because the United States government deposited large sums for the purchase of supplies and payment of soldiers.

In 1815 the Ontario Bank of Canandaigua established a branch in Utica on the west side of lower Genesee, on the site of the Commercial Travelers Association. Reflecting the classical spirit of the time, this building had four stone Ionic columns to support the pediment.

While banks had achieved some success, religious life had dwindled to a very low point in the two decades after the Revolution. Warfare had scattered congregations, disrupted the training of clergy, and sent Tory rectors into exile. None of the denominations had enough clergymen to fill the existing pulpits, much less to follow pioneers. Nevertheless a few missionaries crisscrossed the western settlements, baptizing adults as well as children, marrying couples, and encouraging the faithful to read the Bible. Several years elapsed, however, before the sparsely settled communities could support an organized church.

Jonathan Edwards, the younger, had visited the Oneida settlements in 1791 and persuaded groups in New Hartford and Clinton to organize a church. Jedediah Sanger, a wealthy landowner of New Hartford, offered his barn for a meeting place. The group formed the First Religious Society of Whitestown, which later became the New Hartford Presbyterian Church. Meanwhile the Yankees in Whitesboro in 1793 had organized the United Presbyterian Societies of Whitestown and Old Fort Schuyler, whose pastor held services on alternate Sundays in each village. In Utica the Reverend Bethuel Dodd conducted services in a schoolhouse on Main Street. The rapid expansion of Utica's population led in 1803 to the

founding of the Presbyterian Society of Utica, which was strong enough to erect its own building on the corner of Washington and Liberty streets by 1807. The Welsh Baptist and Welsh Congregational churches had already been formed.

Meanwhile Colonel Benjamin Walker and several other persons of Anglican and Episcopalian background had formed a loose society, which in 1803 became Trinity Church. They decided to put up a church, a goal reached in 1810 when the bishop opened the structure on the corner of Broad and First streets. Baptists in Deerfield had by 1800 organized a society which pledged its members to take care of the poor in their neighborhood.

The scattered and highly mobile population included some members of churches who did not have the numbers or resources to organize a congregation. In Utica John C. Devereux, an ardent Roman Catholic, opened his home to visiting priests who celebrated Mass from time to time. Not until 1819 did the Catholics of Utica feel strong enough to organize the Trustees of the First Catholic Church in the Western District of New York, which sponsored St. John's Church on the corner of Bleecker and John streets. Many Protestants subscribed liberally to the building fund, following the example of Devereux, who had contributed to the construction of several Protestant churches.

Schools in New York had lagged well behind New England during the colonial period. In 1782 Governor Clinton urged the legislature to encourage schools and five

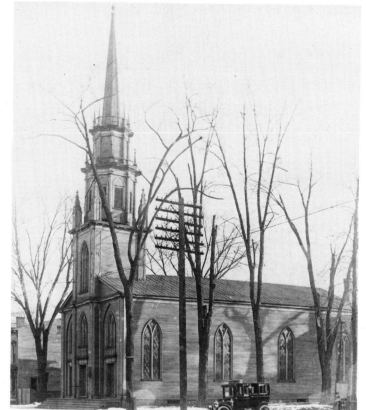

Top
Baroness Hyde de Neuville's painting entitled simply Utica church 1807 *depicts Trinity Church as first constructed. In 1833 the front was extended to the sidewalk and the steeple was rebuilt. Courtesy, The New-York Historical Society.*

Above
Old Trinity Church is shown circa 1920, shortly before it merged with St. Andrew's on Faxton Street. The structure was occupied by an Episcopal Italian mission church, St. Peter and Paul's, until it was torn down in 1926. Courtesy, Architectural Archive, Munson-Williams-Proctor Institute.

years later the Regents of the University of the State of New York called for a public school system. The legislators moved cautiously but in 1795 granted $50,000 for elementary schools. Meanwhile several schools had opened, thanks to the initiative of parents, churches, and individuals. Teachers were usually young men who drifted in and out of the profession. The district school law of 1812 greatly stimulated the formation of public schools by dividing the state into districts that were directed to set up schools. A modest amount of state aid helped keep the tuition low. In 1817 the trustees of Utica opened its school on Catherine Street near Franklin. Most children never saw the inside of a classroom, partly because their parents could not afford the tuition but also because their labor was needed in the shop, store, or farm.

Oneida County enjoyed an unusual advantage in having a secondary school as early as 1793, when Samuel Kirkland founded the Hamilton-Oneida Academy to teach the children of Oneidas along with those of white settlers. This academy became Hamilton College in 1812, the third college chartered in New York State. Whitestown Academy

Top
John C. Devereux was co-founder of both St. John's Roman Catholic Church and The Savings Bank of Utica. A pioneer merchant from Ireland, he became the first popularly elected mayor of Utica. (OHS)

Above
Roman Catholic priests from Albany celebrated some of the first Masses in Utica in the John C. Devereux house on Broad Street at Second Avenue. Later occupied for many years by the Lowery Brothers cotton business, this historic home was torn down about 1972. A bronze plaque on a boulder remains to explain the significance of the site. Photo by Carl K. Frey. (OHS)

A

NARRATIVE

OF THE

MISSIONS

TO THE

NEW SETTLEMENTS

ACCORDING TO THE APPOINTMENT

OF THE

GENERAL ASSOCIATION

OF THE

STATE of CONNECTICUT:

TOGETHER WITH

AN ACCOUNT

OF THE

RECEIPTS and EXPENDITURES

OF

THE MONEY CONTRIBUTED BY THE PEOPLE OF CONNECTICUT,

IN MAY, 1793,

FOR THE SUPPORT OF THE MISSIONARIES,

ACCORDING TO AN ACT OF THE GENERAL ASSEMBLY OF THE STATE.

NEW-HAVEN—PRINTED BY T. & S. GREEN. 1794.

Above
The reports of early New England missionary societies are a valuable source of information about life on the New York frontier in the late 1700s. (OHS)

opened its doors in 1813. The merchants and political leaders of Utica delayed secondary education until that same year, when they petitioned the legislature for a charter. They decided to have the academy share quarters with the town hall and court in a building on Chancellor Square, an arrangement that later proved awkward for all parties involved.

Utica received its second charter in 1805, which enlarged its boundaries although it remained within Whitestown. Male citizens met in the schoolhouse and elected five trustees who served one-year terms, an office which carried no salary but considerable "status." Their major duty was to appoint 25 firemen. The firemen's party at a tavern run by George Tisdale in 1808 consumed one gallon of beer, three pints of gin, three pints of brandy, and 13 bottles of wine. When a fire broke out, each citizen had to carry his leather bucket and join the bucket brigade to the town pump or the river. Women and children passed the empty buckets back to the pump. The president and the trustees acted as fire directors and each carried a wand with a gilded flame on the top. Fire wardens wore leather hats with a white crown and a black rim. The larger Utica became, the greater the number of fire companies, whose rivalry sometimes led to pitched battles for the honor of putting out the conflagration.

The village trustees also had to regulate the public

market, a necessity but also a giant nuisance. Butchers and victuallers had to pay a license fee for the right to have a stall. Residents near the market complained of odors and filth; a reasonable grumble, further heightened by hogs wandering in the streets. Trustees tried valiantly to prevent this unpleasant problem. And in answer to a charge that dealers were cheating citizens as to the weight of items, they regulated the price and weight of bread, a regulation similar to that in Albany, New York, and Boston. Because yeast was difficult to secure, many householders had to forego homemade bread and buy baker's bread instead. Signs of Utica's growth were apparent in 1804 when houseowners on Genesee, Whitesboro, and Main streets were required to provide sidewalks (although the village paid for crosswalks), and to number the buildings on Genesee Street.

The family household was the primary social unit and carried on many functions—economic, governmental, and religious. All members, whether the patriarch, womenfolk, children, servants, or apprentices, had specific duties. *Rhymes for the Nursery,* a local publication in 1815, urged boys and girls to work hard. It stated:

The little girl who will not sew,
Should neither be allow'd to play.

The New England Primer, reissued in 1810, paraphrased the Fifth Commandment: "I will honor my father and mother. I will obey my superiors." Male authority was supreme. Only adult males could vote or hold office. And when officials of the Oneida County fair awarded prizes for needlework, they gave them to the men, who then turned the prizes over to their womenfolk.

Although Utica with its mixed population had less of a New England flavor than Whitesboro, it subscribed to the basic moral values of Connecticut. The village charter of 1817, for example, upheld the sanctity of the Sabbath, established just prices, and opposed vice.

The citizens of Whitestown experimented at an early date with such newfangled ideas as voluntary associations that stood apart from church, village, and family. In 1806 the Whitestown Charitable Society was formed and in the next decade other groups—Presbyterian, Methodist,

Baptist, and the Welsh—founded benevolent and missionary societies. Mrs. Sophia Clark of Utica founded the Female Charitable Society, the first of several societies organized by the frontier generation of women. The Female Missionary Society of Oneida County (1814) stood on its own financial feet, the first such organization free from male supervision.

The Oneida country became a bastion of Federalism partly because its residents relied upon the national government for protection. Furthermore landed proprietors along with their advisors tended to favor the Federalist party. When Jefferson imposed the embargo on exports, merchants and farmers complained that this action reduced farm prices. In 1810 the remnants of the old Federal party chose Jonas Platt of Whitesboro as their candidate for governor. Platt attacked France (and Napoleon) as the main foe of the United States, but Governor Daniel D. Tompkins defended the strong measures taken against Great Britain by Presidents Jefferson and Madison. Platt lost by a wide margin but won a major victory when he persuaded De Witt Clinton to support the proposal for a canal from the Hudson to Lake Erie. The War of 1812 delayed the proposal, but in 1815 Platt and others organized a public meeting in New York City which appointed the committee to draw up a petition to the legislature. When news of this meeting reached Utica, a group of interested citizens met in Bagg's Hotel to send a supporting petition to the legislature. Their hopes would be realized in a decade.

The Upper Mohawk country by 1817 had developed a prosperous economy and a fairly sophisticated society boasting churches, courts, schools, and banks. Its surging population made up of hard-driving citizens, the expansion of commercial agriculture, the turnpike network, and the emergence of factories generated a spirit of enterprise. De Witt Clinton in 1810 captured this ebullient feeling when he noted that Utica "arrogates to itself being the capital of the Western District," constituting well over half the state. And this unbuttoned optimism was partly justified. Would not the proposed canal linking the Hudson with Lake Erie open the cornucopia of the West, fill Utica's warehouses, and attract hundreds of country storekeepers to Genesee Street?

"The Genteel Society."

Utica and its neighboring villages had come a long way in creating a "genteel" society by the opening years of the new century. The recollections of Alexander Bryan Johnson give us a fascinating glimpse of the hearty appetites and bibulous habits of the traders of the Upper Mohawk.

Our food, consisting in part of fine poultry, was superior to the food I had been accustomed to, and fresh butcher's meat was plenty at all times, with good bread, butter, and cheese. Even groceries were abundant, including loaf sugar and good teas and coffee. . . . I found, however, the manners of the people worse than the food. The habit of loud eructation was prevalent to an extraordinary degree. . . . Swearing was much less prevalent than I had heard it in

England, and it was more confined to men than in England. Obscene conversation among men at their social feasts was probably a fault of the age in question and it was the ordinary source of mirth and good fellowship. . . . In all such gatherings madeira wine was often the only beverage, except occasionally hot punch, and the great point of all the company was to make as many intoxicated as practicable. The mode consisted in drinking toasts in bumpers from which no one was excused except on the penalty of singing a song or telling a story. . . . As far as I could judge, chastity of conduct was far more generally practiced in America than in England, and any deviation therefrom was deemed a public offense which a whole neighborhood would resent, especially when implicating married persons.

CHAPTER THREE

CANAL CENTER AND THE REFORM IMPULSE
1817-1840

In 1817 officials turned over the first spadeful of earth at Rome for the Erie Canal, the most ambitious and successful undertaking in state history. A population explosion followed, marking the quarter century. The thriving turnpike village was propelled by canal boat and locomotives into a prosperous city bursting with commercial enterprise and poised for the industrial revolution of factory production, which had already taken root along the Sauquoit and Oriskany creeks. Matching these revolutionary changes were religious revivals and humanitarian reforms. Energized by Pentecostal fervor, believers revitalized old denominations, founded scores of schools and colleges, spawned dozens of charitable reforms, nourished many journals, and transformed the position of women. A middle-class society was emerging from the welter of flux and change.

The village of Utica in 1817 contained 2,861 residents who lived and worked in 420 dwellings and shops. It had several churches, two banks, many taverns, printing offices, and an abundance of lawyers and land agents. Stores lined Genesee Street as far south as Catherine, beyond which private residences predominated. Most inhabitants lived between the river and Liberty Street.

Utica was a city of wooden structures, although a few of the wealthier citizens had built brick mansions and establishments. Whitesboro Street was the business center, characterized by the Bank of Utica and the Manhattan Branch Bank as well as many inns and stores. Streets such as Seneca, Washington, and Broadway extended only as far as Liberty. Main Street near Bagg's Square had several stores and offices, but farther east merchants and lawyers had built attractive mansions. Water Street had warehouses for wheat and other products that used the boats on the Mohawk. The area called Corn Hill remained wilderness as far as the clearings of New Hartford. A short distance to the west of Genesee one stepped into another forest. Travelers passing to Deerfield and points to the north had to cross the bridge over the Mohawk and follow the muddy causeway, which the spring floods often covered with water.

The village of approximately 3,000 in 1820 rose to about 5,000 residents in the next five years and to 8,323 by 1830. In the following decade population rose half again to 12,782. Providing shelter and work places for all these people

became the major activity of Uticans. Wealthy merchants and lawyers erected fine mansions on Broad Street and Genesee while thousands of workingmen packed boardinghouses. Craftsmen with families acquired modest dwellings.

At first most Uticans worked, ate, and slept in the same place. Rich and poor lived in the same neighborhood, often in the same building. Employers expected apprentices and servants to live in the shop or behind the store. Custom, church sanctions, and state law made employers responsible for the conduct of their entire household.

In the 1820s masters were putting social and

Above
To determine the tolls for canal boats, the state built several weighlocks, including one on the south side of the canal near John Street in 1829. The canal was wider here to allow boats to maneuver. Courtesy, Savings Bank of Utica.

geographical distance between themselves and their workers. They were becoming more interested in the purchase of raw materials and the sale of finished goods. Furthermore they tried to discipline the apprentices by forbidding drinking in the shop. When the master walked to his home on a side street, he was entering a middle-class environment in which an evangelized housewife set standards of sobriety.

The increasing number of young men living in boardinghouses found male companionship at taverns, food stores, and variety shops. Grog sellers dispensed their wares on every street. Distinct neighborhoods were emerging where boardinghouses predominated. The wealthy also began to congregate around Chancellor Square, on upper Genesee Street, and on John Street. But even the rich could not escape the noise of the brawling Erie boatmen or fail to see the fights and reeling drunks on the streets.

"A pretty country town." So foreign observers described Utica, whose livelihood depended upon an exchange of goods with the surrounding countryside and farmers to the west. Actually the great majority of male Uticans were engaged in blue-collar occupations; in fact

over 40 percent of them belonged to the category of craftsmen. The census of 1845 recorded another 20 percent as unskilled laborers or factory laborers. Meanwhile the old mercantile elite was losing both in numbers and in prestige. Their percentage of 17.4 in 1817 declined to only 2.7 in 1845. During the same period the percentage of shopkeepers inched upward from about 9 percent to about 11 percent. The number of clerks and other white-collar employees doubled but in 1845 only one in 10 belonged to that group. Utica's adult males worked with their hands—in shops, along the canal, or in construction.

Youthfulness characterized both Utica's and Whitestown's population throughout this period. Two out of three persons had not reached the age of 25 in 1820. During the next two decades the youthful contingent rose to over seven out of ten. Although at first males outnumbered females by a small margin, this ratio was reversed by 1840.

The population changed constantly, a characteristic noted by historians in many cities such as Rochester and Boston. Each year hundreds of newcomers arrived; each year a somewhat smaller number left. Bagg's *Pioneers of Utica* records a constant stream of persons who had made Utica a way station before heading for Detroit, Chicago, and New York City.

Top
This woodcut entitled View from the Car House *(the Utica & Schenectady Railroad station) appeared on an 1836 map of the city. It shows the taverns and shops that faced Bagg's Square and lined lower Genesee Street prior to the Great Fire of 1837. Nearly all of the buildings shown except Bagg's Hotel (left) were destroyed in the fire. (OHS)*

Above
When Judge Morris Miller built this house at the head of John Street in the 1820s, people called it ''Miller's Folly'' because it was so far from the center of Utica. In 1867 it became the home of Senator Roscoe Conkling. This photo was taken about 1890, prior to alterations by the Kernan family. (OHS)

Most Uticans were engaged in manufacturing although the factory did not arrive until the late 1840s. A great number of articles were "made by hand" by scores of skilled craftsmen such as hatters and woodworkers. Some artisans expanded their operations into large enterprises. Similarly some merchants invested their money in shops that made goods. A new breed of manufacturers gradually emerged, a considerable number of them immigrants from Great Britain where the industrial revolution had taken firm foothold before 1800. Newcomers from New England were also prominent in the development of manufacturing in Utica.

In West Utica William Smith made wrought-iron nails on Nail Creek. In 1813 Joseph Masseth acquired some notoriety by using two dogs to power the bellows in his nail factory. Tanneries sprang up because cows were slaughtered and farmers and stage operators needed harnesses, saddles, and boots. Shoemakers arrived at an early date and they required leather softened by immersion in hemlock vats. David Hoyt from Connecticut opened a shoe store on Genesee Road but his tannery was located on Whitesboro Street beyond Broadway. He built a warehouse on the south bank of the Erie Canal and he ground hemlock bark by using the power of a gigantic windmill on Hoyt

Street. His tannery, the largest in the state in 1824, had 237 vats.

William Inman, an English gentleman who powdered his hair and wore knee buckles, settled in the village in 1792. A dozen years later he began to brew English ale. His three sons attained high honors in several fields. William rose to commodore in the United States Navy, Henry became famous on both sides of the Atlantic for his miniatures and portraits, and John became editor of leading New York papers such as the *Commercial Advertiser.* Michael McQuade bought the Gulf Brewery from John C. Devereux and ran it for half a century before his death in 1879. During that time he produced a famous "Mountain Dew" whiskey made from barley malt.

Starch Factory Creek in East Utica took its name from the business begun in 1809 by John Gilbert, another English gentleman. He secured power from dams on the south side of the Erie Canal, employing about 40 men to work at the task of mashing corn, wheat, and potatoes. This enterprise, the largest in the state, declined when Oswego and western cities established more efficient plants.

Making pots and stoneware from clay became a profitable enterprise. Noah White took over a small pottery founded by a man named Nash and subsequently developed

Above
Alfred Munson (1793-1854), businessman, philanthropist, and patron of Grace Church, was founder of the Munson-Williams-Proctor family fortune. The bust was made by noted sculptor Erastus Dow Palmer, who began his career in Utica. Courtesy, Munson-Williams-Proctor Institute.

Above
William Williams (1787-1850), in addition to his record as a printer and publisher, fought in the War of 1812 and led the Utica volunteer fire department. He also cared for victims of the cholera epidemic of 1832 until he contracted the disease himself and nearly died. (OHS)

by Samuel Addington on Whitesboro Street. By 1840 White had added many buildings on his 400-foot front on Whitesboro Street. There he made stoneware, firebrick, and later sewer pipe.

Alfred Munson, from Connecticut, opened his shop on Hotel Street in 1823 and also began to manufacture burrstones, mainly used in gristmills to grind wheat into flour. Munson, who amassed one of Utica's major fortunes, contributed heavily to charitable causes and especially to Grace Church.

Several small foundries (five in 1835) sprang up to handle the needs of local firms such as the textile mills along the Sauquoit Creek. The manufacture of soap and candles naturally developed to serve the local market. The leading manufacturer was John Thorn, who took Isaac Maynard as his partner in 1837. Thorn expanded his plant on the north side of Water Street near Division.

William Williams remained the foremost printer, his imprint appearing on dozens of schoolbooks including Webster's *Spelling Book* and the *New England Primer.* He served as trustee of the village of Utica and proudly published the first *Utica Directory* in 1817. Every printer in that generation took an active role in politics and Williams was no exception. A supporter of De Witt Clinton, he edited and printed a new newspaper called *The Sentinel* between 1820 and 1824. *The Sentinel* attacked Martin Van Buren and the Albany Regency on every occasion. The abduction of William Morgan stirred up popular indignation over the Masons' threat to personal liberty. Williams reprinted Bernard's *Light on Masonry* and the *Elucidator,* a journal that crusaded against the fraternal order.

John H. Lothrop purchased from William McLean his interests in the *Western Sentinel,* a paper published in Whitesboro. Lothrop changed the name to the Utica *Patriot* in 1805. The *Patriot* continued until 1816 when it was combined with the *Patrol,* a paper begun by Seward and Williams. Five years later the *Utica Sentinel* took its place. Samuel D. Dakin and William G. Bacon bought the paper and combined it with the *Columbian Gazette* in 1825 under the title *Utica Sentinel and Gazette.* Bacon soon withdrew and Dakin in 1829 sold to his printers, Northway & Porter.

The confusion in New York State politics reflected

itself in the local press. Allies of Martin Van Buren and Bucktail Democrats sponsored the *Oneida Observer,* which was published and edited by Augustine G. Dauby after 1823. For his ardent support of the national party of Andrew Jackson, Dauby was appointed to the office of postmaster, serving from 1829 to 1840. Eli Maynard was thereafter proprietor of the paper for many years.

When the Whig party emerged in 1834, it received the support of the *Oneida Whig,* which inherited the subscribers of the *Elucidator* (Anti-Masons) and the *Sentinel and Gazette.* This paper was published by Mr. Northway until 1853 when the Whig party began to disintegrate. Another paper, the *Oneida Standard,* moved from Waterville to Utica in 1833 but machine Democrats disliked its antislavery stand.

Oneida County remained a Democratic bastion from 1832 to 1844 but Uticans consistently gave their support to parties opposing the Democrats. The Whigs attracted most of the wealthy and many of those who favored the religious revivals and temperance. The Democrats favored state rights over national programs such as the national bank and protective tariffs. They also opposed efforts to regulate private morals by such means as restricting the sale of hard liquor.

The textile industry, which utilized the power of the Sauquoit and Oriskany creeks, made a slow recovery after its postwar collapse in 1816. Benjamin Walcott sent William Copley to work in a Rhode Island mill so that he could learn the secret of the power loom. Copley returned with the information and the Walcott mill had the first power loom in New York State.

The Oneida Manufacturing Society (later Cotton Factory) in 1827 had 63 employees, most of whom were boys and girls. Five years later its labor force had risen to 190 persons who made one million yards of cloth. Benjamin Marshall, an English investor, helped finance in 1825 the largest venture, New York Mills, which Benjamin Walcott, Jr., managed. In 1828 it had 180 workers, a figure that rose to 265 within four years. The mill stood in the midst of family cottages, a boardinghouse for boys, and another for girls. Walcott, a Presbyterian elder and temperance champion, actively encouraged attendance at Sunday

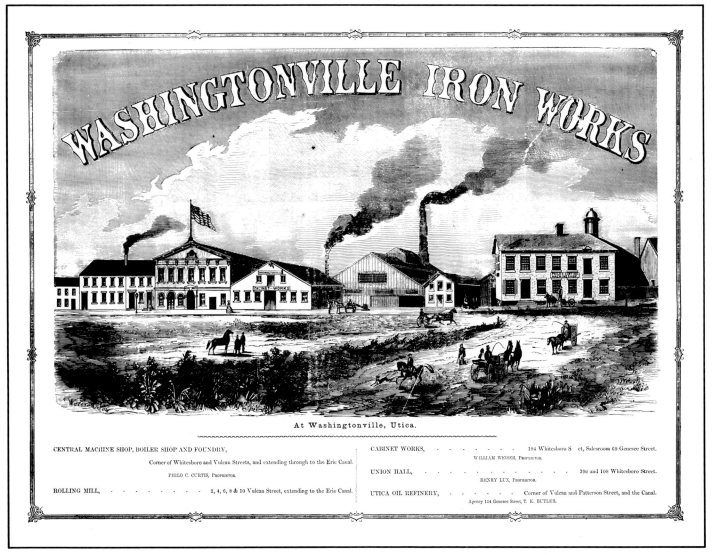

At Washingtonville, Utica.

CENTRAL MACHINE SHOP, BOILER SHOP AND FOUNDRY,
Corner of Whitesboro and Vulcan Streets, and extending through to the Erie Canal.
PHILO C. CURTIS, PROPRIETOR.

ROLLING MILL, ... 2, 4, 6, 8 & 10 Vulcan Street, extending to the Erie Canal.

CABINET WORKS, ... 194 Whitesboro S et, Salesroom 69 Genesee Street.
WILLIAM WEISER, PROPRIETOR.

UNION HALL, ... 106 and 108 Whitesboro Street.
HENRY LUX, PROPRIETOR.

UTICA OIL REFINERY, ... Corner of Vulcan and Patterson Street, and the Canal.
Agency 114 Genesee Street, T. K. BUTLER.

services and at revivals. Walcott built a stately mansion near his mill and bought out his partners so that he could take his sons into the business.

The McLane report on manufacturers of 1832 provides an excellent summary of the various factories in Oneida County, most of them within a few miles of Utica, which lacked water power. The 20 mills employed 1,075 workers in 1832. The census for 1840 shows that the number of mills had fallen to 13 but operatives had risen to 1,302. Utica's capitalists invested in these enterprises.

Alexander Bryan Johnson, perhaps the ablest banker in Utica's history, spent many weeks in the winter of 1815-1816 in Albany lobbying for a charter for a new company, the Utica Insurance Company. Secretly Johnson planned to open a bank but the Ontario Bank and the Bank

of Utica had enough political power to thwart him. With the cunning of a man who later wrote a book on the meaning of words, he secured a charter whose vague phrases gave his company the right to exercise banking privileges. Johnson rounded up a group of friends, erected a building on the corner of Division and Whitesboro streets, and offered banking services. His rivals persuaded Martin Van Buren, attorney general of the state, to seek a court injunction, and the legislature also passed an act limiting corporations from banking. Embarrassed and contrite, Johnson dissolved his bank in 1818.

Meanwhile the Ontario Bank had fallen into serious difficulties because of bad management. Its board recognized Johnson's talents and offered him a position of director. Soon he became president, a post he held for 38 years. He restored public confidence in the Ontario Bank, which did more business in Utica than in its headquarters in Canandaigua.

Uticans plunged into wild speculation in the 1830s. The favorite speculation was real estate, since everyone expected that the city would continue to grow at an explosive rate. Other Uticans put their money into railroad ventures as well as western lands. When President Jackson required all purchasers of public lands to pay for them in gold or silver, the boom collapsed. The Panic of 1837 hit

Facing page
In the early 19th century, the front pages of Utica newspapers were almost entirely devoted to advertising. (OHS)

Above
One of the first industrial establishments in Utica and perhaps the oldest factory still used is the building at the right of this circa 1862 print. Built by Philo C. Curtis in 1832 at Whitesboro and Lafayette streets, it still houses part of the Utica Steam Engine & Boiler Works. (OHS)

Utica somewhat harder than most cities and forced many young businessmen into bankruptcy.

Canal workers, many of Irish origin, needed a safe place for their savings. They trusted the Devereux brothers who had a reputation for honest dealing and who paid them regular dividends on their savings. The legislature in 1821 granted a charter for the Utica Savings Bank run by the Devereux family, but this business remained small scale. In 1839 the Savings Bank of Utica was incorporated with John C. Devereux as president and Stalham Williams as treasurer. Williams served in this post for 34 years. None of the directors or officers received any salary or loans from this bank, which grew very slowly.

Few undertakings have so completely fulfilled the highest claims and the fondest hopes of its sponsors as did the Erie Canal. When De Witt Clinton and his associates first proposed to dig a ditch 40 feet wide and four feet deep for some 364 miles through the wilderness, they were greeted by a chorus of scoffers. Where were the engineers to direct the work and build locks? How could New Yorkers (fewer than one million) pay for such a project?

Clinton convinced his fellow citizens to undertake the risky venture. Oneida County gave enthusiastic support to the canal, whose benefits to its citizens did not need to be spelled out. On July 4, 1817, state and local officials turned over the first shovelfuls of earth at Rome, which the commissioners had wisely chosen as the starting point. The soft alluvial soil between Utica and Salina (Syracuse) required no locks, though both the eastern and western sections did.

Benjamin Wright, a Rome surveyor, took charge and advertised for sealed bids. By October a thousand men were hard at work. Surveyors staked out a path 60 feet wide. Next axmen felled trees. Once the logs and brush had been collected and burned, diggers broke up the mass of roots with iron-tipped plows and shovels. The contractors, almost

Above
John C. Devereux opened his first store on Bagg's Square in 1802. In 1821, with his brothers, he built a new store next to the Erie Canal and in 1845 replaced it with the Devereux Block (shown here circa 1890) which still stands. At one time it housed the office of Senator Francis Kernan along with a saloon in the basement that was a favorite of Senator Roscoe Conkling. (OHS)

Engineer of Rome, a craft 61 feet in length. The excursion reached Whitesboro in about 40 minutes and a number of smiling ladies climbed on board. From bridge to bridge, guns saluted the voyagers and church bells rang. After spending an hour in Rome, the party rode back to Utica on the *Chief Engineer.*

The next year the commissioners opened the middle section from east of Utica to Montezuma on the Seneca River. Individuals ran boats for hire and carried all kinds of goods from church bells to oysters, not to mention cases of liquor. The commissioners then turned to completing the eastern and western sections where they faced serious physical obstacles.

In October 1825 Uticans joined enthusiastically in the ceremonies celebrating the opening of the Erie Canal. The *Seneca Chief* bearing Governor Clinton and distinguished guests left Buffalo to the salute of cannon whose echo was picked up by other guns stationed at intervals of four to five miles all the way to Albany and New York City. The gunners in Manhattan sent the same signal back to Buffalo. A procession of boats reached Utica on a Sunday morning and Clinton, a staunch churchman, attended afternoon services at the First Presbyterian Church. The party spent the night at Bagg's Hotel and the following morning local leaders greeted Clinton with the flowery oratory of the day.

all of whom were nearby farmers, hired diggers, supplied them scrapers and shovels, and gave them their daily grub and whiskey. Canvass White, grandson of the pioneer, discovered that a certain kind of rock in Madison County could be converted into a cement equal to the hydraulic cement imported from England. For good reasons the Erie Canal was called America's first school of engineering.

The canal commissioners in October 1819 opened the section from Rome to Utica to placate citizens who were complaining of delays, waste, and bungling. Cautiously they opened the sluice gates feeding water into the canal from the Oriskany Creek. Governor Clinton, accompanied by a large party of dignitaries, embarked upon the *Chief*

Top
Stalham Williams (1773-1873) was 66 years old in 1839 when the Savings Bank of Utica was chartered. He remained active in the bank into his nineties and still held the title of treasurer at the time of his death, only six months short of his 100th birthday. (OHS)

Above right
Five times mayor of New York City and thrice governor of New York State, DeWitt Clinton was considered the "father" of the Erie Canal and the political force behind its financing. Courtesy, Library of Congress.

Above left
Medals bearing the figures of Pan (representing the inland region of the Great Lakes) and Neptune (representing the Atlantic Ocean) were struck to commemorate the completion of the Erie Canal, which linked these great natural waterways. Boxes to hold the medals were made from fine wood transported from Buffalo to New York on the Seneca Chief. *(OHS)*

Clinton replied with a eulogy to Jonas Platt of Whitesboro. That evening floating barrels of flaming tar illuminated the water. Citizens bought chinaware decorated with canal scenes. Medals were struck for the occasion.

The city's center shifted southward as both people and business establishments moved away from the river. Merchants built warehouses, taverns, and stores on the canal bank. Where Ballou's Creek flowed into the canal, a large basin took shape between Third Avenue and Mohawk Street. The canal commissioners erected a weighlock building on the southern side of the canal at John where state officials collected tolls. As a result of this shift, the old York House lost clientele but the coming of the railroad in 1836 saved Bagg's Hotel as a major hostelry.

During the 1830s Uticans favored almost any canal or railroad that would bring trade to the city. In 1833 the legislature voted to build a canal from Utica to Binghamton and in three years workers had dug the Chenango Canal. Its first lock was located on Columbia Street near State and another eight locks were needed before Burrstone Road. The legislature also voted to enlarge the Erie from a depth of four to seven feet, a task not completed until 1862. The success of the Mohawk and Hudson Railroad stimulated a wave of railroad promotion. By 1836 Alfred Munson, Nicholas Devereux, and Henry·Seymour joined other capitalists to build a railroad from Schenectady to Utica, a

line that for a short time was the longest in the world. Hardly had this line reached Utica when other promoters began work on a railroad from Utica to Syracuse. All these transportation links tied Utica into the maturing national economy.

Egbert Bagg, the architect, observed that the domestic architecture of Utica reached its peak in the 1820s and perhaps for a few years thereafter. Merchants had accumulated enough wealth to afford more comfortable dwellings. The elite—Varicks, Stockings, Doolittles, Camps, Ostroms, Harts, Hubbards, Denios, Bacons, Kirklands, Lothrops, Johnsons, Beardsleys, and many others—wanted to display their wealth and to live in comfort if not luxury. They generally constructed their dwellings of brick and their houses came close to the street. Quite often they put up a high wall to permit their families

Above
The earliest known view of the Erie Canal in Utica was painted in 1822 to illustrate a travel diary. The Canal Hotel or Canal Coffee House (center) opened in 1820 at the southeast corner of the canal and Genesee Street. Courtesy, New York State Library.

Above
The Marquis de Lafayette, French hero of the War for Independence, visited America in 1825. "The nation's guest" rode into Utica in an elegant carriage driven by Theodore Faxton and accompanied by a military escort. Entering the village on Fayette (now Lafayette) Street, the party passed under a triumphal arch erected over the canal bridge on Genesee Street. The general visited the home of Alexander Bryan Johnson, whose wife was the niece of President John Quincy Adams. Then, with the militia firing a 24-gun salute and small boys throwing flowers from canal bridges, the French nobleman departed on his packet drawn by three white horses. Courtesy, Savings Bank of Utica.

and guests to enjoy private garden parties. But the gardens had utilitarian uses as well because the head of the house and his lady liked to serve fresh vegetables to their guests. Each house also required huge woodpiles in order to heat the high-ceilinged rooms. Although each room had a fireplace, few rooms were really warm in winter. Large folding screens were used to keep drafts away and individuals had to snuggle in the large sofas.

These mansions required a large force of servants who were often the daughters of farmers or artisans and, after 1840, many Irish girls worked as domestics. The servants had much work: tending the garden, keeping the fires going, taking care of the children, preparing the meals, and getting the house ready for the parties and dinners of friends and relatives. Just reading the 10 to 14 courses sometimes offered to guests is enough to make most modern observers shudder, though a few might feel slightly envious.

Among the more elegant houses were those lived in by Samuel Stocking, Ephraim Hart, and Samuel Beardsley. Almost all of these houses have disappeared, victims of the high cost of energy, servants, and business development. Broad and Whitesboro streets have long since lost any

Above
The boyhood home of Governor Horatio Seymour, built about 1815 on Whitesboro Street at Hotel Street, is shown circa 1890. It still stands, with a warehouse addition in the rear, as a rare survivor of early Utica. The magnificent elm tree was typical of the thousands that lined the city's streets until Dutch elm disease struck after World War II. Courtesy, Architectural Archive, Munson-Williams-Proctor Institute.

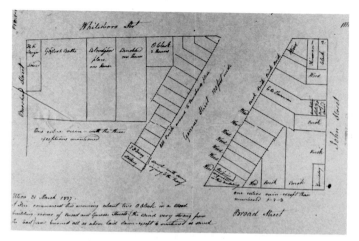

claim to fashion.

Utica became on February 13, 1832, the first city west of Schenectady to receive a city charter. The city was divided into four wards by Genesee Street and the Erie Canal. Each ward elected three aldermen who formed the common council. The council selected the mayor, four justices of the peace, a supervisor, treasurer, and other officers. The city tax had a limit of $8,000, but a majority of taxpayers could approve additional sums.

The new council met March 13, 1832, and promptly appointed Joseph Kirkland as first mayor. After his move from New Hartford to Utica in 1813, this young lawyer devoted his life to civic improvements and charitable agencies. He took an active role in the Presbyterian Church, the Utica Academy, the Ontario Branch Bank, and several industrial corporations. The council passed several ordinances dealing with the prevention of fires, the regulation of public nuisances, the construction of buildings, and the use of streets. They even prohibited swimming in the Erie Canal or the Mohawk River between 5 a.m. and 8 p.m. within most of the city.

Hardly had the city government become organized when it faced a massive threat to public health. In 1832 Asiatic cholera surfaced in Canada and this news caused the council to create a Board of Health. Five physicians had authority to make any regulations necessary to stop the spread of the plague. The council also instructed aldermen to examine houses, streets, and outhouses. The Board of Health examined all canal boats, especially those from

Canada. Boats were detained and cleansed with lime.

On August 13 the Board announced the grim news that four cases of cholera had been found. Citizens became almost hysterical and an estimated 3,000 fled to the countryside. Newspapers suspended publication because of the flight of printers. Churches closed their doors. A total of 65 people died out of 206 cases. By mid-September the epidemic had run its course and the Board of Health discontinued the temporary hospital set up in the Academy.

Many Uticans acted heroically during the crisis. Among them were Dr. John McCall, William Williams, and Mayor Kirkland, who helped bury the dead and kept essential services going.

The prevention of fires continued to absorb much attention by the aldermen. Six fire engines and one hook and ladder company served the city. When the council discovered that free refreshments to fire fighters led to drunken parties for all their friends and onlookers, it stopped paying the bills. Late in March 1837 flames broke out at two o'clock in the morning on the east side of Genesee north of Broad. Flames spread down to Bagg's Square and consumed all the buildings on Broad as far as John as well as the buildings on the west side of John Street. Flames jumped Genesee to the store of Stocking & Hunt and rapidly licked their way down to Whitesboro Street. From that point the fire raged up Whitesboro to Burchard Lane. Some 50 tenements were destroyed in Utica's greatest fire and scores of inhabitants shivered in the snow.

The maintenance of law and order became more serious because of the larger population. In 1832 the council appointed two constables. Neither wore a uniform but each had a shield and a long club. In addition 12 men served as the night watch from 9 to 2 a.m. The constables managed to overawe most troublemakers but they could not deal with mobs. The *Utica Observer* of 1840 reported rowdies emerged from the old rookeries between the packet basin and Bleecker Street and near Charlotte where "rummeries"

Above
Joseph Kirkland (1770-1844), nephew of the Reverend Samuel Kirkland, was a lawyer, a general in the militia, and served as the first mayor of the City of Utica. This oil portrait is by F.R. Spencer. (OHS)

Above
Almost all of the area included in this manuscript map was burned in the fire of March 31, 1837. Today the area is under the new Bagg's Square bridge and its approaches, and the new connection between Whitesboro and Broad streets cuts through the triangular area at left. (OHS)

and a filthy brothel were located. Two years later boatmen engaged in a brawl with railroad men at the Utica Railroad Station. In New Hartford citizens formed an association in 1830 to fight horse thieves.

The Utica Academy got under way in 1818 under many difficulties. Since it was housed in the same building as the courts, the students interrupted court proceedings with their shouts while at the same time the throngs of jurymen, witnesses, and attorneys created a constant hubbub. Trustees agreed to visit the school each month and to provide the people with public exhibitions of the students' work at the end of the school year. Captain Charles Stuart, a retired officer of the British East India Company, became principal in the early 1820s. Earnest and eccentric, Stuart was a charismatic figure who dominated the academy. David Prentice, who served as principal and teacher of classics from 1825 to 1836, brought rigor, discipline, and order.

Charles Bartlett, a graduate of Union College, founded the Utica High School in 1827. This boarding school for boys was located on the farm of Dr. Solomon Wolcott at the east end of Broad Street. About 40 boys paid $200 a year for charges. For this they received instruction in English, lectures in various sciences (Asa Gray taught botany there), and genteel arts of horseback riding and gymnastics. A staunch Presbyterian, Bartlett required all to attend church on Sunday and Bible class on Sunday evening. A

fire in 1835 destroyed the main building and Bartlett moved to Poughkeepsie. Other private schools sprang up such as the Classical and Commercial Lyceum, which Messrs. Phillips and Kingsley conducted on the east side of Washington Street between Whitesboro and Liberty. Although it attracted the sons of many good families, it did

Top
Most of these buildings on lower Genesee Street in 1841 replaced those destroyed in the Great Fire of 1837. The one at left, facing Bagg's Square, was among those standing until demolitions in 1971 made way for the new Bagg's Square bridge. From Barber and Howe, Historical Collections of the State of New York.

Above
The first Oneida County Court House in Utica was built in 1818 on the east side of John Street just south of Bleecker. It also served as the first Utica Academy (forerunner of Utica Free Academy) but the combined quarters proved impractical and by 1852 separate buildings were constructed back-to-back on the same site. This lithograph was made circa 1835. (OHS)

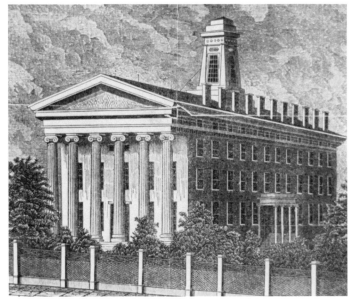

gracious arts and ladylike deportment in her short-lived school on Broad Street. City leaders began to demand an academy for their daughters equal to that for the boys. A society brought the four lots lying between the corner of Washington and Genesee streets with the buildings on them. They constructed an academy building of brick, three stories in height, and appointed Miss Urania E. Sheldon the first principal.

Scores of small private schools were opened by young ladies and college graduates but the schools usually did not last. In 1829 there were 31 of them in the village. Because the law did not require attendance, many youngsters never did see the inside of a schoolhouse. They received their education from fellow workmen, from their parents, or from their church school.

The trustees had the authority to establish elementary schools for which they received some state aid, but the city did not support these schools generously. The buildings were usually overcrowded with scholars.

Oneida County's major distinction lies in its role as the nursery of religious revivals and humanitarian reforms. Not only did the most important revival in 19th-century America originate there but many of the dominant figures in both religion and reform—Charles Grandison Finney, Theodore Dwight Weld, Gerrit Smith—launched their crusades in central New York.

The soil for spiritual growth had been well prepared by

not survive the hard times following the Panic of 1837. In 1832 the Roman Catholics began a school on John Street above Bleecker.

Several schools were opened expressly for girls. Montgomery R. Bartlett in 1818 opened his institute for young females. Madam Despard sought to impart the

---

Above
The imposing Greek Revival Utica Female Academy, built in 1838, stood on the site of today's YMCA. Burned in 1865, it was replaced by a Mansard-roofed structure later known variously as the Balliol School and Mrs. Piatt's School. (OHS)

Top
This view of "the Gymnasium of Utica" (a later name for Charles Bartlett's Utica High School) appeared on a city map published in 1835. The school first opened in a converted farmhouse, possibly the building at right. The round-roofed building at left may be the unique half-round schoolhouse in which students sat in two semicircular tiers of stalls, unable to communicate with each other, but in plain view of the teacher who sat in the center. The school closed after one of the buildings burned in 1835. (OHS)

CONSTITUTION
&c.

****

THE subscribers, believing that a portion of the bounties of Providence can be applied in no better way than in administering to the spiritual necessities of our fellow creatures, and convinced of the utility and importance of Missionary Societies, by whose benevolent exertions the glad tidings of redemption are carried to multitudes who are perishing for lack of knowledge: and wishing to contribute our mite towards the advancement of so good a cause, do agree to associate ourselves for that purpose under the following REGULATIONS:

I. The society shall be composed of females, associated under the name of the *Female Missionary Society of Oneida.*

II. There shall be an annual meeting of the members of the society for the purpose of choosing trustees, who shall be elected by a majority of the votes of those present: The meetings to be on the first Tuesday of September, at two o'clock in the afternoon, at the place to which the previous meeting shall have adjourned.

III. The society shall appoint ten trustees, whose duty it shall be to manage and transact all business relative to the institution, for which purpose said trustees shall meet at least twice a year, at such times and places as they shall agree.

clergymen and women. In 1814 the First Presbyterian Church had won 65 persons to the Lord. Five years later another 90 individuals joined while in the same year the Presbyterian and Baptist churches in Whitesboro had reaped a harvest of 135 converts. The more plentiful the harvest, the more earnestly did clergymen seek to gather in the adults and particularly men, a majority of whom did not practice family prayers or attend church. When clergymen mounted the pulpit, they looked at a congregation overwhelmingly female in composition. Women headed almost half of the families of members. They composed two-thirds of the converts in the early revivals.

The spectacular revivals of 1825-1826 began in Western, a tiny village northeast of Rome. Here George Washington Gale had retired to recover his health worn down by years of preaching in the North Country. In Adams he converted Charles G. Finney, a handsome young lawyer and choirmaster who was ordained in 1824. The next year Finney visited Gale and the two evangelists began a revival in the local Presbyterian Church. The excitement spread to Rome, then to Utica, Whitesboro, and other churches. One observer declared that Oneida County was "overthrown by the Holy Ghost" and that the theatre "has been deserted, the tavern sanctified."

Prior to 1825 elite families, lawyers, merchants, and landowners, had predominated among the saved. The Van Rensselaer family joined the church in 1814. Federalist families—John Ostrom, Thomas Walker, Arthur Breese—experienced saving grace five years later. The great revival of 1825-1826 brought in many artisans and shopkeepers. Few laborers joined, possibly because they felt uncomfortable among the commercial elite who paid substantial pew rents.

Many women who belonged to the Female Missionary Society (1814) had husbands who maintained business addresses separate from their residences. These ladies had both time and freedom to experiment with new roles. Eunice Camp, for example, ran a school for black children. The ladies also contributed to the support of missionaries who were bringing the Gospel to pioneer homes. Educated women began to write memoirs and stories for the evangelical magazines published in Utica.

Maternal associations sprang up at the same time as those founded in New England but before such societies emerged in other states. In 1824 a maternal association took form in Utica, its members pledging themselves to pray for

Above left
The Reverend Charles G. Finney (1792-1875) was known as a master of dramatic gesture, with eyes that "could pierce the individual and compel the masses." (OHS)

Above
The constitution of the Female Missionary Society set forth the ideals on which the group was founded. (OHS)

each child daily, to attend fortnightly meetings, and to read Scripture. In contrast to the earlier missionary society, this association enrolled many wives of artisans and shopkeepers. Women prepared their children for conversion and also persuaded (one critic used the word "harassed") their husbands to join the church. Moses Bagg, the wealthy innkeeper, accepted the Lord in 1826, a dozen years after Sophia Bagg had professed her faith. Charles Finney relates how Sophia Clarke trapped a Hamilton College student into attending a revival service and kept him from leaving her pew in the First Presbyterian Church. The young man, Theodore Dwight Weld, wrestled with his conscience, yielded his will, and soon became the greatest organizer of temperance and antislavery societies.

The revival not only added hundreds to the church rolls in Utica but it also increased the percentage of church members in the village. The increased numbers and the emergence of scores of dedicated leaders spawned a large number of benevolent societies concerned with missions, Sunday observance, Sunday Schools, adult education, temperance, and the abolition of slavery. Utica became the capital for many voluntary associations that published magazines and hosted quarterly meetings. During the first week of May, delegates attended the annual meetings of several societies: the Oneida Evangelical Society, the Oneida Bible Society, Utica Tract Society, Western Educational Society, Western Domestic Missionary Society, and the American Sunday School Union. Some delegates attended more than one conference and some Uticans served as directors of more than one society. The *Utica City*

Above
The Oneida Institute in Whitesboro was praised for its success in training ministers for frontier missions, but conservatives condemned it for its strong support of the abolitionist movement. (OHS)

Directory for 1832 lists 26 religious and charitable associations, more than one third limited to women.

Women collected money for missions and for the poor. They distributed Bibles and tracts to every household. They also organized the Female Moral Reform Society in 1837, which crusaded against prostitution and the seducers of young women. Sophia Clarke, Fanny Skinner, and Paulina Wright, veteran reformers, led this drive, which annoyed some Uticans.

The Oneida Academy, later called the Oneida Institute of Science and Industry, was another offshoot of the revivals. Pastor John Frost appealed to his fellow clergymen in the Oneida Presbytery to purchase a farm in Whitesboro and set up a labor institution where each student could pay part of his expenses by working on the farm or in the shops. In 1827 the Presbytery bought the farm and influential Uticans contributed money for the school. By 1830 the institute accepted 60 students but it turned away 500.

When Gale retired in 1833 from the leadership of Oneida Institute, the trustees selected Beriah Green, a fiery and hot-tempered reformer. Green took an advanced position on the slavery issue and indeed became the first president of the American Anti-Slavery Society. Oneida Institute admitted blacks, one of the very first colleges or schools to take this radical step. Gerrit Smith of Peterboro helped support these black students. Among the most distinguished graduates were Henry Highland Garnett and Amos Beman, both Negro ministers. Garnett demanded equal rights and eventually became American ambassador to Liberia, where he died.

Green kept moving to ever more radical positions. When the Presbyterian Church refused to denounce all slaveholders within the church, he attacked Presbytery. His vitriolic language led to a church trial and his secession from the Presbyterian Church. He and his followers then formed the Whitesboro Congregational Church. The panic of 1837 led to a drop in enrollments and a decline in financial support. By 1841 Oneida Institute closed its doors.

Most Uticans opposed abolition in general and

abolitionists in particular. The Utica Common Council on January 10, 1834, deplored agitators after Green had urged abolition in a public debate. Early the next year the abolitionists flooded the mails with millions of pamphlets calling for everyone, including women and children, to join the crusade.

Tensions reached a new peak when the antislavery chapters picked Utica for their first statewide meeting. Congressman Samuel Beardsley organized a gathering to prevent the abolitionists from convening. A political ally of Martin Van Buren, Beardsley felt that Southern Democrats would abandon Van Buren unless New York Democrats took a firm, even violent, stand against abolitionists. Augustine Dauby, editor of the *Utica Observer* and local postmaster, wrote that he would prevent the meeting "peacably if I can, forcibly if I must."

At first the common council agreed to allow the delegates to meet in the city's courtroom, but on October 18

they reversed their stand. This opposition and the open threats of violence aroused another group of Uticans to declare in favor of freedom of assembly and freedom of speech. On October 21 some 400 or so delegates assembled in the Bleecker Street Presbyterian Church. Their enemies, led by many of the commercial elite, marched on the church and rushed into the sanctuary. The delegates scattered and many adjourned to Clark's Temperance House, where Gerrit Smith invited them to Peterboro. Smith announced his conversion to abolition and for the next 30 years he lent his talents and opened his coffers to the cause. That evening a mob invaded the offices of the *Oneida Standard and Democrat* and threw the type into the street.

The "gentlemen of property and standing" who led the mob had stores on Genesee Street and belonged in exceptional numbers to the Episcopal Church. Abolition attracted artisans and manufacturers such as Benjamin Walcott, Spencer Kellogg, and Samuel Stocking. Both

Above left
Beriah Green (1795-1874), clergyman, educator, abolitionist. From Cirker, Dictionary of American Portraits, *Dover, 1967.*

Above right
Gerrit Smith (1797-1874) was born in Utica, the son of pioneer merchant and land speculator Peter Smith. He added to his father's fortune and generously supported many reform movements, especially abolitionism after 1835. (OHS)

Above
Samuel Beardsley (1790-1860) was an able and respected lawyer. He was influential in the Democratic Party and held a number of important legal posts in addition to his service in Congress. (OHS)

Facing page
The Second Presbyterian Church was built in 1826 on the corner of Bleecker and Charlotte streets and became a Baptist church in 1845. The New York State Anti-Slavery Society met here in 1835, provoking a riot from its opposition. (OHS)

camps, however, enlisted merchants, lawyers, and manufacturers. Women and clergymen tended to favor abolition as did immigrants from Wales and England. The Irish opposed this crusade, partly because its leaders often opposed Catholicism, and partly because blacks competed with them for unskilled jobs.

Sabbath observance also proved a troublesome issue. The noisy and sometimes disorderly behavior of stage drivers, boatmen, and hostelers at taverns shocked those accustomed to the traditional Puritan Sunday. They urged individuals not to patronize firms running boats or stages on Sunday.

Temperance enlisted the greatest number of followers. Alcohol was pervasive among all classes who drank at home and abroad, alone or together, at work or at play. Whiskey and other hard liquors were very cheap and helped to wash down poorly cooked, greasy, and sometimes rancid food. Heavy drinking had disastrous effects upon the health, morals, and family life of citizens.

In 1829 the newly formed Utica Temperance Society invited Alexander Bryan Johnson to deliver an address.

Top
A view of Liberty Street in 1846 shows Mechanics Hall (at right with dome) and the First Presbyterian Church steeple. Mechanics Hall was the site of countless fairs, political rallies, revival and temperance meetings, art exhibitions, and theatrical productions throughout the mid-19th century. Minus the dome, it still stands at the corner of Hotel Street. The First Presbyterian Church on Washington Street burned in 1851 and was replaced by a new church on the corner of Washington and Columbia streets. (OHS)

FAMILY TEMPERANCE SOCIETY.

AS FOR ME AND MY HOUSE, WE WILL SERVE THE LORD.

We, the undersigned, do agree,

that we will not use intoxicating liquors as a beverage, nor traffic in them; that we will not provide them as an article of entertainment, or for persons in our employment; and that in all suitable ways we will discountenance their use throughout the community.

> This little band do with our hand,
> The pledge now sign, to drink no wine,
> Nor brandy red, to turn our head,
> Nor whisky hot, that makes the sot,
> Nor fiery rum, to turn our home
> Into a hell, where none can dwell,
> Whence peace would fly—where hope would die,
> And love expire, 'mid such a fire;
> So we PLEDGE perpetual hate
> To all that can intoxicate.

This society was made up largely of upper-class gentlemen who believed that if they gave up consumption of spirits "ordinary" people would follow their example. Manufacturers could see the advantage of having a sober work force that would appear for work on Monday morning.

The temperance movement gained strength during the 1830s. The more ardent members of temperance societies agitated for total abstinence. The Presbytery of Oneida passed several strong resolutions in 1833. The more numerous the pledge signers, the more militant became the leaders, who moved from temperance to prohibition.

The last straw for conservatives came in the 1840s when reformed drunkards took major roles in the crusade and formed the "Washingtonian" movement. That movement attracted much support among Uticans who collected over 8,000 signatures for the pledge of total abstinence. The Total Abstinence Convention met in Utica on February 22, 1842, with over 2,000 in the audience. Temperance parades by the Cold Water Army had many units representing women, children, Irish, blacks, workingmen, and others. Women composed well over half of

the membership and Elizabeth Cady Stanton lectured in churches, to the dismay of old-line conservatives.

The crusade did cause many members of the evangelical middle class to give up drinking. It led to bitter disputes in families, churches, and business. Uticans were to continue to play a leading role in the campaign against Demon Rum. In 1851 a group of printers organized the Order of the Good Templars, a fraternal order, which by 1900 had 100 grand lodges all over the world and boasted a membership of 403,287.

Utica experienced severe growing pains during this period. Most residents were newcomers who felt like outsiders. Municipal officials had to deal with new problems of crime, disease, poverty, and urban planning. Businessmen had to adjust to many shocks: the opening of the Erie Canal; speculative frenzy; the panic of 1837. While merchants and artisans were working to provide shelter, clothing, and food, they were also seeking to find personal salvation and to establish the Kingdom of God along the Mohawk.

Facing page, bottom
Converts to the cause of temperance swore an oath or signed a form such as this in which they renounced the use of intoxicants. (OHS)

Above
Probably the best-known early views of Utica are the prints based on English artist William H. Bartlett's sketch of Genesee and Washington streets about 1838. The 1827 First Presbyterian Church on lower Washington Street is at left and the Utica & Schenectady Railroad depot at Bagg's Square is at right. (OHS)

CHAPTER FOUR

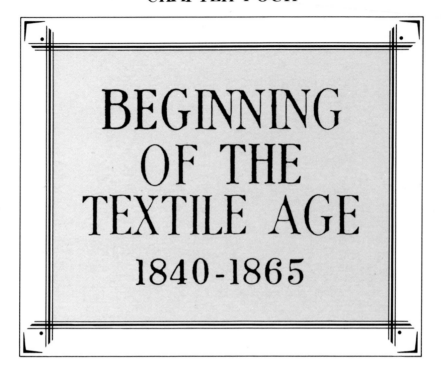

BEGINNING OF THE TEXTILE AGE
1840-1865

Utica emerged as an ungainly factory city from the chrysalis of a commercial center. In the quarter century after 1840, population almost doubled, most of this gain taking place between 1845 and 1855. Irish, German, and British immigrants by the thousands crowded the boardinghouses and tenements surrounding the factories or fringing the canal. Democracy made another stride forward in 1840 when Uticans voted for mayor the first time. The election of John C. Devereux, a Roman Catholic, symbolized the relative decline of the old native Protestant stock, who thereafter shared power with newcomers.

Transportation remained as before the key to economic development of the Upper Mohawk. The thickening network of canals, railroads, and roads broke down the localized economy in which craftsmen serviced the farmers in the neighborhood. The transportation revolution was creating a national economy.

Uticans hoped that the Chenango Canal would bring additional business and enable residents to buy coal from Pennsylvania. They also hailed the state legislature's action in 1835 in authorizing the deepening of the Erie Canal channel from four to seven feet. They even expected

to reap some benefits from the Black River Canal, which probed north from Rome into the Watertown region. The panic of 1837 and extravagant spending on public works impaired the state's credit. In 1842 the legislature ordered a stop to all public works and stalled further efforts to enlarge the Erie. But in 1853 Governor Horatio Seymour of Utica called a special session of the legislature to submit an amendment providing for more funds for canal enlargement. The public approved overwhelmingly because they charged the newly organized New York Central with setting unfair rates.

Meanwhile Alfred Munson, vice president of the Utica and Schenectady Railroad, and other Utica directors, Nicholas Devereux and Henry Seymour, were pleased with the business of their company. Two western links, the Syracuse and Utica and the Auburn and Syracuse began to operate trains in 1839. Although Utica's hotels and merchants benefited from the expanding passenger traffic to and from these points, they were not entirely happy when the railroads established through trains from Albany to Buffalo in 1842. For many travelers Utica became a mere way station. The state ban on freight carriage naturally

irked railroad managers and some merchants and manufacturers. After much agitation the legislature agreed in 1847 to allow the railroads paralleling the canal to carry freight provided they paid the equivalent of canal tolls to the canal fund. Four years later the legislature repealed this provision but also appropriated large sums for canal enlargement. During the 1850s almost all freight except timber and grain products deserted the canal boats to the railroads.

Railroad fever spread to the villages and towns north and south of the Mohawk. Farmers wanted speedy transport of their milk to market. Businessmen in Utica

Above
After a series of incendiary fires in the early 1850s in which some volunteer firemen were implicated, the city attempted to start a part-time paid fire department, one of the first in the country. This proved unworkable, however, and the volunteer system was reinstated in 1857. One of the elite units formed in 1857 was the Tiger Hose Company, seen on parade on Broad Street just off Genesee in 1866. They served until the establishment of a full-time paid department in 1874. Courtesy, Richard M. Lockwood.

hoped to bring more customers to their doors, especially when they heard that Syracuse entrepreneurs were planning rail lines to the North Country and south to Binghamton. In 1853 Theodore Faxton and associates formed the Black River & Utica Railroad Company and urged Uticans to buy stock in this venture. They even persuaded the city council to buy $250,000 of stock. Poorly managed and wastefully constructed, the railroad had hardly reached Boonville before it ran out of cash. In 1861 John Thorn and another group of capitalists raised more capital and slowly pushed construction toward Lyons Falls and Carthage, reaching the latter point in 1870.

Meanwhile Alfred Munson and allies were planning to penetrate the region south of Utica but the project bogged down because of rivalries over the route. Interest was renewed in the early 1860s when two routes to Sherburne were proposed, one following the Chenango Canal, the other advancing up the Sauquoit Valley, thence to Waterville, and on to Sherburne. A massive campaign took place in 1866 to convince Uticans to support this enterprise and the citizens voted to purchase $500,000 in bonds.

John Butterfield and associates organized the Utica,

Clinton & Binghamton Company whose first goal was to connect Clinton with New Hartford, Utica, and Whitesboro. By 1863 horses were pulling cars from Utica to New Hartford along Genesee Street. By 1870 steam trains were chugging to New Hartford along a route paralleling the Chenango Canal.

The canals and railroads did little to aid farmers on short hauls. Mud mired their wagons because town officials had neither the funds nor the knowledge to construct all-weather roads. In the late 1840s the plank-road movement reached Oneida County. Cheap and easy to build, plank roads served local users well. In January 1847 a group of Utica's leading citizens held a meeting and offered $50,000 for the construction of plank roads. Six months later they formed an association to build a plank road northward from Deerfield to a point some five miles north of Remsen. The road was speedily constructed and prospered. Other associations built roads to Rome, Schuyler, and Frankfort, and others to New Hartford, Clinton, Waterville, and Burlington. Plank roads, however, quickly deteriorated because the timber, usually hemlock, rotted. The holes between the planks caused horses to break their legs or suffer injury. The heavier the traffic, the sooner the planks wore out. None of the roads brought in enough revenue to pay for upkeep, and the panic of 1857 made it difficult to raise additional funds. After heavy rains most roads

became mudholes in spring, resulting in seriously limited transportation.

Although Utica's trade expanded within the region of central New York because of improvements in canal and rail transport, it lost its former position as the jumping-off point for the west and the supply center for western storekeepers. Canal boats, once the main support for Utica's commerce, more and more became carriers of through freight, which passed under the Genesee Street bridge without stopping. Furthermore by 1842 passengers could board a train in Albany and ride to Buffalo without changing. The manufacturers of New England began to make cheap shoes, textiles, tools, and machine products in their factories and shipped their goods westward over the Erie Canal and the railroads. These goods forced craftsmen in the Upper Mohawk region to go out of business or to copy their rivals' new methods of production.

The census of 1845 reported that Utica had lost about 700 inhabitants or almost five percent of its population. After the heady gains of the previous two decades, this loss shocked the business and political leaders. Real-estate values were falling and many storekeepers were closing their businesses. In July 1845 the *Utica Gazette* asked why was it that "in western New York, in Cleveland, Detroit and Chicago . . . prosperity . . . is so much higher than in Utica?" Benjamin Cooper, the son of Judge Apollos Cooper,

---

Above
The Globe Woolen Mill's second complex, shown circa 1915, was located at Court and Stark streets. The original building on the site burned in 1871. Today part of the complex houses the State University College of Technology. (OHS)

Facing page
In 1845 Spencer Kellogg, Andrew Pond, and Edmund Graham were appointed to investigate the usage of industrial steam power. Their report was a catalyst in transforming Utica from a mercantile to a manufacturing city. (OHS)

REPORT

OF THE

COMMITTEE APPOINTED TO INVESTIGATE

THE RELATIVE DIFFERENCE OF THE COST OF THE

MOTIVE POWER

OF

WATER AND STEAM,

AS APPLICABLE TO

MANUFACTURING.

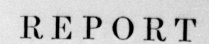

UTICA:

R. W. ROBERTS, PRINTER.

1845.

wrote several articles urging Uticans to overcome the economic crisis. Businessmen called public meetings to discuss remedies and they appointed a committee of three to determine the feasibility of utilizing steam power for manufacture. Spencer Kellogg, a leading merchant; Andrew Pond, a manufacturer of ironware; and Edmund Graham, a lawyer, railroad promoter, and philanthropist, set off for New England where they observed several factories powered by steam engines. They recommended the promotion of factories that could use coal transported over the Chenango Canal.

Efforts to organize a steam cotton mill received the full support of the local press. Because the general incorporation law limited capitalization to $100,000—a restriction not suitable to costly cotton mills with machinery—Mr. Graham had to travel to Albany to seek an exemption from the legislature. The principal backers included Alfred Munson, who had experience in making burrstones and ironware; Silas Childs, who had served as a partner in Parker's staging company; and Theodore S. Faxton.

Faxton deserves additional mention because of his many business and charitable activities. Originally a stage driver, he became a partner of Jason Parker. In 1845 Faxton promoted the telegraph company that built a line from New York City to Buffalo. He became president of the Second National Bank, mayor in 1864, and benefactor of many causes including a home for the aged and a hospital. Graham and his associates did not secure the charter until February 1848, but they immediately started construction and the plant began operations in 1850. It employed 165 hands who tended 180 looms powered by a Corliss steam engine. This company occupied the oblong block bounded by State, Columbia, and Court streets. The Chenango Canal bordered it on the west.

Meanwhile other capitalists including Andrew Pond, Nicholas Devereux, and Dolphes Skinner decided to open a woolen mill, which required less capital than a cotton mill. This mill at the southeast corner of Columbia and Schuyler streets employed about 100 workers and used a steam engine of 50 horsepower built by Utica's Vulcan Works. In 1847, a year after the Utica Steam Woolen Mill began operations, the Utica Globe Woolen Mill came into production. Investors included Theodore Faxton, Judge William Bacon, and Horatio Seymour. This enterprise ran into many difficulties and required reorganization in 1855. Robert Middleton took over the management in 1857 and turned it into a profitable business. The company occupied the block bounded by Court, Stark, and Warren streets and Sunset Avenue.

Clothing and shoe production gradually shifted from small shops in which customers ordered their own suits or shoes to factories that made ready-to-wear goods. In 1846 James Martin began to make clothing and his firm continued for many decades despite many changes of ownership. James M. Wiswell and James W. Thompson were among the first to lease sewing machines developed by various inventors to speed the process of sewing soles to the uppers of shoes. Although output rose sharply in the needle trades after 1840, only the cutting of cloth was undertaken in central shops. Here skilled workmen cut cloth and leather, after which managers distributed materials to the homes of Welsh and German immigrants for further

processing. In 1860 clothing and leather working had a combined work force of 2,332.

Oneida County was the only county west of Albany to boast of many large-scale mechanized factories prior to 1855. Large numbers of small service shops and mills remained in the towns outside Utica, employing almost one-third of the 5,392 men and women in the industrial work force. During the next 10 years this share in Utica firms rose to approximately one half. What was happening was a rapid increase in the average size of the companies in Utica employing more than 50 persons.

Although manufacturers had made important progress toward adopting steam, most mills in 1860 still relied upon waterpower. Utica's factories, however, had made a substantial breakthrough toward the modern factory system. Of the companies employing 50 or more persons, the largest were Walcott and Campbell, Palmer Kellogg and Co., J.N. Rice and Co., R.V. Yates, and Utica Steam Cotton Mills.

The foreign-born constituted a higher percentage of Utica's population during this period than at any time before or since. In 1845 some 40 percent of the residents and over 60 percent of the local heads of households had birthplaces in foreign lands. A decade later almost 43 percent were born abroad. Ireland sent the largest number (3,417), almost one in six. One in eight hailed from England,

Above
Theodore S. Faxton, always a promoter of new enterprises, made a fortune in transportation, communication, and manufacturing ventures, and gave generously of his wealth to found local institutions that still bear his name. (OHS)

Scotland, and Wales, and a similar number from the German states. If one adds the children born in this country, one finds that upward of two out of three residents had close foreign ties. In this city of immigrants one would hear Irish brogues near the locks, the lilt of Welsh voices in song, and the guttural tones of Germans in shops and stores.

The foreign-born in Whitestown and New Hartford, textile suburbs of Utica, totaled over 30 percent in 1855. Of Whitestown's population of 4,838, some 1,516 had foreign birthplaces; almost all from the British Isles. Whitestown had 495 English, 133 Scots, 451 Irish, and 256 Welsh. The composition of New Hartford's population was almost identical. A large majority of the operatives in the mills were born in Great Britain or were of British-born parents. If one deducts the Irish contingent (about nine percent) as

Above
The Utica Steam Woolen Mill opened at the corner of Columbia and Schuyler streets in 1846. Closed in 1877, it stood vacant until 1902 when it was taken over and remodelled to become the Utica Knitting Company's No. 2 Mill. This photo was taken in 1954 when the West End Brewing Company bought it as a site for their garage. Courtesy, Utica Newspapers.

Top
The original Utica Steam Cotton Mill on State Street opened in 1850. The No. 2 Mill at right was added in 1868. (OHS)

distinctive in religion and culture, one finds these two townships overwhelmingly British in origins.

High rents by absentee landlords, a rapidly expanding population, and the potato blight forced millions of Irish to leave their lovely homeland. The steady stream of Irish immigrants of the 1830s became a torrent after the mid-1840s, when blight destroyed the potato crop year after year. Captains crammed hundreds into sailing vessels bound for the North Atlantic ports. Although most remained in New York, Boston, and Philadelphia, several thousand followed the transportation routes to the interior. Utica attracted a large number because of the abundance of construction jobs (canals, railroads, factories and houses). "Colleens" could also find work in the mansions on Broad, John, and Genesee streets. Many Irish settled in the fifth ward where they could attend St. John's Roman Catholic Church. Hundreds rented flats and rooms in West Utica near the canals and textile mills. On St. Patrick's Day, 1850, the bishop directed the Reverend Patrick Carraher to organize a new parish in honor of their patron saint. Within a few years the faithful had contributed funds for a large

Above
This circa 1854 ambrotype of the east side of Genesee Street north of Bleecker Street may be the oldest existing photograph of a Utica scene. Courtesy, Broome County Historical Society, Binghamton.

brick building and school on the corner of Columbia and Huntington streets.

The Irish gravitated to the Democratic party, which had welcomed immigrants since the 1790s. No doubt the election of John C. Devereux as mayor in 1840 encouraged other Irishmen to enter politics. Every year Devereux on St. Patrick's Day wore a green sash and shamrock in the parade. The Irish did not forget their homeland, and many joined clubs that called for an independent Ireland.

The well-established Welsh community was large enough to support four churches, several societies, and publications. By mid-century Bethesda Congregational and the Calvinistic Methodist (Presbyterian) churches had over 200 members as well as large Sunday Schools. The Welsh Baptist church was losing membership because of bickering and the defection of young people to English-speaking

churches. Welsh Methodists arrived in sufficient numbers to organize Coke Memorial in 1849. This congregation met on Washington Street until 1886 when it moved to its new brick structure on the corner of Hopper and Union.

In Wales the ancient *eisteddfod* (literally, "session") was revived in the early 19th century and evolved into its modern pattern of literary and singing competitions. The first *eisteddfod* in Utica was held in 1856 and for the next century choruses vied in singing Handel or Bach and individuals competed for prizes for poems, recitations, and solos. In 1861 *Y Drych* (The Mirror) moved from New York City to Utica, its home for the next century. Meanwhile Evan Roberts, Thomas J. Griffiths, and other printers published hymnbooks, tracts, and religious journals that made Utica the center of Welsh-American cultural activity. The Presbyterians established *Y Cyfaill* (The Friend) in

Facing page, bottom
The program for the 1940 Utica eisteddfod *reflects the continuing tradition of Utica's Welsh residents. (OHS)*

Above
The City Hall at Genesee and Pearl streets was designed by Richard Upjohn and completed in 1853. The county clerk's office moved from Whitesboro Street to the small building at left in 1848. (OHS)

1857 and this journal continued until 1933.

A sampling of names in the *Utica City Directory* for 1865 shows that two-thirds of the Welsh lived west of Genesee Street in the old flats near the canals. But a considerable number were buying homes on Corn Hill, which in the next half century became the center of Welsh community. Over a third of the men listed themselves as craftsmen and their skill as stonecutters was prized. Girls and widows worked as domestics; some housewives did work for clothing manufacturers. Strongly evangelical in religion, the Welsh favored the temperance movement, opposed the expansion of slavery, and joined the Republican party. They blended in well with the old Yankee-Yorker stock, which regarded them as natural allies against the tremendous influx of Irish and Germans who tended to be "wet," Roman Catholic, and Democratic.

Although English immigrants outnumbered the Welsh by a considerable margin, they left relatively few traces on the institutional life of the city. One historian of immigration has called them the "invisible immigrants." Many English families took up residence in the second ward close to the textile mills. English men and women had worked in the Lancashire mills, and supervisors, often English or Scots, employed them readily. The Odd Fellows, a social organization imported from England, enrolled many immigrants but also attracted native Americans. During the 1840s this fraternal association spread rapidly in Utica.

In Germany people repeated Goethe's famous line: "Amerika Du Hast Es Besser" (America you have it better). Millions of disgruntled craftsmen and peasants decided to seek a new life in America and several thousand landed in Utica. The Germans not only brought skills as bakers, carpenters, tailors, and cobblers but also introduced the art of brewing beer, and gradually they came to dominate the brewing business. Bierbauer's brewery, later absorbed by Matt's West End Brewing Company, enlisted a loyal following. Most Germans settled in West Utica but after 1850 several hundred drifted to Corn Hill and East Utica.

A majority came from Bavaria and the Rhineland, strong centers of Roman Catholicism. In 1842 a small group of German Catholics founded St. Joseph's Church, which in 1852 built a large sanctuary with a school. Germans in East Utica in 1870 founded St. Mary's Church on South Street. Lutherans also settled in Utica in much the same districts as the Roman Catholics. The Reverend Andrew Wetzel held services in various homes as early as 1832 but he had to wait until 1842 to found Zion Evangelical Lutheran Church. After a fire destroyed its first quarters, the congregation moved to a new building on the corner of Cooper and Fay. When some members moved to Corn Hill, Zion sponsored a mission on South Street which became St. Paul's in 1860. Pastor Wetzel was the first to introduce the

Above
Founded in 1882, the Utica Turn Verein or Turner Society was a local branch of a German organization devoted to physical and intellectual culture. This ladies' class, photographed about 1919, was directed by Fritz Nicke, standing in rear. (OHS)

A small contingent of Jews settled in Utica after 1847. Most came from Poland, which was under the control of Russia. A majority were young men who carried packs on their backs as they displayed their wares to farm housewives. Some bought a horse and buggy, added more items, and extended their rounds. Soon several Jews had opened small shops and stores on Whitesboro Street, which retained a Jewish flavor until World War I.

Utica's Jews remained loyal to the Orthodox tradition for many decades. In 1848 a *minyan* (quorum) began to meet. Led by chairman Harris A. Hershfield, they organized Beth Israel, a congregation of about 20 families. This group soon gave way to another synagogue, Adas Jeshurum. Jews founded a Hebrew School as early as 1850 and in a few years bought their first cemetery.

The Jewish community suffered from its transient constituency, a characteristic that affected all groups, native or foreign-born. In the late 1860s another wave of Jews from western Russia came to Utica and in 1870 they founded Congregation House of Jacob, the first permanent synagogue in Utica.

The influx of immigrants to Utica tended to upset some members of the old native stock, who feared the growing strength of "Popery." Whigs and Republicans disliked the additions to Democratic voting power by the Irish and Germans. As a result a nativist feeling swept across the Northeast with thousands joining the Native American Party. In 1856 this party, sometimes known as the Know-Nothings, won a plurality in the state and carried many counties. The citizens of Oneida County and Utica, however, showed slight interest in the nativist movement and only a tenth of them voted for nativists, a percentage among the lowest in the state. Apparently these citizens were more receptive to newcomers than were most voters in the Empire State.

In 1850 Utica had 190 blacks out of the county's non-white population of 672. Utica's Negroes did not receive

Christmas tree at a Sunday School celebration. The Moravians, a denomination of German background, arrived in Utica in this period and in 1856 they built their church on the corner of Cornelia and Cooper.

The German community established clubs, athletic associations, and singing societies. Perhaps the most famous was the Maennerchor, founded in 1865 and still an important center of German-American life. The Germans also felt the need of a newspaper to keep track of events in Europe and America and to voice their opinions. In 1853 a group founded the *Central New York Demokrat,* which underwent several changes before it became the *Utica Deutsche Zeitung and Oneida Demokrat* in 1865.

Above
The Modern Hebrew School operated in 1912-1913 in an old house on the southeast corner of Whitesboro and Seneca streets, in the days when the triangle between Genesee, Liberty, and Whitesboro streets was the "Jewish quarter." Led by Rabbi Louis J. Haas, the school offered courses in Jewish history and culture in English, a radical experiment at the time. Courtesy, Utica Public Library.

Above
Designed by noted architect Alexander Jackson Davis, this house was built for banker John Munn in 1857. During the Civil War, when Remington Arms of Ilion had a factory in Utica, it was occupied by Samuel Remington. It was later the home of the Walter Jerome Green family. Courtesy, Architectural Archive, Munson-Williams-Proctor Institute.

equal treatment in jobs, public accommodations, and in social life. In 1834 Alexander Bryan Johnson described a Negro's situation as follows: "He cannot enter a church, a canal boat, a tavern, a steamboat . . . he is practically excluded from every post of honor and profit which usually stimulate other men to virtue and industry.'' There were, however, a minority of Uticans who fought for abolition of slavery and treated their servants kindly. In 1863 Philemon H. Fowler, pastor of the First Presbyterian Church, appealed to influential citizens to aid the Negro population. Theodore Faxton, Judge William Bacon, and James Sayre led a drive to build Hope Chapel on Elizabeth Street.

Youthfulness continued to characterize Utica's population. Almost half of the residents of Utica and Whitestown in 1855 were minors. Only 31 percent of Uticans had reached the advanced age of 30, but Whitestown had a somewhat higher percentage of people over 30. Foreign-born women bore on an average two more children than native women who averaged a little over three children.

The managers of the mills drew most of their workers from the ranks of the foreign-born. A majority of native-born men and women held positions within the middle class—artisans, shopkeepers, professionals, or white-collar workers. Only one in eight was listed as unskilled or factory laborer. The sons of shopkeepers and artisans often shifted

Top
John Butterfield built this house just south of today's Parkway in 1865-1866. His 300-acre estate stretched from Genesee Street to Oneida Street. (OHS)

Above
John Butterfield (1801-1869) came to Utica as a young man and worked for Jason Parker as a stagecoach driver. In addition to farming, promoting railroads and the telegraph, and developing real estate, he established the Butterfield Overland Mail. He served as mayor of Utica in 1865. (OHS)

"High-Handed Outrage at Utica" by Artemus Ward

At the beginning of a Cabinet meeting Abraham Lincoln read to his colleagues a sketch written by Artemus Ward, a leading humorist of the "By Gosh" school of writers. While Secretary of War Edwin Stanton fidgeted and Secretary of State William Seward inwardly fumed, Lincoln read "High-Handed Outrage at Utica."

In the Faul of 1856, I showed my show in Utiky, a trooly grate sitty in the State of New York.

The people gave me a cordyal recepshun. The press was loud in her prases.

1 day as I was givin a descripshun of my Beests and Snaiks in my usual flowry stile what was my skorn & disgust to see a big burly feller walk up to the cage containin my wax figgers of the Lord's Last Supper, and cease Judas Iscarrot by the feet and drag him out on the ground. He then commenced fur to pound him as hard as he cood.

"What under the son are you abowt?" cried I.

Sez he, "What did you bring this pussylanermus cuss here fur?" & he hit wax figger another tremenjis blow on the hed.

Sez I, "You egrejus ass, that air's a wax figger—a representashun of the false 'Postle."

Sez he, "That's all very well fur you to say, but I tell you, old man, that Judas Iscarrot can't show hisself in Utiky with impunerty by a darn site!"

with which observashun he kaved in Judassis hed. The young man belonged to 1 of the first famerlies in Utiky. I sood him, and the Joory brawt in a verdick of Arson in the 3d degree.

---

to professional and white-collar work. The daughters of the natives took jobs outside the home more frequently than the daughters of immigrants. Native women were also eager to increase the family income by taking in boarders.

Citizens of Utica and Oneida County normally voted for the Whigs and Republicans during this period. When Horatio Seymour ran for mayor, assemblyman, and governor, his neighbors rallied to his banner. The emergence of Seymour and Roscoe Conkling as state and national leaders was the most important development in politics.

Seymour inherited status and wealth from his father, Henry, who served as mayor in 1833. The young Horatio received the post of military secretary to Governor William Marcy, and in Albany he courted Mary Bleecker, whose grandfather had owned over 5,000 acres of Cosby's Manor. Their marriage brought him additional land as well as powerful political connections. Dignified and conciliatory, Seymour belonged to the conservative or Hunker branch of the Democratic party. He regarded antislavery advocates as troublemakers and a threat to the union. Nevertheless as mayor, Seymour defended the right of abolitionists to speak in Utica.

Seymour first ran for governor in 1850 but lost by a narrow margin. Two years later, however, he won and promptly pushed for more state funding for canal enlargement. He opposed a bill imposing prohibition of alcoholic beverages, a veto which brought on his shoulders a torrent of abuse. When he sought reelection, he lost by a scant 300 votes. He returned to private life but in 1862 he won the governorship again. Highly critical of Lincoln's coercion of the South and the draft, Seymour sent in troops to quell the draft rioters in New York City in July 1863.

Conkling rose to national prominence in the Whig and Republican parties. A forceful orator and a handsome figure, Conkling attracted a devoted following but also made many enemies by his sarcasm and arrogance. Although Seymour opposed his suit, Conkling won the hand of Julia Seymour, Horatio's sister. Conkling, elected mayor in 1858, won a seat in Congress in 1859. After two terms, however, he lost to Francis Kernan, a Democrat who later became United States Senator.

Abraham Lincoln in 1860 carried Utica and Oneida County. His supporters, the "Wide Awakes," paraded in uniforms with blue capes and blue caps. Calling themselves the "Little Giants" in honor of Stephen Douglas, ardent Democrats sported red attire and headdress. As the winter advanced, reports that secession was sweeping the Deep South disturbed Uticans. The overwhelming majority, preoccupied with private concerns, the shaky economy, and political turmoil, had little use for "troublemakers" such as abolitionists. When Beriah Green announced that Elizabeth Cady Stanton, Susan B. Anthony, and Samuel May would stage a rally on January 14 and 15, editors and politicians denounced the proposal. The common council in special session ordered a ban on the meeting and apparently few citizens objected to this violation of civil liberties. A large throng of citizens on February 18 greeted Lincoln who offered a few pleasantries from the rear platform of his eastbound train.

The attack on Fort Sumter aroused a surge of patriotic fervor and unity. When Lincoln called for 75,000 volunteers, the public responded with enthusiasm. Captain William Christian organized a battalion of four companies and hundreds enlisted. Every volunteer received a bounty of $100 for a three-year enlistment. On April 17 the Utica Citizens Corps, a unit formed in 1808 and always present on public occasions, announced its readiness to serve for two years. Led by Captain James McQuade, the corps soon left for Albany where it became the nucleus for the Fourteenth New York Volunteer Infantry, commonly called the First Oneida. This regiment took part in action in the summer of 1861 and later served at Fredericksburg and Chancellorsville. Many of its members reenlisted in May 1863 when it was mustered out. This corps provided 61 officers including 14 generals. Among the major generals were Daniel Butterfield, Charles A. Johnson, H.S. Bradley, John W. Fuller, James McQuade, and J.J. Bartlett. Three other regiments—the 97th, 117th, and 146th—were organized in Oneida County.

Major General Butterfield composed the bugle call used at military posts and known as "Taps." After the battle of Gaines' Mill, Butterfield became dissatisfied with the bugle call to "Extinguish Lights." A haunting melody

Top left
Hundreds of Uticans stood in the rain the evening of April 26, 1865, waiting for President Lincoln's funeral train, which stopped at the old New York Central station about 8:15. The Utica Brass Band played "The Dead March from Saul" and the newly organized Utica Maennerchor offered appropriate choral selections. At 8:35 the train eased quietly away to continue its long, sad journey to Illinois. (OHS)

Top right
General Daniel A. Butterfield, son of John Butterfield, was wounded at Gaines Mills, Virginia, and received the Congressional Medal of Honor for gallantry in action. He was wounded again at Gettysburg, where he was chief of staff of the Army of the Potomac. Following a distinguished career in business and government services, he was buried at West Point beneath an elaborate marble monument. (OHS)

came to his mind and he had an aide jot down the notes. With the help of his bugler, Oliver Norton, Butterfield polished his sad refrain, which is today played throughout the world.

The roll of Civil War dead in every village and city of the Upper Mohawk is by far the longest of any of our wars. In fact 19 of the 26 towns and cities in the county lost population between 1860 and 1865 largely due to the enlistment of thousands in the army, many of whom never returned even if they survived camp fever and battle death. It is estimated that over 700 died in service. We have a fine record of an average soldier in *Back Home in Oneida: Hermon Clarke and His Letters,* edited by Harry F. Jackson and Thomas F. O'Donnell. His letters reveal how a Waterville youth became a mature young man during the tedium of camp life and the fury of battle. The home front was also the scene of much sacrifice and dedicated service. Public-spirited citizens collected funds to aid needy families, especially those of recruits. The sharp increase in prices caused a decline in the standard of living for most citizens although some businessmen reaped great profits. In 1861 the banks had to stop payment of specie and the scarcity of hard money caused great inconvenience. Some companies and the city of Utica issued "shinplasters" or paper notes to meet the need. Unfortunately unscrupulous individuals began to print bogus notes, creating confusion and distress.

The shortage of cotton caused the cotton mills to run on short time, but the woolen mills ran full speed because of government orders for blankets, uniforms, and clothing. The clothing firm of Palmer V. Kellogg on Hotel Street was flooded with orders. It hired 65 men to hack and cut the cloth, after which it was sent out to housewives for sewing.

The government also needed more shoes, and several firms in Utica, notably that of James M. Wiswell, filled many orders. Hardly had the first shots been fired when Secretary of War Edwin Stanton ordered another 5,000 rifles from the firm of Eliphalet Remington of Ilion, whose guns enjoyed a fine reputation for accuracy. Remington opened a plant on Franklin Street in Utica, and employed 150 men and 35 boys. In 1865, however, the war came to an end and all contracts were cancelled. Remington closed his plant and moved the machinery back to Ilion.

In spite of grim news from the front, many residents still sought diversion and entertainment. In 1863 a thousand people came to City Hall to see the first stereopticon show, and in the same year the State Fair was held in Utica. Mechanics Hall staged concerts, lectures, minstrel shows, and other forms of entertainment. The Holman family gave lantern slides and concerts. Billy Birch, a native of Utica, toured the country with his minstrel show and was always popular in Utica. The most famous event was the concert by Ole Bull in 1864. The Norwegian violinist received almost as warm a welcome as Jenny Lind had in 1851.

Shocks of seismic proportions buffeted Utica's economy, politics, and society in this period. The rapid development of textile mills bolstered the sagging economy and reversed the drop in population. A tidal wave of Irish, Germans, English, and Welsh swamped the community and challenged Yankee-Yorker supremacy. The intensifying struggle over slavery inflamed political debate, divided Democrats, destroyed the Whig party, and created the Republican party. But when the Confederates fired on "Old Glory" at Fort Sumter, citizens and aliens alike marched off to defend the Union.

Facing page, bottom
The Civil War draft for the City of Utica was held at Mechanics Hall on August 28, 1863. With a detail of soldiers on hand to keep order, names were drawn from a box by Albert West, a blind man who was nevertheless blindfolded for good measure. There was no violent resistance to the draft, although a broadside was printed on October 24 listing the names of 68 men who had failed to report for duty. Utica's quota was 594 men. (OHS)

Above
Prior to the establishment of Syracuse as the site for the New York State Fair, the fair was held in different cities throughout the state. Utica hosted the New York State Fair for the first time in 1845 on grounds just west of Oneida Square, then on the outskirts of the city. A new fairground was opened for the 1852 state fair. Shown here in 1863, it extended east from Genesee Street to Oneida in the area of today's Grand Union Shopping Plaza and Holland Avenue. (OHS)

CHAPTER FIVE

NURSERY
FOR
POLITICAL
LEADERS
1865-1895

During the last third of the 19th century Uticans and residents of the Upper Mohawk region won high places in state and national politics. Horatio Seymour, who had served two terms as governor, won the Democratic nomination for President in 1868. Unfortunately for Seymour he was running against Ulysses S. Grant, who capitalized on his career as Civil War hero. Interestingly enough, Grant leaned heavily upon another Utican, Roscoe Conkling, for political advice. Opposing Conkling were the followers of James G. Blaine, who infuriated Conkling by attacking him for his "grandiloquent swell" and "turkey-gobbler strut." In 1881 Conkling resigned his Senate seat because President James Garfield stripped him of control over New York patronage. Conkling expected reelection by the state legislature but his enemies, led by Blaine's allies, rejected him.

Did Conkling take revenge in 1884 when Blaine ran for President? Oneida County normally voted Republican but in that year Cleveland won a bare majority of its votes. Since Blaine lost the state by only 1,149 votes, his allies charged that Conkling and his "Unconditionals" had knifed his foe. Of course other factors played their part.

Cleveland, who had spent his boyhood in Holland Patent and Clinton, had many friends in Oneida County. Furthermore Blaine had failed to repudiate the speech of Dr. Samuel Burchard, whose slur on Catholicism offended Irish-Americans. Political analysts up and down the country, however, speculated on the role of Conkling and Oneida County in defeating Blaine.

The Upper Mohawk region produced other political leaders who exercised much "clout" on the state and national scene. Francis Kernan of Utica, a prominent figure in Democratic circles, served as United States Senator between 1875 and 1881. James S. Sherman, Utica's mayor in 1884, held the local congressional seat from 1886 to 1908, except for a two-year interlude. "Sunny Jim" worked his way into the upper echelons of the Republican party, which rewarded him in 1908 with the nomination for Vice President. Sherman presided over the Senate with skill and affability.

Probably the outstanding figure to grow up in Oneida County during this period was Elihu Root, whose father and brother, teachers of mathematics at Hamilton College, were known by students as "Square" and "Cube." Root

became a leading lawyer in Manhattan where corporations paid high fees for his legal acumen. Root, however, kept close ties with his birthplace and spent most of his summers in Clinton. President William McKinley appointed Root Secretary of War, in which position he reformed the army, set up the Army War College, and organized the General Staff. President Roosevelt made Root his Secretary of State from 1905 to 1909. Root won the Nobel Peace Prize in 1912 for his efforts to create an international organization for arbitration.

No other region of comparable population in that period produced so many political leaders of prominence.

Above
James S. Sherman (on platform) was officially notified of his nomination to the vice presidency in 1908 in ceremonies at his home on the east side of Genesee Street between Clinton Place and Jewett Place. The "Sherman Notification Days" in both 1908 and 1912 were among the largest celebrations ever held in Utica. (OHS)

On the whole they made constructive contributions and carried Utica's name throughout the nation.

Utica and the Upper Mohawk region provided the backdrop for several authors, some of whose works attracted national attention. A century after Alexander Bryan Johnson's death in 1867, more than a score of scholars from Europe, Canada, and the United States met in a conference in Utica to honor his contributions as a philosopher, semanticist, and economist.

The output of novels, essays, sketches, and poems by Oneida County women reached impressive numbers. A listing for the Columbian Exposition of 1893 recorded over 140 "notable" women authors in this county, a figure that includes several with considerable talent. Frances Miriam Berry, who married an Episcopal minister, Benjamin W. Whitcher, began to publish satirical sketches of her neighbors in Whitesboro. When they appeared as *The Widow Bedott Papers* in 1855, the public bought the book by the tens of thousands until the end of the century. Emily Chubbuck, a teacher at the Utica Female Academy, submitted light fiction to the *Mother's Magazine,* a local periodical. A chronicler of village life, Chubbuck became

A LEGITIMATE QUESTION ABOUT HOME RULE

U.S. Republic. "To whom do you owe your first allegiance?" Hon. F. Kernan (from New York[!]). "This is a very embarrassing position to be placed in."

Top
This natty group was the Jacksonians, Utica's Democratic marching club, organized in 1894. Like their Republican counterparts, the Conkling Unconditionals, they were organized to add life, color, and noise to political campaigns. Marching down Genesee Street with their ragtag escort of small boys, they were probably on their way to the railroad station to entrain for a rally in some neighboring town. (OHS)

Above
Francis Kernan (1816-1892) served in the United States Senate in a period when few American Roman Catholics held high public office. This cartoon expresses the suspicions that some Americans felt concerning the loyalties of Roman Catholics, particularly after the proclamation of the doctrine of papal infallibility in 1870. (OHS)

one of the most popular American authors in the 1850s. In the next decade Mary Clemner Ames, a full-time authoress, made a good living writing newspaper columns and best-selling novels. Grover Cleveland's youngest sister, Rose Elizabeth, lived in Holland Patent and wrote literary criticism, a novel, and children's books.

Harold Frederic, the only local author who achieved international recognition, was born on South Street in 1856. He became a reporter, and by the age of 24 editor of the *Utica Observer.* Local traditions and neighbors' activities— draftdodging in the Civil War, Irish-American picnics, the Battle of Oriskany—sank deeply into his consciousness and provided material for his stories and novels. An admirer of Horatio Seymour, Frederic became a close friend of Governor Grover Cleveland. After serving as editor of the *Albany Journal,* he became European correspondent of the *New York Times* between 1884 and 1898. London literary circles accepted him as a jovial companion and a writer of distinction. His novel, *In the Valley,* contains a graphic description of the Battle of Oriskany. *The Damnation of Theron Ware,* his outstanding novel, depicts the drudgery of rural life and the impact of Darwinism upon a Methodist minister who came to live in Utica. Students of literature have written scores of articles and several books on Frederic's significance.

The Utica *Saturday Globe* was founded in 1881 by William T. and Thomas F. Baker. An early illustrated newspaper, the *Globe* quickly attracted readers and by 1886 occupied its commodious quarters on Whitesboro Street. In 1891 its circulation averaged 165,354 copies. This paper published scores of local editions in all parts of the nation. By 1896 it installed a rotary press for halftones, anticipating the Pulitzer and Hearst press.

One should also note the *American Journal of Insanity,* the first journal (1844) in any language on that subject. The founder, Dr. Amariah Brigham, was the superintendent of the New York State Lunatic Asylum. After Brigham's death Dr. John P. Gray edited the journal for 30 years. Copies of this journal circulated in all parts of the world.

Many Uticans attended the theater and most of the great actors and actresses of the period performed on the local stage. In 1891 the Lafayette Street hall of the Mechanics' Association was renovated and renamed the Utica Opera House. Considering the fact that 1894 was a depression year, its entertainment fare was impressive. Audiences could see *Lady Windermere's Fan, Macbeth* with Modjeska and Otis Skinner, *Faust, Dr. Jekyll and Mr. Hyde* with Richard Mansfield, or *Rip Van Winkle* with Joseph Jefferson. Those with somewhat less formal tastes could listen to Cleveland's Minstrels, watch Hermann the Magician, or view Sandow, the strong man. Spellbinders such as William Jennings Bryan, Robert Ingersoll, and Theodore Roosevelt spoke to packed audiences in the Opera

House. The great days of the Opera House came to an end in 1899 when Charles Frohman declared that he would no longer allow his actors to appear in such a dirty firetrap. His description was accurate.

After stillness came to Appomattox, Utica resumed its steady growth, although the depression years of the 1870s slowed immigration. The pace of growth then quickened for the rest of the century with population increases exceeding 24 percent in each decade. Although Utica doubled its population between 1865 and 1900, the rest of the county showed no gain. Villages lost population because their water-driven mills could not compete with cheap products made in factories. Many farmers abandoned their holdings because cheap butter and cheese from Wisconsin were undercutting marginal producers. The bright lights of Utica and other cities lured farm youth who disliked back-breaking labor and low returns.

The population structure remained basically the same as late as 1890. In that year the foreign-born population in Utica numbered 11,767, approximately one-fourth of the total of 44,007. The Irish, the largest group between 1850 and 1870, had yielded first place to the Germans. Meanwhile the British (English, Scots, Welsh, English Canadians) climbed above the Irish figure.

Roughly two out of three Uticans (29,452) belonged to what is called "foreign stock," that is immigrants and their children. The major elements in 1890 were as follows: German (8,831), Irish (7,201), Welsh (2,334), English (2,188). Because many immigrants came as young couples, their birthrate continued to exceed that of the native stock.

The census recorded 58 Poles, but most of these newcomers and also the 307 from Russia were probably Jewish. The Tsarist government had in 1881 begun its bloody pogroms, setting in motion a massive migration. In the 1880s Jews organized more synagogues (mostly short-lived), fraternal, and social organizations.

The emergence of the Italian colony of 709 is perhaps the most significant development. To be sure Dr. John B. Marchisi had settled in Utica in 1815 and opened an apothecary shop, but only a handful of Italians found their way to Utica before 1880. When the contractors were building the West Shore Railroad in 1883-1884, they imported many laborers from Italy who later found work in the mills, brickyards, and in construction. In 1895 a group of laymen met with Bishop Patrick Ludden to organize a new Roman Catholic parish. Michael Kernan and his wife Cecelia Rapetti Kernan helped lead the campaign to raise money. At first the people had to worship in the basement of the church but by 1901 work on the main structure of St. Mary of Mount Carmel had begun.

A vanguard of Poles organized the Benevolent Society of St. Stanislaus in 1889 and formulated plans for a church. In 1896 they bought a house and lot on Lincoln Avenue,

Facing page, bottom left
This picture of Horatio Seymour (1810-1886) is one of a series taken at his home in Deerfield for the 1868 presidential campaign. The telescope reflected his interest in natural science. Courtesy, Library of Congress.

Facing page, bottom center
Senator Roscoe Conkling (1829-1888) was an able attorney, a flamboyant, sometimes sarcastic orator, and a shrewd political power broker. Happiest amid the action of the United States Senate, he spent little time at his home in Rutger Park and refused appointment to the United States Supreme Court. He died in New York City of complications from a cold caught during the Blizzard of '88. (OHS)

which became the nucleus for Holy Trinity Church. More Poles, chiefly from New England cities, came to work in the foundries and knitting mills. Their contributions enabled the parish to construct a Gothic building that was dedicated in 1899. Membership grew so rapidly that by 1910 the parish replaced it with the present impressive structure. The Polish people formed many societies and clubs for cultural as well as entertainment purposes.

Meanwhile German Catholics in East Utica formed St. Mary's of the Immaculate Conception in 1870. Almost immediately this church on South Street organized a parochial school and established a cemetery. The Irish were also moving southward into the area of Corn Hill. In 1877 St. John's sponsored a new parish, which by 1888 had completed a large church on the corner of Eagle and Summit Place and took the name of St. Francis De Sales Church. Enough Irish settled in East Utica to justify the establishment of a new parish that would include all the area east of Mohawk Street. On Christmas Day 1887 the first Mass was celebrated in the basement of St. Agnes Church on the corner of Blandina and Kossuth Avenue.

The movement of people to the outskirts also inspired Protestants to follow their members. The Welsh Presbyterians moved from Seneca Street to Park Avenue and Dakin Street and constructed Moriah Church by 1882. Westminster Church started a mission on Howard Avenue in 1876, which 10 years later became Olivet Church. Another Westminster mission on Albany Street in East Utica became Bethany Church in 1869. First Presbyterian

established a Sunday School in West Utica and this mission became Sayre Memorial Church.

Episcopalians also responded to the needs of people drifting to the outskirts. As early as 1850 Calvary Church had received a charter and its parishioners worshiped on South Street. Its stone church on the corner of Howard Avenue and South Street was erected between 1868 and 1872. Episcopalians, especially some from England, favored the "high church" movement and in 1862 they organized St. George's Church on State Street. Grace Church encouraged three missions in various parts of the city. In 1869 it opened its mission in West Utica which eventually became St. Luke's Church. To the east its mission developed into the Memorial Church of the Holy Cross, and to the south it assisted a group which in 1891 became St. Andrew's on Faxton Street. Meanwhile old Trinity on Broad Street was losing membership because the neighborhood had become largely industrial and commercial. Its members in 1922 joined up with St. Andrew's which thereupon took the name

Above
Downtown streets at the turn of the century were filled with trolley cars, horses, wagons, bicycles, and pedestrians, all vying for space without benefit of traffic lights. This is Genesee Street just north of the Busy Corner. (OHS)

TIME TABLE

OF THE

Globe Woolen Company.

Arranged to make the Working Time throughout the Year 11 Hours per Day.

Commence Work at 6 :30 A. M.   Leave off Work at 6:30 P. M.

Saturday Evenings at 5 P. M.

Dinner at 12 M.   Commence Work after Dinner at 12 : 45 P. M.

BELLS.

Morning Bells.	Dinner Bells.	Evening Bells.
First Bell, 5:00 A. M.	Ring out, 12:00 M.	Ring out, 6:30 P. M.
Second Bell, 6:00 A. M.	Ring in, 12:35 P. M.	Saturday, 5:00 P. M.
Third Bell, 6:20 A. M.		

Three taps of the Bell will be given as a signal for Starting the Engine, and three minutes thereafter the Yard Gates will be closed ; and it is expected that every employee will be ready to begin work at precisely 6:30 A. M., and 12:45 P. M.

By Order of the Board of Directors,

ROBERT MIDDLETON, President.

UTICA, May 1st, 1876.

Speed will be checked Three Minutes before time to leave the rooms at noon and night but no person will be permitted to leave the Room they are at work in until the Shafting comes to a dead stand, which will be precisely at 12 M. and 6.30 P. M.   **R. M. Pres.**

Above
The work days in the early textile mills were long and closely regulated. One large steam engine drove all of the mill's machinery through a system of line shafts, pulleys, and leather belts, and the workers' comings and goings were governed by the operation of the engine. Courtesy, Utica Public Library.

of Trinity.

The First Baptist found that many of its young people could not speak Welsh, so in 1885 it merged into Tabernacle Church. The Second Baptist (later Tabernacle) moved in 1865 from Broad Street to its present site on Hopper. Meanwhile a Baptist offshoot in 1847 bought the building of the defunct Second Presbyterian Church on Bleecker Street, where it held services until 1888. Following the pattern of several other churches, it moved uptown to the corner of Rutger and West streets and took the name of Park Baptist. In 1930 it disbanded and its members joined Tabernacle. Meanwhile Tabernacle in 1889 sponsored a mission in East Utica, which became Immanuel Baptist on Eagle Street. Four years later Baptists in West Utica organized Calvary Baptist Church.

The First Congregational Church (Welsh) moved in 1872 to a new brick structure on upper Washington Street. It took the name Bethesda. Shortly thereafter, in 1883, a group of Congregationalists, including some young people from Bethesda, organized Plymouth Church. This fellowship constructed a small chapel on the corner of Plant and State streets. In 1905 it employed Frederick H. Gouge to design the present structure.

German immigration led to the formation of more Lutheran churches, which like the Welsh churches had to cope with the language issue. Should they adopt English in order to hold the young people? And how soon? Zion Lutheran in the old German neighborhood of West Utica did not introduce English until 1921. On the other hand St. Paul's on South Street, where the neighborhood included many non-Germans, introduced one English service a month in 1885, a concession doubled within five years. Meanwhile John C. Hieber in 1877 called together Lutherans who wanted church services in English. They formed the Evangelical Lutheran Church of the Redeemer, which opened its building in 1884 on Columbia Street. Because some Moravians had moved to East Utica, the First Moravian Church opened a mission on South Street opposite Leeds, which in 1913 took the name of Trinity.

Many immigrants worked in textile mills, whose directors and managers were drawn from the ranks of old merchant and professional families. The success of textiles led Utica's entrepreneurs and capitalists to found many businesses. Several industries sprang up, flourished for a time, and faded away. Utica had no special resource as Scranton had in coal, or invention, as Rochester had in cameras. It scrambled for its share of light or consumer industries—shoes, clothing, textiles—but other cities were making the same products.

Shoe manufacturing flourished for several decades and by 1890 employed well over 1,000 workers. Thompson and Cloyes took over the Wiswell firm and several other companies also made shoes. The Hurd Shoe Company is a descendant of one of these early firms. In the 1890s, strikes by the Knights of Labor and the grinding depression ruined several companies and caused others to leave Utica.

Clothing factories employed thousands, especially immigrants. The Martin firm passed through several changes until it emerged as Roberts, Butler & Company, which employed about 800 workers. Crouse and Brandegee, later Kincaid and Kimball, made clothing sold throughout the nation. Several other firms—H.H. Cooper and Company, Roberts, Wicks & Company—made ready-to-wear clothing until well into the 20th century. In 1884 the Mohawk Valley Cap Factory had 250 hands.

Utica had a fair number of foundries and manufacturing plants making tools and machinery. Charles Millar opened his business in 1861, concentrating first on dairy apparatus, which local farmers needed. Later he added the manufacture of lead pipes, another product useful in the rapidly growing cities. In West Utica the Foster Brothers Manufacturing Company made spring beds for both the local and regional market.

Textiles continued to expand and prosper. In 1882 a group formed the Skenandoa Cotton Company on Broad Street for the purpose of making cotton yarn. Subsequently it was remodeled to make rayon. Its list of employees hovered around 500. The owners of the Utica Steam Cotton Mills in 1880 decided to build a mill on Broad Street to make sheetings. Soon people throughout the nation knew of Utica Sheets, a trade name famous for quality for decades. Ironically Utica Sheets have been made in the Carolinas for the last 30 years.

Knit goods, a branch of the textile industry, also made Utica famous. During the Civil War S.S. and J.L. Lowery

had begun to make knitted stockings for the army. Their firm prospered but then failed in 1886. Within five years Quentin McAdam and his associates reorganized the company, acquired the mill, and erected another factory on Erie Street. Utica Knit expanded its operations to Clayville, Oriskany Falls, Sherburne, and eventually Alabama. Meanwhile Charles Stewart started another knitting mill, which gradually expanded its operations, especially after Nicholas E. Devereux Jr. became a partner in 1874. The Oneita Knitting Mills employed about 440 operatives in its Broad Street factory. Andrew Frey, who ran the mill as superintendent, developed the union suit, a one-piece undergarment. Utica Bodyguard became another name known throughout the colder regions of the United States. The success of the Oneita and Utica Knitting companies spurred dozens of individuals to enter the business, especially after the economic recovery of the late 1890s.

The railroads dominated all other forms of transport. The New York Central built huge freight yards in Utica and its four tracks carried freight and passenger trains day and night. The Black River & Utica reorganized, pushed northward, and reached Ogdensburg by 1878. Soon its rival, the Watertown & Rome acquired control—only to be absorbed into the New York Central in 1891. In 1892 Dr. William Seward Webb, a Vanderbilt by marriage, built the Mohawk and Malone Railway from Herkimer to Malone,

where it made connections with a line to Montreal. Manhattan businessmen built elegant camps in the western Adirondacks because they could join their families on weekends by taking a sleeping car to Utica, where it would then be attached to trains heading for Thendara, Raquette Lake, and Lake Placid.

Promoters of railroads also aimed to reach the Pennsylvania coal fields. Hardly had the Utica, Chenango, & Susquehanna Valley been completed with the assistance of a half-million dollar loan from Utica when the Delaware,

Top
Southbound trains of the Utica, Chenango, & Susquehanna Valley Railroad approached the Erie Canal (now Oriskany Boulevard West) on a long wooden trestle and crossed on a bridge that could swing open to allow canal boats to pass. This photo was taken about 1872. (OHS)

Above
During Utica's heyday as a cheese marketing center, cheese brokers conducted their business at Bagg's Hotel. (OHS)

Above
Utica produced several champion bicyclists during the late 1880s and
early 1890s. Among them were Frank Jenny (back right) and Emil Georg
(front left). Courtesy, Miss Ruth Georg.

Lackawanna & Western acquired it. Another line, the Utica, Clinton & Binghamton, was leased to the Delaware & Hudson company and later became part of the New York, Ontario & Western. Speculators promoted another railroad up the west bank of the Hudson and then westward through the Mohawk Valley to Buffalo. This undertaking, called the West Shore, reached Utica in 1884 crossing Genesee Street near the present Uptown Theater. When the corporation collapsed, the New York Central bought control and ran freight trains over its tracks.

Railroads brought more customers to Utica's stores, offices, and factories. Farmers along the route turned from making cheese to producing fluid milk for creameries that sold milk to urban customers. Because the Chenango Canal could not compete with railroads, the State abandoned it in the 1870s. Meanwhile low railroad rates, the result of

vicious rate wars in the 1870s, stole almost all the traffic from the Erie Canal. Horatio Seymour and other canal champions tried to rescue the Erie Canal by getting the tolls repealed in 1882. This move made little difference to shippers who found railroad service faster, more convenient, and as cheap.

Horsecars carried a growing number of passengers from downtown Utica to the outskirts. In 1886 the Utica Belt Line got control of all street railways and soon converted them to electric cars. Trolleys ran eastward over Bleecker, Eagle, South, James, and other streets where new houses were being built.

The bicycle craze won hundreds of eager followers. Where previously only daring youths climbed upon the first bicycles with their huge front wheel, after the safety bicycle was developed in the early 1890s, even the more timid learned to ride. Storekeepers, professional men, and workingmen used bicycles to get to work and do their errands, and even matrons took lessons on how to ride so that they could visit their friends. On a summer evening cyclists by the hundreds rode ten abreast over Rutger Street, their headlights glowing in the dusk.

Bicycle races eclipsed horse racing in popular interest. In 1892 thousands lined the street to see Phil Hammes race against time in a relay contest. Thousands packed the stands each Saturday night to watch racers circling the

The Balloon Farm

Just east of Utica, Carl F. Myers of Frankfort operated a balloon farm during the last third of the 19th century. Myers, an energetic little man, was the only person at the World's Fair session on aeronautics in 1893 who had actually run an aeronautics business for two decades at a profit. His wife, Mary, known professionally as "Carlotta," had become the most famous aeronaut of the period.

A born tinkerer with many kinds of scientific experiments, Myers began to study meteorology and he developed small balloons to test the weather. In 1880 Carlotta donned a smart sailor shirt and made her first ascension at the Little Falls fair. Soon Myers was devising rudders and propellers so that Carlotta could control her flight. Myers gradually developed an "Aerial Bicycle," which he later called the "Sky-Cycle." He loved to pedal the craft over the Mohawk flats, changing direction by leaning right or left. In the 1880s he, like Carlotta, demonstrated his Sky-Cycle at county fairs.

Unfortunately few people had the funds or the space to house a Sky-Cycle. Furthermore the machine required absolutely calm weather if the aeronaut was to have some assurance of returning home safely. The main practical use came from the United States Weather Bureau, which bought from Myers over a hundred instrument-carrying balloons of various sizes. In 1898 Myers supplied the army with 21 military balloons.

The birth of Elizabeth Aerial in 1881 did not ground Carlotta who made several ascensions. In 1886 her balloon

"Professor" Carl Myers, circa 1890. (OHS)

"Carlotta" Myers, lady aeronaut, circa 1890. (OHS)

carried her to 21,000 feet, about four miles.

Myers, who published the *Balloon Bulletin,* bought the Gates mansion in Frankfort and used the 30 rooms and large attic for his business. He had a carpenter shop, a machine shop, a chemical laboratory, and a "loft" where he could lay out and cut fabric for balloons. His library had the largest collection of aeronautical books and pamphlets in the country.

The Myers family operated the Balloon Farm until 1910. Carl was still riding the skies with his Sky-Cycle when he was 68 years of age.

One of the Myers' balloons rises above an umbrella-shaded crowd in Bagg's Square, sometime during the 1890s. (OHS)

half-mile track at Utica Park. In 1895 Utica hosted an international meet, and thousands lined Genesee Street to watch over 300 wheelmen from all over the world carry Chinese lanterns and gay bunting. The wheelmen and their powerful clubs stimulated the good roads movement even before automobiles had become more than a toy. Villages put up money for cinder paths in order to attract riders (customers) from the city.

Citizens demanded better law enforcement, especially after crime waves threatened property and violence frightened individuals. In 1862 the common council ordered the 10 patrolmen to wear uniforms as a symbol of authority. According to John Donato, who has made a study of the development of the police department, party chieftains made appointments to the force on the basis of political loyalties. In 1866 a bipartisan board of police commissioners appointed the police chief, but patrolmen also had to obey the mayor, aldermen, and justices of the peace.

When James McQuade, a war hero, became mayor in 1866, he tried to fire patrolmen appointed by the police commissioners. He ran into opposition from the board of aldermen who refused to attend a meeting called by the mayor. McQuade sent patrolmen to round up the aldermen

Above
William Mansfield White, great-grandson of Hugh White, the first settler of Whitestown, posed proudly with his 11 children about 1883. The White family lived in the former Alexander Bryan Johnson house at 194 Genesee Street, later the site of the Savings Bank of Utica. Courtesy, Mrs. Henry Crumb.

who had hidden in the Mansion House. The manager of the hotel called in the sheriff who arrested Chief Baxter and the mayor's messenger. The impasse, however, was broken and a compromise worked out. Patrolmen walked their beats, checked for unlocked doors, and stopped young men from fighting. Drunkenness, vagrancy, larceny, and assaults comprised almost all the misdemeanors and crimes. A major improvement came in 1892 when the city installed 26 signal boxes from which patrolmen could keep in touch with headquarters and ask for assistance. By 1900 the "paddy wagon" had responded to 1,400 calls. The rise in crime and the changing neighborhood drove many families uptown.

Wealthy families were gradually abandoning their former homes on Whitesboro and Broad streets, largely because commercial and manufacturing establishments were encroaching upon their neighborhood. Uptown, comprising Genesee Street south of the Erie Canal, upper John Street, and Rutger Park, offered advantages including distance from the canal, the polluted river, and the crowded tenements, mostly inhabited by immigrants. The elite relaxed in their gardens in the deep lots running to Union and King streets to the east and Broadway to the west of Genesee. If they wanted a change from dining at home, they could go out to dinner in the Butterfield House, an elegant new hotel on the corner of Devereux and Genesee streets. When the Army of the Cumberland held its reunion in 1875, President Grant, General William Sherman, and Governor Samuel Tilden attended the ball in the Butterfield House. Bagg's Hotel continued to attract a substantial clientele, especially among commercial travelers arriving by rail.

What streets to pave and what material to use provided a good deal of the discussion in the common council during the 1880s. Officials experimented with cobblestones, macadam, and wood blocks. They selected

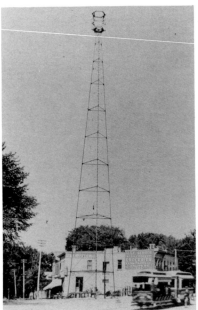

Top
This view of the west side of Genesee Street between Columbia and Lafayette streets was taken about 1870. Modest two and three-story frame and brick stores were giving way to more imposing structures like the Mansard-roofed "Iron Bank" of the Savings Bank of Utica at right. Courtesy, Utica Public Library.

Above left
This electric light tower dominated Oneida Square from about 1887 until 1891, one of about a half dozen erected around the city. Each tower was supposed to illuminate an area of several blocks. Unfortunately they served "only as intensifiers of the shadows in the streets, and temptations to small boys to climb to dizzy and dangerous heights." All were soon replaced by more conventional fixtures. (OHS)

asphalt for Rutger Street and the smooth surface won general approval. Another problem was street lighting. In 1887 the city council made a contract with the Utica Electric Light Company to provide lights for the business district, and gradually major streets and side streets received electric lighting.

Straightening the course of the Mohawk River became the most pressing civic improvement. Spring floods often entered the cellars of homes and business firms on Main, Broad, and Whitesboro streets. If the riverbed were moved a half mile northward by eliminating the huge horseshoe bend, floods would no longer reach the city. Furthermore such an improvement would give the New York Central more ground for a freight terminal, which was to become one of the largest in the nation. In 1891 the state legislature gave its approval and during the next decade the county and city worked on this project.

Like most Americans during the Gilded Age, Uticans pursued the Almighty Dollar with enthusiasm and with success as well. Every group of newcomers could point to some of its members who had achieved wealth. Middle-

class values, which the old native stock had preached and exemplified, were soon accepted by immigrants who also wanted to get ahead or at least see their children climb the social and economic ladder.

But if many Uticans worshiped at the shrine of Mammon, they also displayed compassion for the elderly, the ill, and the poor. Churches tried to help the unfortunates in their congregations or neighborhoods. As early as 1834 St. John's Church supported the Sisters of Charity who tended the many ill and poor Irish. Protestants introduced several institutions to give aid. When they saw youthful workers thronging the saloons, they set up a Young Men's Christian Association where young men could play games, read books, and avoid trouble. Theodore S. Faxton offered the sum of $20,000 for a Home for the Homeless, which occupied a house on Whitesboro Street in 1866. Before long Faxton and Benjamin Jewett offered lots on Faxton Street as a site for a home. Not to be outdone, a group of women in 1884 founded a club which in 1905 emerged as the Young Women's Christian Association, where women of all ages could relax, learn, and display

Facing page, bottom right
Floods like this prompted the removal of the channel of the Mohawk River from just north of Bagg's Square. This picture was taken behind the old New York Central station and looks west. Fortunately for the railroad, the old steam locomotives could run through two or three feet of water, a feat which no modern diesel—with electric traction motors only inches above the rail—can accomplish. (OHS)

Above
The muddy banks of the Mohawk were just across the New York Central tracks from Bagg's Square when this picture was taken in 1874. The building in front of Bagg's Hotel was a remnant of the city's original railroad station which had been replaced in 1869 by a new station farther east. The large wooden gates kept unauthorized wagons out of the station platform area. New York & Oswego Midland trains departed from the American Hotel on the west side of the square. Courtesy, Utica Public Library.

Top
The City Hospital or General Hospital on South Street near Mohawk Street served the people of Utica for nearly a century. Union soldiers were cared for here during the Civil War. (OHS)

Above
The Utica Orphan Asylum built this complex on the northeast corner of Genesee and Pleasant streets in 1861. It served until 1924 when the orphanage was reorganized to become Children's Hospital. (OHS)

Above
The old main building of the Masonic Home was an imposing
Romanesque structure dedicated in 1892. The Daniel D. Tompkins
Memorial Chapel (left) was completed in 1911. (OHS)

leadership. Most women took part in countless church societies that supported humanitarian and religious activities.

Illness and injuries struck fear into the hearts of many Uticans. Each family tried to take care of its members who fell victim to some disease or accident. Although the elite preached the virtues of temperance, frugality, thrift, and industry, they recognized that some individuals could not cope with disasters. The city founded its City Hospital in 1858 on the corner of South and Mohawk streets in a building that was renovated several times before the County Welfare Department took over this facility in 1947.

St. Elizabeth, the first private hospital, began in a tenement on Columbia Street with nurses of the Order of St. Francis in charge. In 1887 it acquired a new building that served the growing Catholic population as well as citizens in general. Matthew Carton and associates organized a campaign to finance a new structure on upper Genesee Street and it opened in 1917. Faxton Hospital, which treated its first patient in 1875, was an outgrowth of Theodore Faxton's benevolence. At first the upper floors were used to house aged men but during the 1890s the number of patients rose and filled the entire building. As a

result the directors constructed a Home for "Aged Men and Couples" across the street. This building was razed and in 1977 a new structure emerged called the Faxton-Sunset-St. Luke's Health Related Facility and Nursing Home, Inc.

St. Luke's Home was expanded in 1872 to provide hospital services but few patients were registered for the first decade. Then in 1882 Dr. Willis E. Ford became medical director and greatly expanded its activities. He established a training school for nurses that was perhaps the first in America's interior. In 1905 Mr. and Mrs. Frederick T. Proctor funded a new hospital on Whitesboro Street. Both Faxton and St. Elizabeth hospitals also set up nurses' training schools. Utica Memorial Hospital was begun in 1895 as a homeopathic institution.

Ill and orphaned children received more than sympathy. In 1830 a group of society women incorporated the Utica Orphan Asylum, which moved several times until 1846 when it acquired a lot and house at 312 Genesee Street. When Benjamin Jewett gave the society a four-acre lot on the corner of Genesee and Pleasant, it erected a model building which was to serve hundreds of orphans for three-quarters of a century.

The Masons of the state selected Utica as the site for their home for elderly Masons. The various lodges contributed to the building, constructed on the site of the Utica Driving Park, and dedicated it in 1892. This unit became the nucleus for a cluster of buildings that were added in the 20th century.

By mid-century a majority of children between the ages of five and 16 were enrolled in schools, although some parents kept their children home to do piece work or help out in the store. A visiting committee in 1842 compared Utica's schools with other cities and found them

"exceptional." Almost all the teachers were women who had received their training in courses given by secondary schools. Only a handful of students enrolled in the Utica Academy and a much smaller number attended college. Nearby Hamilton College attracted young men who planned to become ministers or lawyers.

Utica had 12 ward schools and the Advanced School. The old private secondary school became Utica Free Academy in 1853. A board of six commissioners supervised the system, which in 1853 employed 57 teachers to instruct 3,826 pupils. The Board rebuilt the academy building immediately after a fire destroyed it in 1865. It served secondary students until 1899 when the new building was opened on Kemble Street. Andrew McMillen became superintendent of schools, a post he held for a quarter

century. During his administration he directed the construction of more buildings because of the population growth and the compulsory school law of 1874 requiring children between eight and 14 to attend classes.

By the end of its first century of settlement, the shallow ford on the Upper Mohawk had passed through its commercial stage into a mature economy with manufacturing as its base. Immigrants from southern and eastern Europe joined those from the British Isles, Ireland, and Germany. Its residents had access to a fairly sophisticated cultural fare as represented by traveling troupes of thespians and musicians. Trained and tested in the hurly-burly of regional politics, men such as Horatio Seymour, Roscoe Conkling, James Sherman, and Elihu Root won national recognition and laurels for their talents.

Facing page
Utica Free Academy occupied this building on Academy Street from 1867 until 1899. The building was later used as a grammar school and for school offices. (OHS)

Above
Miss Florence Hicks presided over the first grade at School Number 21 (Lincoln School) in West Utica in 1899-1900. (OHS)

CHAPTER SIX

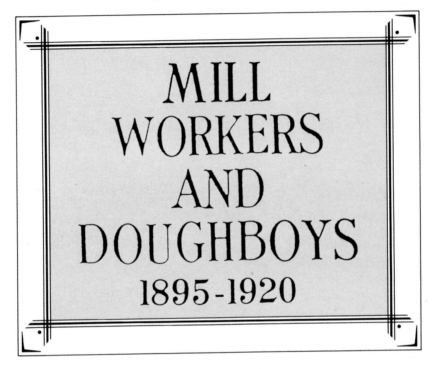

MILL WORKERS AND DOUGHBOYS
1895-1920

The union suit and ladies' underwear provided the foundation for Utica's booming economy and population explosion in the first two decades of this century. Many citizens regarded knit goods as a more solid and permanent basis for prosperity than cameras were for Rochester or light bulbs for Schenectady. In the first decade of the century, Utica added another 18,383 residents, a gain of almost one third. In the second decade population rose by over one fourth. Utica expanded its physical limits, attracted thousands of immigrants, created scores of fortunes, and added an elegant system of parks and civic improvements. When the American Knit Goods Association set up its headquarters in 1917, Utica had become the world capital of this form of manufacturing.

The city fathers gradually rounded out the city's basic boundaries by 1921. Utica acquired the land for the proposed new riverbed before the straightening of the Mohawk River was completed. In 1916 it annexed more acreage in present-day North Utica from the town of Deerfield. To the south the city annexed several parcels from the town of New Hartford: the area south of Prospect Street and between Oneida and Genesee streets and several

small parcels in 1921. Other tracts such as Roscoe Conkling Park (1904), South Woods (1910), and the Tilden Avenue district (1913) were secured.

Developers rushed to buy tracts on which to build houses or to sell lots to families who wanted to construct their dream home. The electric trolley had already stimulated the outward movement of citizens, a trend greatly accelerated by the purchase of automobiles by middle-class families. Politicians were quick to heed the pleas of developers who wanted roads in their section.

Utica in 1900 retained its character as an immigrant city because 64 percent of its residents were foreign-born or had parents born outside this country. Germans held first rank with 3,696 followed by Irish with 2,548. Those born in Great Britain and English Canada numbered 3,484. The Polish total is difficult to determine because some were listed among immigrants from Russia, Germany, and Austria-Hungary.

Some elements such as the Palatine Germans, Dutch, Scots, English, Canadians, many Welsh, and Ulster Irish had become amalgamated into the old Yankee-Yorker stock. Many third and fourth generation citizens of German

and Irish descent as well as the growing number of individuals of mixed ancestry had also slipped into the category of native whites. Persons of Protestant background from northwestern Europe constituted about half of the county's population of 154,157.

After World War I immigration resumed but on a smaller scale. In 1920 Utica contained 23,257 foreign-born, roughly one-fourth of the total of 94,154. The ingredients in the nationality mixture, however, had changed drastically since the opening of the century. The old German-Irish domination toppled before the Italian-Polish surge, which by 1920 comprised more than half of all the city's

Above
Francis P. Miller and Harry Mundy established Utica's first automobile dealership, the Miller-Mundy Motor Carriage Company, in 1901. They began by selling White Steamers and Pierce-Stanhopes and later added other makes. This group of ladies posed in a 1903 Winton in front of the firm's second home on Oneida Square. (OHS)

immigrants. The Italian contingent skyrocketed from 1,661 to 8,435, a gain of more than five times. The Polish figure, 4,091, also represented a quantum leap from the uncertain estimates of 1900.

Clearly the Teutonic and Hibernian population was declining and aging, a trend that the war accelerated. The British total remained about the same although the number of those born in England declined. That loss was more than made up by the rising count from Ontario and other English-speaking provinces of Canada. The Welsh total rose to 1,376, largely because strikes in the slate quarries on the New York-Vermont line stimulated Welsh families to seek work in the construction and defense industries of Utica. Two new groups deserve mention: Lithuanians with 179 and Syrians with 749. Only 354 appeared in the column for blacks.

New nationalities brought additional diversity to Utica. Repressed by the Tsarist and later the Soviet government, the Ukrainians had developed a strong sense of nationhood. A few had reached the Mohawk Valley before World War I and by 1912 established the Ukrainian Orthodox parish of Sts. Peter and Paul. The same

year another minority in Russia, the Lithuanians, formed St. George's Roman Catholic Church on Lafayette Street. Still another minority, the Poles, had become numerous enough in East Utica to found St. Stanislaus in 1911. The Polish National Catholic Church also established a church in Utica and one in New York Mills.

The Syrian-Lebanese community dates before the opening of this century when some Christians fled the poverty and persecution of the Moslem Ottoman Empire. Most families settled around Third Avenue but others took residence in New York Mills, Clark Mills, and West Utica. At first many took jobs in the mills but soon several opened small groceries and farm produce stands. These immigrants prized education and sent many children to college and professional schools.

Most Syrians and Lebanese belonged to eastern rites of the Roman Catholic Church. The Maronites, most of whom came from the neighborhood of Beirut, established St. Louis Gonzaga Church in 1911. Originally located on Albany and Elizabeth, this Lebanese parish built a larger building in 1937 at the corner of Rutger and Conkling. Somewhat less numerous were the Melkites whose rite is in Arabic and who came from the city of Aleppo in Syria. Their church, St. Basil's, was founded in 1916 at the corner of Third Avenue and Lansing Street.

The Jewish community received reinforcements chiefly of skilled workers such as cap makers, cigar makers, and tailors. In 1906 these men organized a Workmen's Circle. Alexander Rosenthal, an officer in the cigar worker's union, took an active role in the Utica Trades and Labor Assembly. The failure of the Russian Revolution of 1905 and more pogroms sent another wave of migrants to America, some of whom ended up in Utica. By 1917 the

Jewish population had risen to approximately 1,600. Three years later another estimate assigned it a figure of 2,517.

Overwhelmingly Orthodox in religion the community continued to support the House of Jacob but also sponsored several other synagogues, usually short-lived. Although a Reform temple was organized in 1904, it soon died. A Conservative Congregation Beth El opened in 1909 but soon closed until 1919 when it attracted greater support. Because most Jews were moving from the old neighborhood around Whitesboro Street toward Corn Hill and South Utica, the members of Temple Beth El bought a lot on Genesee Street and erected a large building with many facilities. Meanwhile Jews had organized a Hebrew Community Building, which opened in 1915. Jewish women organized several societies including the Young Women's Hebrew Association. No group of immigrants sponsored such a wide array of benevolent, religious, cultural, labor, and fraternal societies.

Above
Brothers Michael, Yorhaky ("Rocky"), and Raymond Chanatry came to Utica from Aleppo, Syria, between 1911 and 1913 and established large families and long-lived grocery businesses. The trio was photographed in their store at 519 Bleecker Street in the late 1920s. Courtesy, Miss Nellie Chanatry.

Above
Utica's leading businesses proudly joined forces in 1909 to proclaim the return of prosperity following the Panic of 1907. The allegorical picture on the cover of the tabloid they produced combined the rich foliage of the Art Nouveau style with the smoking chimneys that spelled prosperity during the age of steam. Courtesy, Utica Public Library.

Hind's British Guiana Stamp

Arthur Hind of Wyck, a small town in Yorkshire, made a good living selling plush fabric to American firms making women's coats. Then Congress passed the McKinley Tariff of 1890, raising the rates so high Hind could no longer make a profit. He persuaded H.B. Harrison, a finisher and dyer, to join him in setting up a new operation in America behind the tariff walls. He selected Clark Mills near Utica where a textile company had just abandoned a large factory.

Scores of English families came over to work in the mill that at peak periods employed as many as one thousand. The firm put up a hundred houses and provided its workers with a fine clubhouse. Meanwhile Hind spent much time traveling abroad and collecting stamps for a hobby. He made the front page when he bid $37,500 for the British Guiana stamp, a one-center of 1846, the only one of its kind. Hind received so much publicity that even George V of England, another famous collector, invited him to Buckingham Palace to talk stamps.

In 1933 Hind died and the Utica First Bank and Trust Company, his executors, spent a year cataloguing his collection, which brought over one million dollars at auctions in New York and London. Hind had given his British Guiana stamp to his wife who permitted it to be displayed at New York's World's Fair in 1933. She later sold it for $50,000 to an unknown buyer. In the 1970s it was rumored that a syndicate of investors purchased this stamp for the sum of $500,000.

The company that Hind had begun subsequently went out of business and today part of the old factory in Clark Mills is a showroom for a furniture company.

Arthur Hind is said to have taken up stamp collecting to pass quiet evenings in Clark Mills. A bachelor and bon vivant, *he reputedly spent over two million pre-inflation dollars on his collection. (OHS)*

By 1920 the religious pattern of Utica had been established. The Roman Catholic faith enlisted 42,496 souls or approximately 64 percent of the church membership. The Protestant Episcopal Church claimed 5,195 members or about 5.5 percent. Because most other churches did not include children under 12 or thereabouts in their totals, we need to adjust upward the figures for the church community. Presbyterians numbered about 5,000, the three Lutheran groups 3,350, the Baptists 3,000, and the Methodists about 2,000. The three Congregationalist churches served a community of about 1,750.

The railroad steam engine symbolized the supremacy of rail transport in this period. When the trunk line railroads signed an agreement granting more favorable rates to Philadelphia and Baltimore than to New York City, the Manhattan businessmen campaigned for a revival of the canal system. They urged a barge canal, and in 1903 the voters approved an appropriation of $101 million. The final cost was more than double this amount. Workers and contractors in Utica received some benefits from this massive undertaking. The new channel, almost a mile north of the old Erie Canal, was 12 feet deep and 100 feet wide at the bottom. When the state opened the canal in 1918, Uticans hailed a new harbor in the city. Tonnage, however, never reached the rosy estimates of canal champions.

Meanwhile the common council was fumbling with the plans and financing of a new channel for the Mohawk River to the north of the old river course. After several starts and halts, the firm of Harry W. Roberts completed the job in 1907. Closely allied to this project was an overhead bridge to carry Genesee Street over the railroad tracks where dozens of trains each day created long delays in road traffic. The New York Central agreed to pay for half the cost and to build a new station provided the city gave it the old river channel. It planned a large marshaling yard on the channel and on 40 acres which it had bought north of the riverbed. In 1913 the railroad company began work on its new passenger station to cost over one million dollars. This striking example of Renaissance Revival architecture also served the Delaware, Lackawanna and Western and the New York, Ontario & Western railroads.

The electric trolley reached the peak of its popularity during this period. Cleveland traction interests in 1901 bought control of the Utica Belt line, the Bleecker Street company, which ran east to Utica Park, and the Deerfield line which still used horsepower. They merged these lines into the Utica & Mohawk Valley Railway Company. Soon a line to Clinton was added and in 1902 an extension to Rome and also one to Frankfort. The Utica & Mohawk Valley began to run through cars from Rome to Little Falls and at Mohawk connected with a line to Oneonta. In 1907 the company began an electrified (third rail) service on the West Shore tracks to Syracuse. In 1912 all the streetcar lines in Utica, Oneida, Syracuse and Rochester were taken

Top
After putting up with a makeshift railroad station for nearly half a century, Uticans hailed the completion of Union Station in 1914 as a great step forward. Travelers bound for the Hotel Utica were met at the station by the hotel's own bus. (OHS)

Above left
Factories lined the Erie Canal through Utica, including the stretch between Cornelia and State streets, shown here around the turn of the century. Barges hauled grain, lumber, sand, stone, pig iron, coal, hay, and other bulky commodities. Courtesy, Utica Public Library.

over by the New York State Railways, a subsidiary of the New York Central.

Trolleys provided rapid transportation to points outside as well as inside the city, permitting people to live on the outskirts and in the suburbs. Although primarily carriers of passengers, trolleys also served businessmen with freight service. In 1910, 23 members of the Utica Boosters boarded a green car equipped with wicker armchairs. This car took them on a two-weeks' trip to Kentucky and Indiana where the Boosters displayed Utica sheets, underwear, and other products.

The full impact of the automobile revolution did not make itself felt until after World War I, when more and more Uticans were buying cars. Oneida County in 1921 had 15,667 car registrations and commercial vehicles numbered 2,736.

At first only the wealthy could afford to own automobiles, which could require many trips to the garage for repairs. Car owners were a hardy breed who often entered races to Syracuse and Albany. By 1907 the state imposed speed limits, 15 miles per hour within city limits. In 1910 the Automobile Club of Utica replaced the old social clubs and headed up the drive for better roads. Oneida County became the center of this movement because of the activities of William Pierrepont White, the county road superintendent. White attended conferences, wrote articles, and lobbied in Albany. The state government slowly took responsibility for some trunk roads such as Routes 5 and 20. Meanwhile the common council of Utica made efforts to pave all the streets with asphalt.

While enjoying growth in transportation and roads, Utica remained predominantly a manufacturing center of

Facing page, bottom right
Car 502 led the first train when the Oneida Railway "third rail" service was inaugurated between Utica and Syracuse on June 15, 1907. A group of "Utica Boosters" chartered this car in May 1910 for a promotional tour as far west as Indianapolis and Detroit, a trip made entirely over electric interurban railways. (OHS)

Above
Franz Rath's orchestra provided music for dancing at Utica Park, a popular amusement area located at the end of the Bleecker Street trolley line near the eastern boundary of the city. Utica Park, (later called Forest Park) and Summit Park in Oriskany kept the trolley cars busy on summer evenings and weekends. (OHS)

consumer goods such as underwear, sheets, and clothing. In 1900 its 311 manufacturing establishments employed approximately 9,000 workers. Textiles, especially the knit-goods branch, showed amazing growth and prosperity. By 1902 over 4,000 workers entered the doors of 19 knit-goods factories every weekday. Two giants emerged: Utica Knitting Company with two mills in the West End and some 700 to 800 operatives, and the Oneita Knitting Mill on Broad Street with over 1,000 workers. Entrepreneurs rushed to rent empty lofts and old mills in order to share in the boom. In 1909 Utica Knit doubled its capital stock and a year later Frisbie & Stansfield Knitting Corporation was incorporated with a capital of $2 million. Thus Utica had the two largest knit-goods corporations in the world.

The cotton mills kept increasing their size and hiring more hands. In 1901 Utica Steam Cotton Company merged with Mohawk Valley Mill and dominated the industry. In a couple of years the Globe Woolen Mill passed into the hands of J.F. Maynard, F.T. Proctor, and Joseph Rudd, but in 1916 they sold out to the American Woolen Company, the giant woolen trust. The takeover is significant because it marks the beginning of outside control of local firms. Before this merger Utica residents had collected capital, built the factories, and managed their manufacturing establishments.

The knit-goods boom was largely responsible for the addition of another 5,000 jobs by 1910. Although the number of clothing factories fell by more than half, employment rose a bit. During the next decade employment gained only 2,000 because of the slackening in the knit-goods market. The number of clothing firms declined with a drop in their work force. On the other hand the census of 1920 recorded eight plants making automobile parts.

Utica's industrial leaders were generally men of energy and ability, and who had a sense of civic responsibility. Most came from the old native stock but there were numerous exceptions, such as the Kernan and Devereux families. Whenever civic projects needed aid, businessmen or sometimes their wives supported them with money and talent. Perhaps their successful careers as well as self-interest made them somewhat insensitive to the needs of immigrants who came to work in the mills. Were they not

providing work for people fleeing from poverty? Were there not numerous examples of thrifty workers who had become foremen, opened stores, and founded new businesses? Indeed there were. Everyone could point to immigrants who had become wealthy and to thousands of industrious working families who had bought houses and achieved a solid middle-class status.

Nevertheless working conditions then can only be described as grim. The operatives, chiefly immigrant women, worked long hours for wages that barely kept body and soul together. Textile mills paid about $320 a year, a level considerably below that in clothing factories and foundries. Managers regarded unions with fear and loathing, and they opposed any action by the state legislature to limit the hours of labor.

It is no accident that the famous Lochner Case originated in Utica. Joe Lochner, a baker on South Street, fought the state law banning bakers from working more than 10 hours a day. In 1905 the case reached the United States Supreme Court, which ruled this law interfered with the constitutional guarantee of freedom of contract. Justice Oliver Wendell Holmes wrote a fiery dissent charging that the majority opinion accepted the doctrine of laissez-faire as part of the Constitution. Holmes argued that this regulation was a proper exercise of the State's power to protect the health of its citizens. Most students of constitutional law and the Supreme Court itself in later decisions have accepted Holmes' interpretation.

When Assemblyman Edward Jackson of Buffalo introduced a bill to reduce the hours of labor for women and children to 54 hours a week, the business community of Utica protested indignantly. Attorney Thomas D. Watkins,

Above
The Utica Knitting Company was established in 1892 and soon boasted a number of plants. In addition to the main mill on Erie Street and the former Utica Steam Woolen Mill on Schuyler Street, the firm had branches in Sherburne and Oriskany Falls. (OHS)

November 1913

THE good service of Utica Sheets to three generations of particular housewives makes them the choice of a fourth generation

UTICA
Sheets and Pillow Cases

Established 1848
Times change but "Utica" remains a standard

RUBBING and wringing and ironing—a sheet has a pretty hard time of it. There is a reason for making sheets and pillow cases as good as the "Utica" Brand.

Sold by leading stores everywhere

Our "Mohawk" Brand is a good sheet, not quite so heavy as "Utica"

Utica Steam & Mohawk Valley Cotton Mills   Utica, NY

who represented the mill owners, claimed the bill would cripple the textile industry, and a spokesman for New York Mills declared his mill would have to move more departments to Georgia where 66 hours a week was permitted.

But the Triangle Shirt Waist Company fire in 1911 had shocked public opinion because 146 young women had died in the inferno. The legislature set up the Factory Investigating Committee, which held hearings throughout the state. They found that several mills in central New York, including those at Little Falls, were hiring women on the night shifts and were paying young children to do piecework in their homes. The legislature banned work for more than 10 hours a day for women. Night work for women was also banned.

Some mill owners cut wages 10 percent when the legislature reduced hours of labor by that amount. As a result strikes broke out and paralyzed factories in New York Mills in 1911. The workers joined the union and walked the picket line. A.D. Juilliard Company evicted strikers from company houses. Workers organized relief baskets and held dances in Union Hall, the center of resistance.

These harsh conditions led to a rash of strikes and union organization similar to those that spread through the factory towns of New England. The workers fought hard for better wages and shorter hours and in 1916 the Polish women in New York Mills won a memorable victory after nine months of picketing. Little did they realize that their success convinced many mill owners that they would have to shift the seat of manufacturing from this area to the southern states.

Banks and other financial institutions benefited from Utica's prosperity. The Savings Bank of Utica and the Utica City National Bank built new structures to take care of expanding operations. Oneida National Bank continued its cautious policy on loans to businessmen and homeowners. John L. Train helped found in 1914 the Utica Mutual Insurance Company, which was to become a major company in that field. Commercial Travelers Mutual Accident Association, founded in 1883, continued to prosper and built a skyscraper on lower Genesee Street. Utica Fire Insurance Company (1903) has developed into a profitable operation. In addition to these underwriters, hundreds of Uticans were engaged in the business of selling insurance to homeowners, business firms, and private associations.

The tremendous growth of home ownership in the newer sections of Utica was partially financed by the banks but also by such companies as the Homestead Aid Association founded in 1884. In 1910 it had 5,290 members and assets of over $2.5 million. Somewhat smaller in membership and assets was the Corn Hill Building and Loan Association, which made most of its loans to buyers of

Left
The name of Utica was so associated with quality cotton sheets that even after the J.P. Stevens Company acquired the Utica Steam & Mohawk Valley Cotton Mills and closed the local operations during the 1950s, it continued to use "Utica" as a trade name for products made in the South. This ad is from 1913. (OHS)

Hearst Derailed

In 1906 Charles Evans Hughes and William Randolph Hearst were running neck and neck for governor of the Empire State. Using his *New York Journal* as a bludgeon, Hearst browbeat the New York City Democratic chieftains to support him for governor. He called the bearded Hughes "an animated feather duster," a comparatively mild example of his vituperation. When it looked like Hearst would win, President Theodore Roosevelt sent Secretary of State Elihu Root to Utica to torpedo Hearst's candidacy. A frosty corporation lawyer, Root spoke in the Majestic Theater, guarded from Hearst's bully boys by a platoon of Hamilton College students. Root flayed Hearst as a hypocrite, a false progressive, a tax-evader, and a "corruptionist." He even charged Hearst was responsible for the murder of President William McKinley in 1901 by an anarchist deranged by Hearst's appeal to violence. The charge was actually not true but Roosevelt and Root branded Hearst as an unprincipled demagogue. This sensational speech, which the Republicans circulated widely, caused thousands to split their ticket and Hearst lost by 58,000 votes, the only Democrat on the state ticket to lose.

Of course Hearst was also knifed by Tammany chieftains, but it was Root's speech that struck the fatal blow. One can still speculate that if Hearst had won in 1906, he might very well have received the Democratic nomination in 1908 and beaten Taft, a rather weak candidate. The thought is still a provocative one.

William R. Hearst (1863-1951), newspaper publisher, capitalist. From Cirker, Dictionary of American Portraits, *Dover, 1967.*

homes in the southeastern part of Utica.

About 300 printers were employed in publishing. Utica had two national journals as well as the Utica *Observer-Dispatch* and the Utica *Daily Press. Y Drych,* the Welsh weekly, published by T.J. Griffith and Sons, had over 12,000 subscribers throughout North America. The *Saturday Globe* ran its presses six days a week to supply its subscribers who numbered over 200,000 in some years. The *Globe,* however, began to lose circulation largely because of the competition of daily newspapers, which, like the *Globe,* had increased their use of pictures. The Baker family and other owners sold out their interests in 1920 to new owners whose attempt to publish a daily paper failed. Four years later the *Globe* printed its last issue.

Musical activities reached a new high. In 1903 a group of ladies organized the B Sharp Club, which sponsored musicales and encouraged musical talent among children. The club brought in famous orchestras and soloists, among them Fritz Kreisler, Lawrence Tibbett, Lily Pons, and Rosa Ponselle. Mrs. William B. Crouse headed this society for 22 years. Meanwhile the *eisteddfod* was filling the Armory for its annual musical and writing competitions on New Year's Day. The Haydn Male Chorus traveled to Washington in 1909 to perform at the inauguration of James S. Sherman as Vice President. The Maennerchor took part in German activities, which involved thousands of participants before World War I. Ironically the statue of Baron Von Steuben on the Parkway was dedicated the day the German armies were crashing into Belgium.

Amateur dramatics were promoted by the Amusement Club, which put on plays in the New Century Club. The society embarked upon more ambitious productions and "The Players," its offspring, hired a professional director, Frank Stirling.

Uticans also sought to improve conditions for children, both socially and educationally. The first troop of Boy Scouts was formed in 1909 and its success led to the formation of other troops. In 1903 the Parent-Teachers Association began its efforts to improve the schools and to bring about better communication between teachers and parents. In 1910 the Stevens-Swan Humane Society was organized for the purpose of protecting children as well as animals. Each year its activities increased and by 1949 it established its offices and kennels on North Genesee Street.

Leading citizens in 1900 formed a Playground Committee for the purpose of providing children sandboxes, wading pools, swings, and the like. The improvements proved popular and the city took over these functions. The Chamber of Commerce urged a park system similar to those built in other cities in the Northeast, with bigger and better facilities. Meanwhile Thomas R. Proctor was quietly buying large parcels on the outskirts. He also hired Olmsted Brothers of Brookline, Massachusetts, successors to the nation's most famous landscape architect, Frederick Law Olmsted, to make plans for a system of interlocking parks surrounding the city.

Proctor had purchased the old farm belonging to Bagg's Hotel on the Welsh Bush Road, the tract which was

Top
When the textile workers of New York Mills went on strike in 1916, the company retaliated by evicting them and their families from the company-owned houses. Photographic postcards of poignant scenes such as this were made and sold to arouse sympathy and raise money to aid the strikers. Courtesy, New York Mills Historical Society.

Above
On June 23, 1907, Thomas R. Proctor presented the lands he had purchased for parks to the City of Utica. Mr. Proctor (with white beard in first car) and various dignitaries visited the park sites where he formally named each one in honor of a prominent figure in the city's history. (OHS)

to be named Thomas R. Proctor Park. Roscoe Conkling Park, a tract of 385 acres, included Steele Hill and much of the land between Oneida Street to Third Street. Later he added the Jewett farm and also acquired the space between Bleecker and Rutger west of the Masonic Home. On the other side of the city Proctor donated Horatio Seymour Park, a tract of about 15 acres west of Sunset Avenue and across from Faxton Hospital. A parcel of similar size at the south end of York Street was designated Addison C. Miller Park. Gradually the city constructed baseball diamonds, tennis courts, wading pools, and swimming pools. By World War I Utica possessed as fine a park system for a city its size as any in the nation.

Not all of Olmsted's plans were carried out, but the city did construct the Parkway from Genesee to Mohawk Street, opening this section in 1911. After World War I the common council extended the Parkway to Welsh Bush Road.

The Young Men's Christian Association and the Young Women's Christian Association expanded their activities. The YW in 1916 acquired the former building of the Curtis Dancing Academy on Cornelia Street. The Oneida County Child Welfare Committee was formed to help widows and their children. When the influenza epidemic struck Utica in 1919, its resources were strained to the utmost. The Junior League opened its first day nursery for the care of children whose mothers had to work. Other groups such as the Rotary Club, formed in 1915, included among its many functions aid to newsboys, an activity which developed into the Boys Club of Utica. Rotary built shelters for Camp Healthmore, camps for Boy Scouts, and a dispensary for the "Y" camp on Lake Moraine. Later in 1937 when the Girl Scouts needed a camp, Rotary supplied them with a building and other facilities. The Kiwanis, begun in 1916, also assisted the Boy Scouts and supplied a visiting nurse to the schools.

In 1912 the Associated Charities of Utica was formed with the Reverend Octavius Applegate, rector of Grace Church, as president and Dr. T. Wood Clarke as secretary. This organization sought to secure cooperation among the various agencies and to provide a more scientific approach to problems of dependency. Later this agency evolved into the Family Welfare Association.

Women not only took active roles in aiding children in and outside the home but also formed clubs to promote their own interests. Ladies interested in literary and musical interests formed the New Century Club in 1893. The Catholic Women's Club was opened on Genesee Street in 1918. The next year the Business and Professional Women's Club was organized, testimony to the considerable number of women in business and professional occupations. The right to vote became the burning issue for women in this period. Mrs. George Warren in 1899 had promoted a Utica Political Equality Club, which urged an amendment granting women the right to vote. By 1913 suffragettes were holding parades but the liquor interests, reactionaries, and some political bosses opposed them. Miss Lucy Watson of Utica organized the local forces before she became a leader in the state campaign. Carrie Chapman Catt and William

Above
About 25,000 people crowded along the new Parkway on ''Utica Day,'' September 16, 1911, to watch Eugene Godet, a Curtiss pilot, give the city's first flying exhibition. Godet took off from and landed on the Parkway, which was not yet encumbered with statues, fountains, and trees. This photo was taken from the roof of the Utica City Ice Company's icehouse between Oneida and Kemble streets. (OHS)

Summit Park

Happiness was a trip to Summit Park on a warm afternoon in an open trolley. What could be more exciting for youngsters than to ride the miniature train, take a boat trip, and hang on to the roller-coaster bar.

In 1897 the Utica Belt Line extended its route beyond Whitesboro across Bradley's Bridge to Oriskany. There the conductor turned his car to the southwest and guided it up the steep grade to the circular loop in front of Summit Park Station. Youngsters clutched a dime to give to the man at the turnstile. Young people usually rushed to the Pavilion, the largest building, through whose open sides floated the sound of the big bands such as Rath's and Al Sittig's. On the upstairs balcony, older folk (yes, Virginia, there were even some chaperones in *those* days) observed the couples gliding over the highly polished floor that was 90 feet square.

The management banned booze but visitors found plenty to eat and drink. The restaurant served a fine full-course dinner and the soda fountain dispensed sarsaparilla and lemon sour. One could buy ice cream, the homemade kind, at several locations. The open-air theater booked vaudeville acts, musicians, and speakers who, however, had to compete with mosquitoes for the attention of their listeners. Others clambered up the Observatory on the pinnacle where one could pick out Utica's Forest Hill Cemetery, Hamilton College Chapel, Deerfield Hill, and the monument on the Oriskany battlefield. From time to time individuals competed and horses raced on the quarter-mile track before the grandstand. Nearby was a shooting gallery, a penny arcade, and a Japanese shop. The "lake," really a

pond some 50 feet wide behind the old state dam serving as a feeder for the Erie Canal, attracted the venturesome on hot days. One had to clamber down a series of steps more than 100 feet to reach the boat station.

Opening on Memorial Day and closing on Labor Day, the park attracted about a thousand people each evening and more on weekends. Of course holidays, especially the Glorious Fourth with its firework display, attracted crowds reaching 6,000 to 7,000. Seward Baker, the canny manager, enticed various groups such as Sunday Schools, lodges, and Irish and German associations to come to his park. The peak attendance came in 1910 when white-haired veterans of the Civil War held their state convention at Summit Park with ex-President Roosevelt as their main speaker. Over 20,000 people crammed the park, some coming by bicycle, others by carriage, but most by trolley. Sixteen cars, each holding 84 passengers, rolled into the station every hour.

Summit Park, like most urban and suburban parks, declined after World War I largely because people were buying automobiles. Uticans preferred to drive to Old Forge in the Adirondacks or to Sylvan Beach on Oneida Lake. Mr. Baker tried stunts such as balloon ascensions and offered discount fares but attendance dwindled each year. In 1926 he shut the gates.

Older Uticans still remember the 20 mile an hour breeze as the open cars passed Oriskany bluff, the shrieking children on the roller-coaster, and the half-mile ride on the miniature railroad, equipped with a whistle and belching real smoke. But best of all was the ride home when the tired picnickers sang the old songs and watched the moon rise above Bradley's Bridge.

Rowboating on the Oriskany Creek was one of the simple pleasures available to Summit Park visitors "in the good old summer time" about 1910. Courtesy, Battle of Oriskany Historical Society.

Summit Park visitors could enjoy a fine view of the Mohawk Valley from the "observatory." Courtesy, Utica Public Library.

Jennings Bryan spoke to a huge meeting in the Avon Theater just before the election in 1917. The women and their allies overcame their foes and secured statewide ratification of the Seventeenth Amendment.

An increase in wealth expressed itself in both the private and public sector. Business and professional men built elegant mansions on Genesee Street, the Parkway, and in certain parts of South Utica. The growing middle class of skilled workmen, storekeepers, and white-collar workers built or bought comfortable houses on new streets in Corn Hill, South Utica, and other outskirts. The Utica Free Academy reconstructed its fire-damaged building in 1910.

Utica presented an aura of prosperity and good taste on the eve of World War I. Most visitors arrived by train, passing underground to the magnificent new station. Probably they took a taxi to Hotel Utica, which had opened its doors in 1912. Because most trolleys from north, south, east, and west passed through the intersection of Genesee and Bleecker streets, it became known as the Busy Corner. Shoppers boarded the cars each day to ride to downtown Utica where they could visit the Fraser or Roberts

Top
Robert McKinnon, the owner of a knitting mill in Little Falls, wished to give his wife and daughters the social advantages of life in a bigger city and had this mansion built at Genesee and Scott streets in 1898-99. At a cost of about $100,000, it was the most expensive house in Utica at that time. Charles A. Borst, owner of the Clinton Hematite Mines, purchased it after McKinnon lost his fortune about 1910. The First Presbyterian Church bought the property in 1920. (OHS)

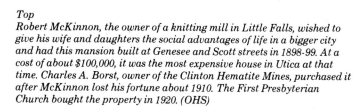

department stores, find specialty shops, attend theaters, and dine in the best restaurants.

The Utica Trust and Deposit company had just remodeled its building on the corner of Lafayette and Genesee, and from its entrance one could see Utica's first skyscraper, Utica City National Bank (1904). Next to Grace Church, John A. Roberts had just opened a modern department store, a friendly rival to Robert Fraser's store. Farther south on Genesee one would pass the Savings Bank of Utica and the brand new Mayro Building, providing offices for lawyers, accountants, and doctors.

If one walked east on Elizabeth Street, he or she would see the new Oneida County Court House. Irregularities in its construction for financial benefit led to jail sentences for the sheriff and the chairmen of the Republican and Democratic parties. The Central Fire Station on Elizabeth Street (1911) had the most modern and elaborate equipment. Labor Temple (1912) on Charlotte housed the offices of trade unions, mostly in the construction trades.

Harry Thurston Peck, self-styled world traveler and author, wrote a travel book in 1910 covering famous cities such as Brussels, Liverpool, Boston, and other centers. Somewhat apologetically he included Utica in his list, saying that what he liked about Uticans was their "true gentility" and that he admired the arcade of elms and the fine shops on Genesee Street.

When Europe lunged into war in the summer of 1914, most Uticans demanded neutrality for this country. Naturally there were some members of various ethnic groups who tended to favor the cause of their motherland and several hundred young men returned home to fight. In

"Where Summer Shopping's a Pleasure"

John A. Roberts & Co
UTICA'S GREATEST STORE.

THE WORLD'S BEST MERCHANDISE attractively displayed, temptingly priced on all Six Floors of
UTICA'S GREATEST DEPARTMENT STORE.

Furs Cared For During the Summer Months.

The moths are very busy this month, and they thrive in a warm atmosphere. They particularly like to house themselves in furs and fur garments which are kept in dark warm closets.
OUR COLD STORAGE VAULT is just the place to store furs, rugs, draperies and anything that moths can damage.
Do not delay, send us your furs and be relieved of their care. We will return them to you next Fall lustrous and free from the odor of any preservative. The vault is on the premises. Visitors are always welcome.

TEA ROOM
Located on the fifth floor, overlooking the beautiful Mohawk Valley, where cool breezes come to make you comfortable. It is the most delightful restaurant in Central New York. The food is the purest and it is most daintily served. The prices are very moderate for such perfection.
Besides the a la carte service from 8 A. M. to 5:30 P. M., specially prepared 25c. and 50c. luncheons are served between 11:30 A. M. and 2:00 P. M.
Most delicious refreshments are served in the afternoon—ice cream, strawberries, etc.

Our Perfect System of Ventilation
keeps our store always cool in summer. Pure fresh air cooled by our ventilating system adds greatly to the comfort of customers trading at JOHN A. ROBERTS & CO.'S

THE HOUSEHOLD CLUB.
A great help to those who contemplate furnishing a home and who find it inconvenient to pay the whole amount at one time.
If you become a member of our Household Club you can Purchase our
CARPETS, FURNITURE, RUGS and UPHOLSTERIES
at our establishment, and the payments are arranged to suit your convenience.
But note particularly —you are not charged any more for any article you select on the club plan than if you paid cash down.
Inquire of any salesman in the Furniture, Carpet or Upholstery Department, or at the Charge Office.

ALL TROLLEY CARS LEAVE PASSENGERS AT OUR DOORS.

Street Cars leave the N. Y. C. depot for John A. Roberts & Co.'s New Store every 5 minutes.

Eighth Year of Early Closing and the First Year of Early Closing in Our New Store, as usual, during July and August. This Store will close daily at 5 o'clock and at 1 o'clock on Saturdays.

(Employes' Half Holiday Saturday Afternoon and Evening)

1914 Ella Rockwell and friends formed the Red Cross Relief Society for the purpose of sending supplies to refugees and civilians in Belgium and France.

When the United States entered the war on April 5, 1917, Oneida County set up a Home Defense Committee, which elected Harry Roberts its chairman. The Red Cross asked Uticans to become members and in one week over 22,000 signed up. The Home Defense Committee supervised the work of some 40 committees, which accomplished an amazing amount of work. The canteen committee served 78,911 servicemen at various points such as Union Station, while the surgical dressing committee prepared 650,612 dressings, masks, and jackets. Dedicated physicians trained hundreds in first aid.

What the census of 1920 could not show was the great defense boom that came during World War I when employment shot upward. Utica became a major defense center because of huge orders from both the British and American governments for machine guns, underwear,

Facing page, bottom
The Hotel Utica had 10 floors when it opened in 1912; four more were added in 1926. Radio station WIBX had its studios in the hotel from 1926 to 1928.

Above
The Oneida County Court House on Elizabeth Street was originally decorated with pillars and broad front steps, all of which were removed in a later renovation. (OHS)

Above
John A. Roberts & Company built a new department store on the site of the old Butterfield House in 1910. The store placed this ad in a labor publication and pointed out that its employees enjoyed a "half holiday Saturday afternoon and evening." Courtesy, Utica Public Library.

Above
The local committee promoting the sale of Liberty Bonds chose the city's first real skyscraper—the Utica City National Bank building—as a good spot on which to advertise. They also staged parades, placed signs on streetcars, and constructed a graph on the City Hall tower to show the progress of bond sales among the employees of the city's major businesses. (OHS)

uniforms, and the like.

In the 1890s a group of citizens had organized the Savage Arms Company to make sporting rifles in an old factory on Broad Street. The company prospered, built a new plant on Turner Street, and added the manufacture of pistols. When war broke out, the British government ordered 70,000 machine guns from the Savage Arms Company, which had acquired the patents to the Lewis machine gun. In 1915 the directors decided to sell the corporation to Driggs-Seabury Ordnance at a price that enriched stockholders. The new owners enlarged the Utica plant, which became the largest concern in Utica. In one year alone it hired another 3,000 workers. But the Armistice in 1918 brought cancellation of war contracts and the loss of

thousands of jobs. The sporting-rifle division continued but employed only a few hundred workers.

Uticans and their neighbors in Oneida County bought millions of dollars of war bonds. Charles A. Miller of the Savings Bank of Utica headed a committee that exceeded its quota in each of five drives. It also sponsored the War Chest, the predecessor of the Community Chest and later the United Way. Citizens contributed generously in 1918 and surpassed the goal.

Over 3,000 Uticans served in the armed forces and a detailed account of various military units can be found in T. Wood Clarke's history of Utica. When the units returned home, they received a warm greeting. On September 15, 1919, the city held a parade with floats and a clambake. Among the speakers on this occasion was Assistant Secretary of the Navy Franklin D. Roosevelt. After the war many veterans organized American Legion posts and many doughboys joined the Veterans of Foreign Wars.

Uticans entered the 20th century in a spirit of buoyant optimism. On every side they could see evidence of industrial health, cultural advance, and civic awakening. Visitors and residents alike took pride in the cityscape—new skyscrapers, Union Station, mansions on Genesee Street, and the thousands of elms gracing every avenue.

Above
Uticans cheered a contingent of troops marching down Genesee Street to board a train for camp or embarkation to go "over there." (OHS)

CHAPTER SEVEN

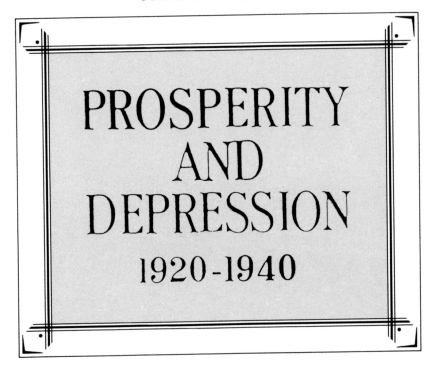

PROSPERITY AND DEPRESSION
1920-1940

Between the World Wars Utica's population slowed its rate of growth and then leveled off around the hundred thousand mark. The foundations of its manufactures began to crack after the Armistice and to crumble under the hammer blows of the Depression. Widespread ownership of automobiles accelerated the movement of residents to the outskirts of the city and to the suburbs. Whereas "Coolidge prosperity" brought an improved standard of living to most Uticans, the Depression spread gloom and poverty.

By 1930 population had risen from 94,156 to 101,740, a gain of 8 percent. Utica was to hover at this figure for the next three decades but its suburbs continued to grow. Despite immigration restrictions, a considerable number of aliens settled in Utica. Most population gain, however, came from the large families of Polish and Italian immigrants who had arrived before World War I. In 1930 Utica had 8,311 Italian-born residents, more than twice the Polish total of 3,871. Meanwhile the English and Germans were losing half of their numbers and the Irish even more. Oneida County showed similar trends, with Italians and Poles accounting for almost half of all the foreign-born. Most Italians (12,780) lived in Utica and Rome; Poles were concentrated in Utica and New York Mills.

Immigration after 1930 slowed to a trickle. In fact many foreign-born sailed home because savings lasted longer in Italy and eastern Europe. Meanwhile unemployment forced many couples to delay marriage and to postpone having children. The census of 1940 demonstrated that Utica was losing its character as an immigrant city since only 17 percent were foreign-born. The census takers began to list the mother tongue of foreign-born residents, which has made it easier to identify minorities—especially those from the Union of Soviet Socialist Republics. The census listed 433 Ukrainian speakers and 231 Yiddish. Only 129 spoke Spanish, indicating that the migration from Puerto Rico had hardly begun.

The Jewish community prospered and many of its members moved uptown to Corn Hill and South Utica. Parents encouraged their children to attend college and enter the professions. Jews took a keen interest in foreign affairs, especially after Hitler rose to power, and a growing number threw their support behind the Zionist movement. To coordinate Jewish activities and to sponsor the United

Jewish Appeal, the Jewish Community Council was formed in 1933, representing the estimated 2,750 persons who belonged to its constituency.

The postwar depression struck Utica with exceptional force because the government canceled its contracts for guns and knit goods. The weaker mills soon closed their doors while those with more reserves operated on half time. By 1922 Utica had only six knitting mills, a sharp drop from the 25 in 1912. The long painful withdrawal from textiles had begun.

Recovery took place in 1922 when the demand for new houses and automobiles sparked another era of good times.

Above
Fifteen thousand people toured the new 14-story First National Bank (right) when it opened on December 3, 1926. Following the 1931 "shotgun wedding" of the First National Bank with two other banks, operations were transferred to the former Citizens Trust building at Columbia and Seneca streets. Although a Kresge's store took over the ground floor, the building remained popular for offices. The Robert Fraser store, center, completed in 1907 to replace the original store that was destroyed by fire, was taken over by Woolworth's in 1939. (OHS)

Thousands of Uticans had accumulated savings during the prosperous years before and during the war. They had the money to buy Model T Fords and to purchase single-family homes. In 1921 Utica annexed most of the land between Prospect Street and the Sauquoit Creek. Various developers bought up tracts, laid out streets, and sold lots. Vernon Davis Company, for example, developed the district from Higby Road to Sauquoit Creek. In 1925 Fay Inman laid out Benton Hills, a tract east of upper Oneida Street. Hugh R. Jones Company acquired the Talcott Road area and the Benton farm east of Genesee Street. He named the latter Ridgewood, landscaped it, and arranged for the construction of attractive homes. Sherman Gardens in East Utica was developed by Harry Roberts, and in a short time prosperous Uticans were enjoying the view from their lawns overlooking the reservoirs and South Woods. In New Hartford and Whitesboro similar developments were attracting homeowners.

By 1929 about 35 percent of families owned their own home, a figure that placed Utica above the national average for urban dwellers. Many families continued to live in duplex houses or flats in which the owner rented out the

upstairs. Most new houses within and outside city limits
were one-family dwellings.

The business community demonstrated confidence in
Utica's future by erecting new buildings or reconstructing
old ones. The Utica Gas and Electric Company in 1922
predicted that Utica would eventually have a population of
330,000. Anticipating greater demands for electricity, it
built a large plant on the corner of Cornelia and Lafayette
streets in 1924 and another at Harbor Point in 1926. The
next year it opened its six-story office building on the corner
of Court and Genesee streets. Most families were installing
telephones in their homes and offices, which required New
York Telephone to string more wires and build new
quarters on the corner of Cornelia and Genesee.

The banks made money lending funds to contractors,
retailers, manufacturers, and homebuilders. The First
National Bank and Trust Company erected a 16-story
building at Genesee and Elizabeth streets. Its president,
Charles B. Rogers, expressed great confidence in Utica's
future.

Commercial travelers, more commonly known as

Top
The Jones Motor Car Company at 318 Elizabeth Street, facing Chancellor Park, sold and repaired Fords. This photo of their shop was taken in 1922. (OHS)

Right
Some of the first traffic lights in Utica also served as directional signs. This one was installed in 1924 at Herkimer Road and North Genesee Street (Deerfield Corners) in North Utica. (OHS)

and vegetable stands, gas stations, garages, and used-car lots. Preachers complained that members would no longer attend Sunday evening services and, even worse, Sunday morning services in the summer months. Daylight saving time, a World War I innovation, became a political football, as did Sunday motion pictures. The Continental Sunday won out; the motoring public overwhelmed the foes of daylight saving time, mainly farmers and motion-picture operators.

Downtown Utica found it difficult to handle the thousands of motor vehicles. The city stationed policemen at the Busy Corner and other intersections, and in 1933 bought its first patrol cars. The Ramp Garage opened in 1928 to accommodate motorists staying at Hotel Utica or driving in for a day's shopping. To reduce taxes, owners of deserted buildings demolished their structures and rented space to car owners.

Shops, stores, and manufacturing plants sprang up in New Hartford, Whitesboro, Deerfield, and other outlying areas where population was shifting and where parking space for workers and customers was available. The New York State Railways began to lose money and gradually shifted over to buses, which proved more flexible and less expensive to operate.

Uticans began to drive to the Adirondack resorts, the St. Lawrence Valley, and New England after the state opened new surfaced roads. Meanwhile Summit and Utica parks saw their attendance fall off, which in turn undermined trolley service. Politicians on every level of government rushed to provide the improved roads the automobile clubs demanded. The State of New York opened the regional headquarters of the State Department of Public Works in its new building on North Genesee Street.

The elegant mansions on lower Genesee Street became less desirable in comparison with the fine new houses on Parkway East, Sherman Drive, Hart's Hill, and South Utica. The huge Victorian mansions required a large staff of servants, but younger Uticans preferred work in offices and stores rather than in homes. Business and professional men coveted the large lots, which they used for parking, and they turned the houses into offices for physicians and lawyers.

The various units of government acquired better quarters. The police department moved into its new building on Oriskany Street West in 1928 and new firehouses were built on Trenton Road (1925), Woodlawn Avenue West (1929), and Madison Avenue (1939). The federal government built its new Post Office on Broad Street and a new armory on Parkway East in 1929. On Deerfield Hill Oneida County erected Broadacres Sanitarium, a much-needed facility since tuberculosis claimed hundreds of victims each year.

Manufacturing plants recovered after 1922 but they

salesmen, visited Utica in increasing numbers. New hotels took care of them but also welcomed tourists and persons attending conventions. As a result Hotel Utica added in 1926 another four floors. The Majestic Hotel (later Hotel Pershing) had opened its doors three years earlier. Across Lafayette Street the Olympic Theater began to show first-run films. Within a year the Stanley Theatre became the showplace of downtown, one of the last great motion-picture houses of the era. Tens of thousands of Uticans recall fondly their graduation ceremonies in this ornate palace. Even more thousands of central New Yorkers remember hearing Fritz Kreisler, Lily Pons, and America's finest symphony orchestras.

Most families bought their first automobiles in the 1920s. Car registrations in Oneida County soared from 15,667 to 41,258, though they did not increase in the Depression. Before the boom collapsed in October 1929 there was one car for every five city dwellers. Drivers had to learn to cope with automatic traffic lights, banked curves, one-way streets, and traffic officers. Along the main highways sprang up a jumble of enterprises—diners, fruit

Top
The Willoughby Company was an important Utica industry during the 1920s. Established as a carriage maker at the turn of the century, Willoughby later built bodies for prestigious automobiles such as Lincoln (a 1928 chauffeur-driven limousine is illustrated), Packard, Cadillac, and Rolls Royce of America. They also made custom bodies for the cars of notables, from the Proctors of Utica to President Coolidge. The firm had some 300 employees at its peak but closed in 1936, a victim of the

Depression and mass production in the auto industry. Courtesy, Harrah's Automobile Collection, Reno, Nevada.

Bottom
Robert Gurley, a Utica trolley buff, took many pictures of the local electric railways during their last years of operation, including this shot on Main Street, Whitesboro, in 1937. He also published a brief history of the lines, entitled Here Comes the Trolley. *(OHS)*

Top
Utica formally entered the Air Age on September 28, 1929, when the Municipal Airport on the old River Road in Marcy was dedicated. Regular service was provided by Colonial Airlines' eight-passenger Stinsons and American Airlines' Ford trimotors. Larger planes made the Municipal Airport obsolete in a few years and it served mostly private planes and a flight school, shown circa 1948. Scheduled air service returned to the Utica area in 1950 when Robinson Airways inaugurated flights to the new Oneida County Airport. (OHS)

Above
Anthracite was still the principal heating fuel in Utica in 1927 and Emil J. Georg and Charles Faass & Company were but two of 39 coal dealers in the area. They delivered coal in horse-drawn wagons from this massive trestle on Erie Street. Similar structures stood at close intervals along most of the railroad lines in the city. Courtesy, Miss Ruth Georg.

Killed in Bootleg War

Louis Malkoon, Utica, left, above, and his son, Rocco, at right, were shot, the victims of rival bootleggers, and their bodies found beside their roadster 12 miles east of this city today. Additional pictures on page 25.

had lost the dynamism of prewar industry. The managers of the textile-knitting goods sector worried about growing competition from mills in the Carolinas, and also about changing fashions. Southern mills paid lower wages, received tax abatements, operated without regulations, and kept union members out of town. New York's state legislature imposed rules on workmen's compensation and kept reducing the hours of employment toward the 40-hour level. Furthermore the state required all children under 16 to attend school, a requirement not imposed or easily evaded in southern states.

During the 1920s Uticans installed furnaces in their homes and included central heating in all new dwellings. Many homeowners found oil cheaper than coal and a lot cleaner and more convenient. More women were taking jobs in offices, which also used central heating. As a result women dressed more smartly. Long underwear was out; short skirts and silk stockings were in. All these trends cut the market for underwear made in Utica's mills. The Skenandoa mill was converted in 1926 to take advantage of the shift from cotton to rayon.

Utica was prospering but not booming. In 1929 its output of knit goods was valued at $19 million and cotton goods at $13 million.

Above
The violence fostered by Prohibition and the competition among bootleggers helped give Utica a reputation as a "tough" city during the 1920s and early 1930s. Louis and Rocco Malkoon were reportedly killed to prevent them from revealing the whereabouts of a still operated by rival bootleggers from Albany. Courtesy, Utica Newspapers.

The Prohibition amendment of 1919, outlawing alcoholic beverages, followed shortly by the women's suffrage amendment, changed the life and habits of Uticans. A majority, especially those of Irish, Italian, German, Polish, and Jewish backgrounds, felt that prohibition interfered with personal liberty as well as ethnic traditions. A new occupation, bootlegging, sprang up to quench the local thirst. Those born in Europe, who had often made their own wine, continued this practice and a few supplied their neighbors and friends. If an outsider muscled in on a bootlegger's territory, he risked a beating or worse. Crime became rampant and payoffs to police became common. When girls began to smoke cigarettes, drink gin, and wear short skirts, clergymen and not a few parents warned of crumbling moral standards.

Most Uticans obeyed the law and never patronized a bootlegger. Alcoholic consumption fell only because booze was expensive and hard to find. Men spent more time at home or driving around the countryside and less in the old-fashioned saloon, now a back-alley speakeasy. Absenteeism fell off and health statistics showed improvement. Other factors—a higher standard of living, better nutrition, and improved medical care—were responsible for most of the gains in health.

Uticans organized more clubs and associations for social, professional, and humanitarian purposes in much the same fashion as George Babbitt's friends did in Sinclair Lewis' famous novel. The Lion's Club (1924) attracted a mixed group of business and professional men who devoted an enormous amount of effort in aiding the blind and its chief agency, the Association for the Blind. The Torch Club (1926) appealed to professional men who listened to experts and questioned them on foreign and domestic issues. The Utica Branch of the Foreign Policy Association (1930) with Mrs. George B. Ogden as first president also brought in speakers who discussed the rise of totalitarian regimes and the threat of war. Meanwhile Rotary, Kiwanis, and Exchange clubs, to mention three of the most prominent, continued their activities especially for the benefit of young people.

The most ambitious organization was the Community Chest, which became a powerful agency despite its shaky start in 1921, when it failed to reach its goal. During the 10 years before 1933, it collected over $200,000 a year, which it distributed to a score of agencies such as the Girl Scouts, Catholic Charities, and the like. While the Depression reduced donors' ability to contribute, the dollars collected went farther in aiding the young and disadvantaged. When World War II came, citizens opened their hearts and pocketbooks. No doubt full employment and overtime earnings helped the agency to reach new goals.

Education made great strides after World War I when most young people began to attend high school until graduation. John DeCamp, superintendent of schools from 1917 to 1941, provided firm leadership. The Board of Education kept abreast of modern trends by providing school nurses and dental hygienists as well as more vocational offerings. When the number of students in Utica Free Academy rose above 4,000, double sessions were inaugurated. Clearly another high school was needed to take care of the swelling numbers. Fortunately Utica was able to secure federal grants for aid in the construction (1936) of Thomas R. Proctor High School in East Utica,

where Rollin W. Thompson became principal.

Dr. T. Wood Clarke's history of Utica contains a detailed account of changes in public health and medical care. In 1925 the Utica Academy of Medicine was formed to bring in specialists for lectures and to provide a better medical library. Physicians helped form the Hospital Plan, better known as Blue Cross, whereby individuals could pay monthly fees in order to insure themselves for hospital expenses. The Visiting Nurses Association brought information and vaccines to stations in seven districts of the city. As a result child mortality fell sharply. Broadacres Sanitarium rehabilitated many patients who were able to return to their families and homes. Fortunately after World War II new surgical procedures and the use of such drugs as streptomycin and PAS brought about a sharp decline in the death rate from tuberculosis. The county government converted Broadacres, no longer needed as a tuberculosis facility, for use as a nursing center for the elderly.

No city in the state matched Utica's long interest in the care of the mentally disturbed. Utica State continued to provide such care even though Marcy Hospital was opened in 1921. At first one superintendent directed both but in 1930 each became independent. Utica State acquired new laboratories, quarters for nurses, a surgical building, and an auditorium. The other hospitals also improved their facilities; Faxton Hospital, for example, added an annex and a new maternity building that became the Children's Hospital Home in 1940.

The Depression, which shook the nation's banking system, threatened Utica's banks as well. Business failures and massive unemployment, often reaching 25 percent, undermined bankers' ability to collect loans and payments on mortgages. Sometimes banks took over defaulting firms and foreclosed mortgages. Burdened with losses and frozen assets, bankers tightened up on loans, fearful that their depositors would demand cash, as in other cities. In December 1930 East Utica residents began to withdraw their savings from the Utica Trust and Deposit Bank. Fearing this panic might engulf the other banks, the Savings Bank of Utica made a large deposit in this institution. The danger of another "run" hung over the city like a cloud.

The collapse of central European banks and the devaluation of the English pound in 1931 led to the suspension of war debts, the collapse of international trade, and the paralysis of credit. These ominous signs frightened Americans who grimly watched the economy stagger downhill. By the fall of 1931 the Utica Trust and Deposit, the First National Bank, and the Citizens Trust Company, which had already in 1930 absorbed the Utica National

Above
The old main building of the Utica State Hospital, opened in 1843, is a nationally recognized example of Greek Revival architecture. It is shown circa 1950. Courtesy, Architectural Archives, Munson-Williams-Proctor Institute.

Bank and Trust, were vulnerable if depositors demanded their savings.

Charles A. Miller, president of the Savings Bank of Utica, organized a group of citizens who decided to head off disaster by arranging a merger of the three banks. He persuaded Mrs. Thomas R. Proctor to guarantee the financial integrity of the new institution, which on October 26, 1931, took the name of the First Citizens Bank and Trust Company. Charles B. Rogers became chairman of the board and Francis P. McGinty became president. The new bank closed branch offices in East Utica, Corn Hill, and James Street. The former Citizens Trust building became headquarters and in later years a large addition was attached on Seneca Street. Because the new institution no longer needed the Utica Trust building, this structure was torn down.

The Oneida National Bank had pursued a cautious policy in making loans and thus escaped the turmoil affecting the other commercial banks. In 1938 Charles W. Hall replaced Albert Niles as president and enlarged its

quarters by adding a wing on Bleecker Street.

The Depression cast a lengthening shadow over all aspects of community life. Almost every family had a member, a relative, or a neighbor who had lost his or her job. Every month more shopkeepers closed their doors. Uticans helped their relatives and neighbors by offering them painting jobs, surplus vegetables, and secondhand clothes. Some parents took in their grown children, including their youngsters; other families invited parents to share their home. Officials granted extensions to taxpayers, and the American Legion and trade unions raised funds for various public projects. Mrs. Thomas R. Proctor not only shored up the banks but paid to have Bagg's Hotel torn down brick by brick. In its place she had a stone building erected, the centerpiece of another park.

In the spring of 1932 the local economy hit a new low. Utica's Department of Welfare reported granting relief to 11,026 families at a cost of $82,426, both figures more than doubling that of the previous year. The Community Chest appealed for help, citing that more than 5,000 families were living on 17 cents a day for food, fuel, and shelter.

To be sure prices had also hit rock bottom. One could buy ham at 13 cents a pound, coffee at 28 cents a pound, and 10 pounds of sugar for 39 cents. For the carriage trade loin lamb chops were only 29 cents a pound. Graffenburg Dairy was selling a half-pint of light cream for 13 cents. The Boston Store offered women coats for $5 and men shorts for 19 cents. Fraser Store, soon to close, conducted a sale with Enna-Jettick shoes for $2.95 a pair. Wicks and Greenman offered Hart, Schaffner & Marx suits for $24.75.

Above
The Utica Country Day School opened on Genesee Street near Golf Avenue in New Hartford in 1921, and offered ''progressive'' elementary and secondary education. Former pupils of the ''Utica Cat and Dog School'' (as some public school students called it) have fond memories of its ''hands-on'' approach to learning, but declining enrollment and competition from improved public schools forced it to close in 1944. The building later served Mohawk Valley Technical Institute and Notre Dame High School before it was razed in 1961. (OHS)

Geffen and Wolf Motors advertised a new Willys 8 Sedan for $795. One could buy a Western Giant Tire for $5.25 with a free tube thrown in. The *Observer-Dispatch* had an ad for a three-room flat at Oneida and Pleasant for only $30 a month including heat and hot water. But coal cost the landlord only $9 dollars a ton. One wonders how sturdy were the end tables offered by J.B. Wells for $2.95. Newlyweds could buy a three-piece living-room suite from E. Tudor Williams for $129.

Life was not all grim. Most recreation was free: swimming in South Woods pond and Addison Miller pool; vacant lots with baseball and ski slopes, and a skating rink on the Parkway. Entertainment was cheap indeed. One could buy the paper for two cents and read the comics, the boys preferring "Buck Rogers 2,432," the girls, "Boots and Her Buddies." The *Observer-Dispatch* carried Dorothy Dix's advice to lovelorn, and a serial with the intriguing title, the *Man Hunter.* Ice cream was only a nickel for a two-scoop cone. You could get into a neighborhood theater for only 15 cents and on Saturday afternoon several theaters ran serials for only one dime.

The unemployed aroused much sympathy. In 1930 Charles A. Miller headed the Emergency Employment Bureau, which tried to collect private funds to hire workers on various projects. The bureau sponsored the construction of a replica of old Fort Schuyler in Roscoe Conkling Park to celebrate the centennial of the city. The tennis, skating, and skiing areas of Roscoe Conkling Park bear the name of Valentine Bialas, commissioner of parks for several years. Bialas became an iceskater who competed in three Olympics, including the Lake Placid contest of 1932. Four years later he qualified once more but a railroad accident cost him his leg. He went on to set an example of courage and determination by competing in tennis and skating competitions with an artificial leg.

As the Depression deepened neither private agencies

nor local governments could handle the mounting relief load. Governor Franklin D. Roosevelt proposed a Temporary Emergency Relief Administration (TERA) to supervise grants to local communities for work and home relief. Home relief was handled by the local welfare commissioner but work relief was directed by an emergency work bureau whose members were appointed by the mayor. Roy C. Van Denbergh of the Savings Bank of Utica replaced Charles Miller as director of the Oneida County Work Bureau.

The New Deal took active steps to combat the Depression. It continued home relief through the TERA until 1935 when approximately one-sixth of the population was receiving public assistance. The Civil Works Administration (CWA) created jobs in the parks and on the highways between 1933 and 1935 and its functions were enlarged under the Works Progress Administration (WPA), which continued into the early 1940s. CWA workers removed miles of trolley tracks from the routes that the New York State Railways had converted to buses and rebuilt the tracks still in use on Genesee Street less than 10 years before they, too, were abandoned. The WPA built tennis courts, wading pools, and baseball diamonds. The ski run on the Parkway and miles of roads in various parks were another legacy. The WPA and the PWA helped finance school improvements such as the gymnasium and

---

Above
Over 35,000 people crowded Roscoe Conkling Park on July 23, 1932, to witness a mock battle staged around the "replica" of Old Fort Schuyler built by the Emergency Employment Bureau. With a cast of hundreds, and much shooting, the pageant made an indelible impression on the spectators. In the words of Dr. T. Wood Clarke, it "made up in dramatic action for its historical inaccuracy, as there is no record of Fort Schuyler ever having been attacked by Indians or anybody else." (OHS)

56

auditorium of Proctor High School. Meanwhile the Civilian Conservation Corps (CCC) enrolled hundreds of young men who built fire lanes and planted trees on abandoned tracts.

Vacant buildings and houses fell prey to vandals and arsonists. The federal government offered grants for slum clearance and encouraged the construction of large complexes of apartments. The Utica Housing Authority started to build public housing units in various districts. Adrean Terrace near the Armory offered apartments at low rent. Subsequently Utica constructed Washington Courts, Gilmore Village, and other public units.

Important changes in the media and the arts took place during the interwar period. The first radio station began in 1922 but its signal was weak and its programming sporadic. Three years later station WIBX opened and occupied some rooms in Hotel Utica. Although many Uticans were buying radios, WIBX found it difficult to make a profit, and not until 1931 when Scott Bowen purchased the station did it achieve firm footing. Soon it joined the Columbia Broadcasting system, which relayed such programs as "Amos 'n' Andy."

The demise of the *Saturday Globe* and its successors left a gap in publishing. In 1922 Frank Gannett, who had acquired papers in Ithaca, Elmira, Albany, Syracuse, and Rochester, bought control of several corporate shells and joined them under the name of the Utica *Observer-Dispatch* with Prentiss Bailey continuing as business manager. In 1935 the Gannett chain bought the Utica *Daily Press,* thus enabling it to use its presses more efficiently. Paul Williams remained editor of the *Press* and William J. Woods after 1937 became editor of the *Observer-Dispatch.* In 1944 Vincent S. Jones of Utica became executive editor of both papers; later he became a top executive in Gannett headquarters in Rochester.

A ray of sunshine flashed through the gloom of 1935 when Uticans learned that Mrs. Thomas R. Proctor had left

---

Above
Munson-Williams-Proctor Institute operated for its first 25 years in the two former Proctor residences, shown here circa 1955. Fountain Elms (left) was built in 1850 for James Watson Williams and Helen Elizabeth Munson Williams and was later the home of their daughter and son-in-law, Rachel and Frederick Proctor. It first served the Institute as the Community Arts Program building and later the Art Gallery, before becoming a decorative arts museum and quarters for the Oneida Historical Society in 1960. The Thomas and Maria Proctor house (right), originally built in 1848 for the Utica Orphan Asylum, was maintained for some years as a house museum but was better known as the Institute's Music Building until it was demolished to make way for the new Museum of Art. The Sidewalk Art Show has been a popular attraction each summer since 1938. (OHS)

The Talkies Arrive

Vitaphone was experimenting with disks to synchronize sound with films and in 1927 a breakthrough occurred. Al Jolson sang and spoke a few lines of dialogue in the *Jazz Singer*.

In April 1928 the Avon Theater advertised a new film starring John Barrymore and Dolores Costello with the title *When a Man Loves.* One could actually hear a cathedral choir, a bell, and a whistle, all at regular prices. The first film using sound throughout was *The Lights of New York,* a gangster picture with Helene Costello and Cullen Landis. Before long all the theaters of Utica were spending thousands of dollars to equip themselves with sound.

No doubt the peak of the motion picture era in Utica came in 1927-1928 when the Stanley Company of America tore down a historic house at 261 Genesee Street and erected a $1.5 million palace. It opened on September 10, 1928, with great fanfare and a parade down Genesee Street. That evening the crowd of customers that formed a line all the way to South Street admired the Byzantine splendor of the interior with its coiled columns, bronzed walls, and glowing lights. Professor George Wald presided at the console of the Wurlitzer organ and guest conductor Phil Spitalny directed the orchestra of 14 on the movable stage.

Uticans took great pride in the Stanley, which a half century later served them as Performing Arts Center.

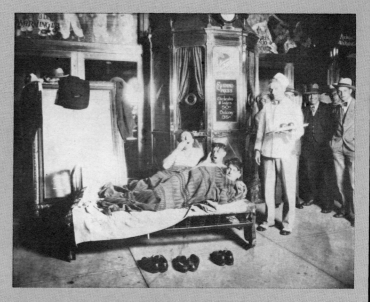

Eager to be first in line for the opening of the Stanley Theatre on September 10, 1928, Joseph Grimaldi, Rocco Asselta, and Anthony Dardano "camped out" the night before on the sidewalk directly in front of the main box office. The trio feigned sleep for the photographer while a dubious waiter from the Morris Coffee Shop next door stood by with either a midnight snack or breakfast in bed. Grimaldi, lying in the foreground, later worked at the Stanley as a projectionist. Courtesy, Joseph Grimaldi and Utica Newspapers.

her fortune to the Munson-Williams-Proctor Institute. The Proctor houses became a museum and a center for music and art. The carriage houses held a School of Related Arts and Sciences, which after 1941 was guided by William Palmer as an art school. Meanwhile Arthur J. Derbyshire had become director of the Institute, which he administered from 1937 to 1943.

The coming of sound movies intensified the distress of musicians already suffering from loss of jobs. In 1932 a group of musicians and interested citizens formed the Civic Musical Society under the direction of Berrian R. Shute, professor of music at Hamilton College. This organization sponsored the symphony orchestra and a chorus whose performances were eagerly awaited.

Oneida County voters regularly gave Republican candidates a solid majority, but Uticans generally favored Democrats. Between 1921 and 1943, Utica had three Republican mayors for a total of six years, but the three Democratic mayors held the post for 16 years. The Republicans elected Dr. Fred J. Douglas (1921), Fred J. Rath (1927), and Samuel Sloan (1933). They stressed Republican prosperity and had a strong ally in Alphonse Bertolini, a powerful chieftain in East Utica. Because the Democrats had Al Smith as governor and Democratic nominee in 1928, they attracted votes among Roman Catholics, labor-union members, and opponents of prohibition. They capitalized on the Depression's having taken place under Herbert Hoover. In East Utica Rufus Elefante rose to power in the 1930s by finding jobs in private business and on government projects for his neighbors.

Most campaigns revolved around personalities and the spoils of office. Businessmen and reformers demanded an

*Above
Rufus P. "Rufie" Elefante once said, "I'm no angel, but I'm not the devil either." Beginning in the 1930s by quietly but quite openly overseeing Democratic patronage and dispensing favors, he became an important power broker in the oldest tradition of American municipal politics. His organization reached its peak in the mid-1950s and continued to wield*

end to the spoils system and more efficiency in government. In 1930 the Chamber of Commerce sparked a movement for adopting the city manager plan which Rochester had accepted by 1928. In Utica Frank J. Baker and Arthur W. Pickard led the forces in favor of this plan. After a petition bearing 3,365 names was submitted to the city clerk, the common council agreed to a referendum. The voters approved the plan by a strong majority. William Bray, a lawyer who later served as lieutenant governor, contested the legality of the vote, charging inadequate publication of the official call for the referendum. The case dragged through the courts and Judge Dowling ruled that failure to observe these requirements invalidated the vote. Disappointed and infuriated by this decision, the supporters mounted another campaign in 1933, but the politicians rallied their forces and defeated the proposal.

Less controversial was the proposal to take over the property of the Consolidated Water Company, a private business, which had supplied the city and some suburbs with water since 1899. The common council agreed in 1937 to the purchase for the sum of $7,900,000. State authorities ratified the proposition and the city set up a nonpartisan water commission with Richard Balch as chairman.

The Depression, which had sapped the city's vitality and discouraged its residents, finally passed. The economy sputtered for years without ending unemployment and bringing back prosperity. For a short time in 1938 employment reached depths close to those of 1932-1933. But slowly, painfully, the economy righted itself, and by 1940 most citizens believed that they had put the Depression behind them.

Looming on the horizon, however, was the specter of war in the Far East and Europe. Japanese advances in China and Nazi victories in the Low Countries and France threatened not only economic recovery but, even worse, the peace and security of the United States.

considerable influence despite the scandals of 1958. Elefante held court for many years at Marino's Restaurant on Catherine Street until it fell to Urban Renewal, then moved to Uncle Henry's Pancake House on Lafayette Street; as a result, both places were known in turn as "Little City Hall." Courtesy, Utica Newspapers.

Above
A sign of upcoming better times as the 1930s drew to a close, Chanatry Brothers opened one of the first modern supermarkets in Utica on December 8, 1938, at 515-517 Bleecker Street. The new store, with bright lights and streamlined self-service counters, was a far cry from its dimly lit predecessor and was the first grocery store in the United States to gross a million dollars in sales in a single year. Courtesy, Miss Nellie Chanatry.

CHAPTER EIGHT

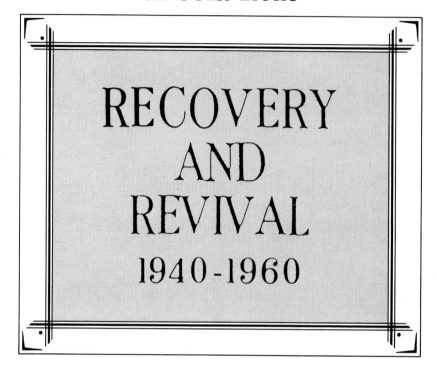

RECOVERY
AND
REVIVAL
1940-1960

From Loom to Boom. That catchy label, attached by one observer to the economic transformation in the Utica-Rome Standard Metropolitan Area in the postwar period, characterized fairly well the changes taking place in Oneida-Herkimer counties. The old economy based on textiles and knit goods collapsed but in its place arose a new economy centered on metalworking, machines, and services. Led by hundreds of energetic and farsighted business, professional, and political leaders, a generation of Uticans showed imagination, enterprise, and hard work in carrying out this revolution. Furthermore their vision stimulated a revival of the spirit best exemplified in the founding of two colleges, the dedication of the new Museum of Art, and the reinvigoration of churches and other associations.

World War II brought a return of full employment and prosperity. The Savage Arms Company once again secured tremendous orders for machine guns and at its peak employed over 8,000 men and women. Savage received the Army and Navy "E" for excellence because its workers and managers filled orders ahead of schedule and produced guns of fine quality. Brunner Manufacturing also received the award and delivered its entire output of compressor

pumps and freezing units to the armed services. Another winner, Bossert Company, turned out 20 million cartridge cases and oxygen cylinders. Divine Brothers won recognition by building bomb-loading devices and fuses for artillery shells. The fifth winner, Utica Cutlery, turned out two million bayonets and millions of knives of every description. Indium Corporation had earlier developed indium, a special metal useful in alloys. When the bearings in airplane engines were coated with it, their useful life was greatly extended. Good wages and lots of overtime attracted workers from neighboring communities. Production soared; almost every worker had a son, brother, relative, or neighbor among the 11,609 men and women who had joined the armed forces.

Civilians worked hard to assist the war effort. Hundreds worked in Rhoads General Hospital on Burrstone Road, built by the Army in 1943 to take care of wounded servicemen. Because of the shortage of nurses, all the hospitals relied on volunteers. Many citizens collected scrap metal and old rubber tires, bought war bonds, and served on rationing boards and in Red Cross stations. Although gas, meat, tires, and sugar were rationed, most

Above
Stores sold government defense stamps to encourage thrift and aid the
country's defense. This girl, dressed in a red sweater, "V for Victory" pin,
white blouse, and navy blue skirt was photographed at Woolworth's a few
weeks before Pearl Harbor. Courtesy, Russell T. Rhoades & Company.

civilians lived better than they had in the grim days of the Depression. Family income rose sharply because housewives, retired people, handicapped individuals, and even high-school students took jobs. Since they could not build houses or buy new automobiles, many citizens saved a great deal of money. Residents of Oneida County purchased a grand total of $260,765,051 of war bonds.

Gratifying as these signs of prosperity were, they did not disguise the fact that postwar Utica could not depend upon arms and textiles when peace returned. Clearly the textile mills had lost their competitive edge over southern factories as early as 1910 and had displayed increasing weakness in the interwar period. Businessmen and political leaders began to make plans for attracting new industry. Their efforts were to be crowned with success; within the next decade the Utica-Rome area added 30,000 jobs during the same time it was losing some 12,000 jobs in textiles.

The collapse of textiles spelled tragedy and hardship for workers, a majority of whom had worked all their lives in the mills. Between 1951 and 1953 three textile firms closed down; within two years another two had ended local operations. Finally A.D. Juilliard left New York Mills in 1959. Whereas in 1951 three of the four largest employers were textile producers, two years later all four were durable-goods manufacturers. Managers of textile factories attributed their decline to a mixture of factors: high costs, old plants, lack of parking, old equipment, cumbersome work rules included in union contracts, high taxes compared with those in southern states, and a lack of semiskilled labor willing to work on night shifts. Outsiders might also assign part of the blame to the failure of management to demonstrate a competitive spirit.

More important than the decline in textiles was the upsurge of new companies making machines and

Top
The Andrews Sisters were playing the Stanley Theatre when Carl K. Frey took this photo for a postcard in 1942. The Central New York Power Corporation building at 258 Genesee Street (tall building at left) and the Stanley were both built in the late 1920s. (OHS)

Above
Hundreds of Utica and central New York women got their first taste of factory work and good wages at the Savage Arms Corporation during World War II. Heat, noise, and 12-hour days were the regimen, as workers

turned out thousands of Browning .50 caliber aircraft machine guns and Thompson submachine guns. Courtesy, Russell T. Rhodes & Company.

Above
In 1941, as the Depression drew to a close, downtown Utica saw its first major construction project in over a decade. The new Boston Store (left) replaced the 66-year-old Arcade Building and its streamlined, windowless facade was a dramatic contrast to the Victorian Oneida National Bank. Courtesy, Russell T. Rhodes & Company.

transportation equipment. Even more significant was the rising employment in service trades and other nonmanufacturing activities. No doubt the outstanding example was the dynamic growth of Griffiss Air Force Base in Rome, which became the largest employer in the Utica-Rome area.

Like the city fathers of the 1840s who faced the loss of trade and a dwindling population, Uticans a century later showed enterprise and imagination in meeting the challenge of dynamic changes revolutionizing the economy.

Hundreds of Uticans and their associates in neighboring communities worked hard to revitalize the economy of central New York. Any listing will overlook important individuals but the following examples will demonstrate that this effort was truly a community undertaking.

James Capps, the proprietor of Wicks and Greenman since 1930, became president of the Utica Chamber of Commerce in 1940, a post he held for the next six years. He discovered that many business and professional men shared his conviction that the city must seek to diversify its manufacturing base. Richard Balch, president of Horrocks-Ibbotson, urged revitalization and served as a conduit to Democratic chieftains. Bankers such as Charles Hall of Oneida National and Francis P. McGinty of the First Bank supplied information and funds when needed. David Hogue, publisher of the two Gannett papers, provided publicity and encouragement. Henry Dorrance, a skilled lawyer who knew his way around the corridors of Albany, was ready to untie legal knots. Former mayor Vincent R. Corrou, an able and energetic personality, became the permanent director of the Chamber of Commerce's committee on industrial-business development. A key figure was Boyd Golder, mayor from 1945 to 1954, who convinced

visiting businessmen that they could expect wholehearted cooperation from the city administration.

The New York State Department of Commerce worked closely with Uticans to identify companies that were looking for new sites. In 1946 a state official learned that the Chicago Pneumatic Tool Company of Cleveland planned to expand and might locate its new plant in Utica if it could find a good site and secure community support. The Chamber of Commerce found a 77-acre location in the town of Frankfort just beyond the county line. Businessmen contributed $30,000 to buy the land and to employ an architect to develop plans for a building of 400,000 square feet. In addition the city officials guaranteed sewer lines and protection by police and fire fighters. Company officials decided to locate in this area because of the availability of labor, the warm welcome of the business community, the cooperation of officials, favorable labor relations, and outright gifts of land. Within a short time CP was employing about 2,000 workers.

During World War II General Electric had set up two small operations. When the company sought a certain building, local businessmen rushed to buy it and lease it to the company on generous terms. Later, in 1951, GE bought the structure and made several additions to it. This plant made home phonographs and radios, the latter in such numbers that Utica claimed to be the radio manufacturing capital of the nation. This claim was soon dropped, however, because GE as well as most American manufacturers moved radio production to foreign countries. In 1951 the Chamber of Commerce achieved its greatest coup when GE selected the area as the site of its new $15-million plant for lightweight military-electronic equipment. The Chamber secured a fine site on the George Hatfield estate in nearby New Hartford. Utica's officials cooperated

Above
James G. "Jim" Capps (1898-1976) was a key figure in Utica's postwar "loom to boom" revitalization. President of the Utica Chamber of Commerce from 1940-1946, he was credited with bringing in more new industry, including General Electric, than had been brought in throughout the previous 25 years. Courtesy, Utica Newspapers.

Above
A Utica newspaper photographer captured the end of the city's textile era in this 1961 picture of the abandoned August Knitting Mill on Niagara Street. Established in 1905, the company ceased operations in Utica in 1958 after opening a plant in North Carolina. Courtesy, Utica Newspapers.

by providing sewers, streets, and police-fire protection. GE managers liked the location because they could supervise this plant from Schenectady and Syracuse. They had already found that Utica's workmen were conscientious and eager to work at fair wages. Almost at once some 3,000 to 4,000 workers were recruited, including many professionals and engineers. By 1960 well over 6,000 people were working for GE in various plants.

In 1946-1947 Continental Can built a large plant on French Road at a cost of about $2.5 million. This operation ran into snags, and in 1951 the plant was sold to Bendix Aviation, which employed about 1,500 workers.

Suddenly a shortage of skilled labor emerged. To be sure, thousands of jobless textile workers wanted another job, but many of them were older women and men who could not perform the skills required in metalwork. In 1952 the State Department of Labor urged the formation of a community employment committee to sponsor training and offer courses. They estimated that about 4,000 jobs were available for persons who could read blueprints and operate machine tools. Utica College offered a special course in electronics for technicians. Mohawk Valley Technical Institute, which became Mohawk Valley Community College in 1962, provided similar courses, using tools and machines lent to them by local manufacturers. Utica Free Academy and some suburban high schools trained technicians in day and evening courses. Some students received loans from Rotary for tuition payments and many returning veterans were able to use the GI Bill of Rights. Newspapers and radio brought to everyone's attention the various courses available and the thousands of good jobs at wages above the prevailing level. The State Department of Education speeded up the training and licensing of teachers. About 1,000 persons secured technical training while many others received in-house instruction. Although few of the older textile workers participated, many moved into unskilled jobs, especially in the service fields.

In 1957 the Chamber of Commerce heard that Sperry-Rand, which owned the important Remington factory in Ilion, needed space for the manufacture of UNIVAC, the computer that had received national publicity. The old Savage Arms plant looked like a possibility, provided some alterations were made. The Utica Industrial Development Corporation agreed to spend $50,000 for the alterations, which convinced Sperry-Rand of Utica's goodwill. By 1961 over 1,200 workers had jobs.

Mohawk Airlines moved its headquarters to the Oneida County airport in 1958. Originally Robinson Airlines, a tiny outfit operating out of Ithaca, the company had expanded at an explosive rate and needed a more central location. County officials with the enthusiastic support of both Utica and Rome Chambers of Commerce offered to build hangars, maintenance shops, and offices as well as access roads, parking facilities, and related services. The county funded its expenditure of $3 million by leasing the facilities to Mohawk for a rent sufficient to pay the interest and principal.

Were the old factories worth adaptation to new users? Some individuals gambled that they could find firms that needed cheap space. A wide variety of enterprises ranging from print shops to automobile dealers settled into the old mills. Perhaps the most unusual was the Upper Division College, which utilized the Globe Woolen Mill for its classrooms and laboratories.

Utica Drop Forge & Tool employed only 450 workers before World War II, but wartime orders and defense contracts after the war led to a remarkable expansion. Willis Daugherty, the president, used the findings of his

Above
General Electric transformed one landmark of Utica's days as knit goods capital of the world—the Oneita Knitting Mill on Broad Street—into a center for the development of sophisticated radar and other military and aerospace electronic equipment. Courtesy, Utica Newspapers.

research team that had discovered new ways to make parts for jet aircraft. When the orders poured in, the company rented quarters in old factories in New York Mills. Its handsome profits attracted the attention of Kelsey-Hayes, which purchased it in 1956. The new owners built a plant in New Hartford for vacuum induction melting of alloys (now Special Metals). They also opened another plant in Whitestown to make jet turbine blades and buckets. By 1959 Kelsey-Hayes employed about 2,000 workers.

Rome was booming at this time because in 1942 the federal government had set up the Rome Air Depot, a base for the storage and maintenance of the Air Materiel Command. During the war the depot employed 10,000 civilians to support about 3,500 military personnel. The base naturally contracted its operations during peacetime

Top
Lathes, drill presses, and milling machines replaced looms, spinning frames, and knitting machines in the hands of local workers as Utica turned from textiles to durable goods in the late 1940s and early 1950s. This picture was taken at Chicago Pneumatic soon after the local plant opened in 1949. (OHS)

Above
The yards of the New York, Ontario & Western Railway lay empty in the spring of 1957 in a picture looking north from the old Burrstone Road bridge. The tracks of the remaining Lackawanna Railroad (right) were later shifted a few yards to the west and most of this strip of land became the route of the North-South Arterial. Courtesy, Utica Newspapers.

and in 1950 had only 1,200 employees. In 1948 it was renamed Griffiss Air Force Base in honor of Lieutenant Colonel Townsend Griffiss who lost his life in a crash.

When the Korean War began in 1950, Congress voted huge sums for defense. The Air Force chose Griffiss as the base for six major air commands, the most important of which was Rome Air Materiel Area or ROAMA, which bought, stored, and maintained ground electronic equipment for all other bases. In 1960 Griffiss had 7,902 civilian and 3,380 military employees. Several small firms which supplied and required electronic parts sprang up around the base. The Pentagon spent millions each year on new construction at the base.

Griffiss had great impact upon the Upper Mohawk region, providing work for thousands of workers within a radius of 30 miles. The city of Rome, however, found it necessary to spend large sums for schools, streets, sewerage and water lines, and for police and fire protection. Although the federal government did not pay taxes on its property, it did provide loans for school construction and tuition grants to schools educating the children of base personnel.

Hardly had Utica-Rome rid itself of its dependence upon textiles than it became the captive of defense industry. Dr. Crisafulli estimated that nearly one-fifth of total employment in 1961 was tied to defense expenditures. A sabre-rattling speech in the Kremlin or a political gaffe in Washington could threaten the well-being of the people in this area. In the winter of 1960-1961, the Air Force proposed to scrap ROAMA and deactivate Griffiss. The threatened

loss of over 6,000 jobs shocked Rome's citizens and indeed disturbed businessmen and citizens throughout the region. Newspapers and civic organizations swung into action, hoping to reverse this decision. They demanded a full report of the cost-effectiveness of the move. Some 35,000 telegrams flooded the White House, the Pentagon, and Congress. Whether these protests proved decisive or whether Russian snarling over West Berlin caused second thoughts in the Pentagon, ROAMA escaped the ax—at least temporarily.

The Utica-Rome metropolitan area had a large percentage of its workers belonging to unions. Membership varied in a range from 50,000 to 60,000, almost half of nonagricultural workers. Michael Walsh was the leading organizer and director of the Labor Temple, where the unions in the building trades centered their activities. As textiles declined and metals and machinery expanded, membership in the textile unions declined and that of machinists expanded. As railroads declined and trucking took over, the railroad brotherhoods lost membership but

Above
Cranes lift steel into place for the Thruway bridge over the Barge Canal just north of Whitesboro. The first section of the Thruway was opened in 1954, a 115-mile segment between West Henrietta, near Rochester, and Lowell, west of Utica. John Pearce of Whitesboro took this and dozens of other pictures of Thruway construction with a camera that he made himself. (OHS)

Above
Dick Clark of "American Bandstand" fame (right) began his television
career in 1951 as a newscaster for Utica's WKTV under the name "Dick
Clay." His father was manager of local radio station WRUN. On one of
several visits to his home city in the early 1960s, he chatted with veteran
WKTV announcer Lyle Bosley. Courtesy, WKTV.

teamsters increased. Rocco F. DePerno, head of Local 182 for 30 years, became head of the New York State Teamsters Council. When large supermarkets and chain stores drove hundreds of small grocers and butcher shops out of existence, Samuel Talarico, a gifted union leader, organized the meatcutters. Talarico later became the national secretary-treasurer of this union that took the name, United Food and Commercial Workers. The local union has erected a handsome building on the Parkway.

Labor leaders worked fairly closely with business leaders on many projects such as attracting new industry and supporting the United Way. Realizing the precarious nature of the local economy, labor leaders did not make unreasonable demands. As a result Utica had the best "no strike" record of any city in the state. Interestingly enough, the trustees of Utica College named one of their buildings on the Utica College campus in honor of DePerno, a distinction seldom accorded to union leaders on any campus. Talarico also supported Utica College and served on its board of trustees.

A "new" economy was emerging in which services and other nonmanufacturing employment were increasing faster than manufacturing. While employment rose more than 10 percent between 1950 and 1960, employment in manufacturing actually dropped almost 4 percent.

Construction employment rose rapidly, partly in response to the demands of manufacturers for space but also because of housing needs. Utica's basic housing stock was old, more than three-fourths of it in 1960 over 40 years of age. The census figures for 1960 showed that 22.8 percent of the housing units, approximately 7,548 units out of a total of about 34,000, were either deteriorated or dilapidated. Renters outnumbered owners by a small margin. Single-family units comprised 10,382 units, slightly less than duplex units totaling 11,725, and slightly more than multifamily units totaling 9,894. During the 1950s Utica added 2,847 units, almost three times that of the previous decade. New Hartford added 2,268 and Whitestown another 1,764. Marcy, Deerfield, and other outlying towns also registered large gains.

Utilities expanded their operations substantially. In 1951 Niagara Mohawk Power completed a pipeline to bring in natural gas. Five years later it began a vast expansion including a new dam at the Prospect Hydro-electrical Station. Most power, however, came over transmission lines from the new dams on the St. Lawrence River. The New York Telephone Company created in 1951 a Northern Area with headquarters on Genesee Street near the Parkway. Extending gas, phone service, and electrical power to new plants and residences generated a good deal of employment. In 1954 the New York State Thruway reached the Utica area but its main impact was more visible in the period after 1960.

Insurance became an important service, with Utica firms serving a national market. Utica Mutual, the largest mutual insurance company in the state, employed 1,257 people in 1961, over half of them in its local headquarters, which moved to its new office building in New Hartford in 1953. The Commercial Travelers' Insurance Company employed 121 people in its home office in 1961.

Utica's banks, which had weathered the Depression without losing a cent of depositors' money, prospered in the postwar years. Businessmen needed loans for expansion; homeowners needed mortgages. The First Bank & Trust in 1954 became affiliated with Marine Midland of Buffalo, one of the largest banks in the state. A Utican, Edward Duffy, rose to the presidency of Marine Midland, which has become an important international bank. Its imposing new structure in downtown Utica enhanced the architectural scene. Marine Midland Trust Company of the Mohawk Valley, the local subsidiary of the parent company, in 1959 had 11 offices including four in Utica. Its main rival, the Oneida National Bank, had 13 offices and approximately the same amount of assets as Marine Midland. To handle all its business, Oneida National constructed an attractive building across from the Stanley Theatre with a large extension on Court Street. The Bank of Utica, which began in 1927 as the Morris Plan, grew at a rapid pace and modernized its building at 222 Genesee Street.

The Homestead Savings and Loan Association (assets of $35 million in 1960) helped finance the large number of new homes. It constructed a handsome new building on the

corner of South and Genesee streets. Cornhill Savings and Loan Association also moved to new facilities on Genesee Street in 1957. The Savings Bank of Utica, with the largest deposits of any bank in central New York, continued its steady growth.

Employment in the various levels and units of government expanded dramatically until it represented about one-fifth of all persons gainfully employed. Of course the expansion of the Griffiss Air Force Base accounted for much of the doubling of government workers in the 1950s, but Utica State, Marcy State, and Rome State hospitals expanded and hired more than 1,000 persons to care for their patients.

Local government units in Oneida-Herkimer counties—towns, 90 school districts, and 36 special districts—required over 9,000 employees. This number of units was unusually high and resulted in duplication and higher costs. Suburbanization led citizens within and outside the limits of Utica and Rome's center cities to urge the county to take over more functions. In 1961 Oneida

Top
Utica's first Urban Renewal area, photographed in 1958, was bounded roughly by Court, State, Columbia, and Washington streets and broadway. Beginning in 1959, dozens of old buildings, from the Moravian Church to "Ma Davis'" brothell, were razed to make way for the new City Hall, Kennedy Plaza Garage, and Kennedy Plaza Apartments. In the process, Spring and Cooper streets were eliminated east of State Street. Courtesy, Utica Newspapers.

Above left
The city razed several rundown buildings between Liberty Street, Oriskany Boulevard West, and Hotel and Washington streets in 1957 and made a parking lot. Note that there is not even a Volkswagen in this picture; the only cars in the lot not made in Detroit were one or two Studebakers made in South Bend, Indiana. Courtesy, Utica Newspapers.

County citizens voted for a new charter with an elected county executive who would administer county affairs. A board of legislators would serve as a policy-making agency.

Utica authorized a comprehensive master plan for future growth. In 1952 it approved Redevelopment Project No. 1, an area of 22 acres of land west of City Hall on Genesee Street. Almost all the residential structures on this tract had severe structural defects or lacked central heating and bath facilities. The funds ($4,180,382) came chiefly from the federal government but the city and state each contributed one sixth. Unfortunately no businessmen were willing to invest money in hotels or commercial undertakings. For years the area looked like a bombed-out section of London.

The uncertain economy of the 1940s and the buoyant recovery of the 1950s were reflected in population trends. During the first decade Oneida County's population gained only 9 percent, the lowest figure for any metropolitan area in the state. The next decade, however, saw population soaring by 19 percent, a rate more than half again as high as that for the state. Young people were moving into the county because they could find jobs there. In 1960 the number of children under 15 years was 30 percent, a tenth greater than the state figure. In addition Rome added almost one fourth to its population and the region between Utica and Rome became an urban sprawl. Although Utica proper lost one percent, its suburbs—New Hartford, Marcy, Whitestown—expanded rapidly.

A higher proportion of Uticans married and had more children, a trend reflecting national patterns. Young couples tended to avoid the old flats of Utica and headed for the outskirts where they could build detached houses surrounded by lawns. They could secure mortgage money at low rates since the government, through the Federal Housing Authority and the Veterans Administration, guaranteed the loans made by banks. Entrepreneurs like William C. Morris set up shopping centers such as the New Hartford Shopping Center. The new plants—General Electric, Bendix, Chicago Pneumatic Tool, Kelsey Hayes—sprang up on open land where space for parking was abundant. Motion-picture operators built new theaters in the outskirts and automobile dealers set up their showrooms and car lots in the suburbs.

The number of foreign-born fell from 17,340 in 1940 to 14,467 in 1950. A decade later it had fallen to 11,404. Greater Utica still welcomed newcomers, notably refugees from Eastern Europe, as well as blacks, Hispanics, and Asians. Ukrainians, many with skills and professions, made their homes in Utica and Rome, and in the early 1950s they organized three more churches. Perhaps the most interesting development was the emergence of the Puerto Rican group (336 in 1960), who of course were already American citizens. St. John's Church established a mission and a community center for these newcomers. Note also that as early as 1950 Utica had 687 persons from Asia, some of them doctors and nurses in the state hospitals. They hailed from many places: Taiwan, Hong Kong, India, Japan, and the Philippines.

The most significant development was the coming of the blacks, who increased to 1,640 in 1940 and to 3,092 a decade later. Most blacks came to Oneida County after World War II to pick potatoes and beans. At first they lived in migrant camps and then returned to Florida and the

Carolinas after the harvest. Some drifted to Utica where they found work in service jobs. The majority lived in the second ward, but as their numbers grew they moved southward to Corn Hill. Like most newcomers, blacks suffered from unemployment and poverty. In 1960 nonwhites earned only 58 percent of the median amount earned by white families, and only 11 percent owned their own houses as compared with about half of white families. Because many blacks had received a poor education in the South's segregated schools, few were able to read blueprints and perform white-collar tasks. They did re-create a set of

Above
Dante O. Tranquille, for many years chief photographer for the Utica newspapers and a master of the aerial photograph, took this view of downtown and North Utica about 1955, soon after the completion of the Thruway. Urban Renewal had not yet begun to clear vast open spaces downtown, while in North Utica much open space remained, later to be filled with housing developments. (OHS)

formal and informal institutions, notably churches. A considerable number of youngsters took advantage of educational opportunities offered by the local schools and colleges.

The people of the Utica-Rome area lagged behind the state in educational achievement. For example, in 1950 only 29.5 percent had graduated from high school. The 4.7 percent of college graduates was the lowest in the state and below the national average. The explanation is obvious. Only a handful of the flood of immigrants had received secondary, much less collegiate, education before their arrival. Moreover Utica was the only city of 100,000 in the nation without a local college where students could cut costs by living at home. Many immigrants believed that their sons should enter a trade rather than seek a college education, the cost of which was beyond their resources. Taxpayers did not believe too highly in education if one can judge by the low salaries they were willing to pay teachers.

In 1960 about 15,000 youngsters attended Utica's public schools—20 grade schools and two high schools. Another 5,000 students attended 13 parochial schools. The old Utica Catholic Academy on John Street was scheduled

Top
Kewpee's drive-in hamburger stand was a 20th-century landmark of Oneida Square and a popular hangout for students of both Utica Free Academy and Utica College before the college moved to Burrstone Road. Opened about 1938, it flourished for a number of years, complete with carhops, until it was torn down about 1972. Courtesy, Russell T. Rhoades & Company.

Above left
Dean Ralph F. Strebel (1894-1959) guided Utica College through its formative years. He came to Utica in 1947 and although he did not live to see the college move from Oneida Square to its new campus on Burrstone Road, he was largely responsible for that development. The student union building, Strebel Hall, honors his memory. Courtesy, Utica Newspapers.

for abandonment. Girls were to be assigned to new quarters on upper Genesee Street and a high school for boys was planned for Burrstone Road. St. Francis De Sales parish continued to offer secondary as well as primary education.

Postwar Utica experienced an explosion in higher education with three new colleges founded in 1946. Moreover expenditures per pupil doubled in the public schools in the decade following 1945-1946. Although this increase left Utica schools behind the state average, the school board did spend more than the state average on buildings, equipment, buses, and furniture. The percentage of high-school graduates enrolling in college shot upward.

In 1943 the New York State Department of Education announced plans for opening five new industrial schools after the war and suggested that Utica adopt the school specializing in merchandising. John L. Train, president of Utica Mutual Insurance, which owned the empty buildings of the Utica Country Day School, offered to rent the facilities. A board of directors was named and appointed Paul B. Richardson as director of the school that opened on

October 15, 1946, under the name of the New York State Institute of Applied Arts and Sciences. Within a year the school had enrolled 500 students. The Institute became part of the State University of New York and in 1953 secured the sponsorship of Oneida County. Operating costs were shared equally by state, county, and students. This college, which took the name of Mohawk Valley Community College in 1963, proved successful in reaching out to the community with an extensive array of evening courses. Dr. Albert Payne, who shepherded this institution through its childhood and adolescence, had the pleasure of seeing his name placed on a major building of the new campus near the Parkway Armory.

In August 1944 Syracuse University proposed the establishment of a branch college in Utica, where it had provided extension courses for many years. Mayor Boyd Golder appointed a committee headed by Richard Balch to negotiate with Chancellor William P. Tolley of Syracuse University who backed the college enthusiastically. Golder, Balch, Henry Dorrance, and Moses Hubbard took an active role in helping the college during its early days. In 1946 the new institution began using the facilities of the Church House of Plymouth Church, Francis Street School, and other buildings in the area of Oneida Square. Winton Tolles became dean and speedily organized a faculty and staff. When Tolles became dean of Hamilton College, Ralph F. Strebel took over the office for the next decade. He helped plan the new campus on Burrstone Road, which opened in 1961. Utica College, a four-year undergraduate college, offered degrees in arts and sciences and in business

Above
Chief among the dignitaries present for the dedication of Mohawk Valley Community College's Payne Hall on September 27, 1969, were (left to right) MVCC Trustee Thomas Kernan, Congressman Alexander Pirnie, County Executive Harry Daniels, former MVCC President Dr. Albert V. Payne, County Legislature Chairman Russell "Tiny" Williams, and former MVCC President Dr. W. Stewart Tosh. Courtesy, Mohawk Valley Community College.

administration. Like MVCC, its evening program enrolled more students than the day session. Governor Thomas E. Dewey announced in 1946 that Rhoads Hospital on Burrstone Road would become Mohawk College in order to accommodate some of the veterans who wanted a college education. Within two years Mohawk enrolled 2,000 students. The state, however, later moved this institution to Sampson base near Auburn.

The Munson-Williams-Proctor Institute greatly expanded its program under the leadership of Thomas B. Rudd and William C. Murray who served as presidents. William Palmer, director of the School of Art, assembled a faculty of gifted artists such as Joseph Trovato. The school offered courses in painting, drawing, sculpture, ceramics, and metalwork, and held special courses for children on Saturday and during the summer. The Art Gallery presented exhibitions of painting and sculpture, lectures, musical programs, and films, and maintained a loan library of records. The Institute made grants to a wide variety of organizations such as the Civic Musical Society, the Players, and the Oneida Historical Society. Roland E. Chesley, who directed the Great Artists Series for decades, had an office in the Institute. Chesley brought to the

structure. President William C. Murray also rebuilt Fountain Elms, a home that for decades belonged to Rachel and Frederick T. Proctor, to exhibit period furniture and decorative arts. The Oneida Historical Society left its building on John, Elizabeth, and Park Avenue and eventually found quarters in the basement of Fountain Elms just south of the Art Museum. Its professional staff catalogued thousands of items in its collections.

Civic leaders promoted the construction of a Memorial Auditorium, which would honor veterans of World War II and make Utica a convention center. They hoped it would host industrial shows, religious gatherings, jazz concerts, and athletic events—and so it has. Unfortunately the arena has seldom met its operating costs.

The campaign to raise $3 million for a new YMCA was successful and the new building on Washington Street served hundreds of young men and scores not so young who wanted to keep in shape. Its swimming pool, gymnasium, dormitory, and other recreational facilities were well utilized.

Health services needed improvement because of the shortage of beds. St. Luke's hospital on Whitesboro Street was an antiquated facility as was Memorial Hospital on

Roland E. Chesley

On May 18, 1971, more than 3,000 people jammed the Stanley Theatre to honor Roland Chesley on his 90th birthday. Roberta Peters, Jan Peerce, and Theodore Uppman had been invited by the Munson-Williams-Proctor Institute to give a concert for the man who had founded the Great Artists Series in 1933 and brought scores of the world's most accomplished artists to Utica. The impressive list included Fritz Kreisler, Artur Rubinstein, Vladimir Horowitz, Isaac Stern, Kirsten Flagstad, Lily Pons, Nelson Eddy, the Boston Symphony, the Cleveland Symphony, and many choruses such as the Vienna Choir Boys.

As a farm lad in Maine, Chesley wanted to hear Paderewski play but he could not afford the trip to Portland. He vowed to make it easier for other young people to hear the finest singers and pianists. At Dartmouth College he sang in the glee club and played piano for the band. He taught school and then sold books for Ginn & Company. In 1928 he risked his own money to bring the New York Symphony to Utica with Walter Damrosch conducting. Five years later he began to sell season tickets, which normally offered subscribers five concerts a year.

Of course problems arose—Lily Pons came down with the flu and Jeannette MacDonald with bronchitis. But Chesley had influence in New York and brought in fine replacements. After 1958 the Institute gave Chesley an office and financial assistance. Although Chesley died in February 1974, the Institute has continued to sponsor the Great Artists Series.

Roland Chesley (1882-1974), at left, greets world-renowned painist Artur Rubinstein following his concert in Utica on January 18, 1972. This was the fourth time Rubinstein appeared in Utica. Courtesy, Great Artists Series.

Stanley the finest musicians, symphony orchestras, and ballet groups.

The trustees decided to tear down one of the Proctor houses and engaged Philip Johnson to design a modern three-story structure with an art gallery, offices, and two basement floors for storing its holdings. Opened in 1960, the building won acclaim and many awards as an outstanding

Genesee. In the late 1950s the boards of the two institutions got together on a plan for a new 218-bed center on Champlin Avenue. William C. Murray, the chairman of the drive, persuaded and cajoled his co-workers to solicit gifts, and a total of more than $5.5 million was raised. A few years later they added another wing with 100 beds. Meanwhile Faxton and St. Elizabeth hospitals held similar campaigns to

extend and improve their facilities.

The Republicans almost always won a majority of votes on the county level whereas the Democrats normally kept control of Utica. In 1941 Vincent R. Corrou won over 60 percent of the votes in his bid for a fourth term. Two years later Richard Balch lost out to J. Bradbury German, Jr., a popular Republican. The Democrats stormed back into City Hall in 1945 behind the banner of Boyd Golder, who held the title of mayor for the next decade. Golder threw his energies behind the campaign to revitalize the economy. Another Democrat, John McKennan, won the post for the next two terms. In 1959 the Republicans elected Frank Dulan who rode the wave of popular disgust over the scandals in city government.

If Uticans basked in favorable publicity arising from their success in attracting new industry, they winced at embarrassing charges in *Newsweek* and New York City newspapers that Utica had become the "Sin City" of the East. The *Press* and the *Observer-Dispatch* hammered away at graft and their investigations and editorials won for the Utica papers the Pulitzer prize for "meritorious public service." Mason Taylor, the publisher, and William Lohden, a reporter, provided most of the energy behind the campaign. What the papers charged and what investigations showed was that prostitution, gambling, and other illicit activities did exist with at least the acquiescence of some city officials.

Top
In 1950, the Citizens Hospital Committee recommended that Utica's six hospitals—Faxton, Children's, St. Luke's, General, Memorial, and St. Elizabeth—be combined into two new institutions. Medical politics prevented the plan from being realized as originally presented, but within a few years the General Hospital was abandoned, St. Luke's and Memorial were merged, and all of the hospitals embarked on ambitious construction programs. St. Elizabeth undertook its first major expansion in 1954, adding 100 beds and other new facilities. Courtesy, Utica Newspapers.

Above
Among the most memorable results of the crime investigations of 1958 was the closing on April 10 of several houses of ill repute, of which the best known was Irene Burke's, shown on the front page of the Observer-Dispatch. *Located at 219 Pearl Street, the house had operated almost literally in the shadow of the old City Hall. A sensational trial in May 1959 sent Irene and her sister to prison and led to the removal of several city officials. The house was later torn down for Urban Renewal and even Pearl Street itself has been eliminated. Courtesy, Utica Newspapers.*

Power Centers

Almost every village and city has its power centers where leaders get together, make deals, and get things done.

In the lively years after World War II, most of the industrial, business, and professional men (sorry, women had little clout then) lunched at the Fort Schuyler Club on the corner of Genesee Street and Court Street. Most came to have a good lunch, others to play billiards or backgammon, and still others to belt down a couple of drinks after a hard day at the office. One would find at various tables important individuals making plans for the next United Way campaign or discussing the financing of new buildings or plants. When the Chamber of Commerce mounted its campaign for revitalizing the city's economy, its leaders often devised their strategy at the Fort Schuyler Club.

A quarter of a mile or so to the north, in the old section of Utica, another group of powerbrokers met at Marinos, a restaurant with good food and drink. Here chieftains of the Democratic party gathered almost every noon for lunch and planned party strategy. Charles Donnelley, former mayor and Utica's postmaster, talked politics with other party notables including Rufus Elefante, the leader of East Utica. Joe Davoli, education director of the Textile Workers Union, often stopped by. Richard Balch, head of Horrocks-Ibbotson, sometimes skipped luncheon at the Fort Schuyler to confer with his friends who had put him up for mayor.

In the 1970s if one wanted to see Rufus Elefante, he could find him at another favorite spot—Uncle Henry's Pancake Restaurant on Lafayette Street.

Local preservationists mounted a last-ditch effort to save the tower of the old City Hall when it was scheduled for demolition in 1968. Utica newspaper editor William Lohden produced this composite picture and offered the tongue-in-cheek suggestion that the landmark tower be transplanted to the roof of Utica's "little city hall," Marino's. Courtesy, Utica Newspapers.

In 1957 state troopers raided the convention of crime bosses held at Appalachin. The New York *Journal-American* sent a reporter to investigate crime and corruption, which the presence of several Uticans at Appalachin suggested. Governor Averell Harriman came under pressure to make an investigation and appointed a special prosecutor to supercede the district attorney. Other agencies—the Department of Justice, the New York State Criminal Commission, the State Police, the Joint Legislative Commission on Government Operations—made several investigations.

Throughout the spring of 1958 a mountain of evidence piled up showing considerable vice, gambling, and illegal activities. Seven persons were indicted on vice charges and 13 for bookmaking. The police chief resigned when he could not explain the origin of $10,000 in a tin box. Seven detectives and a deputy police chief were convicted of perjury and conspiracy.

These revelations shocked many citizens who demanded reform. The Republicans used the scandals as ammunition in electing Frank Dulan. Reform Democrats elected Tom Gilroy county chairman of their party and he and his friends ousted Elefante's allies from the executive committee. Although Elefante lost some of his power, he remained a strong influence in selecting and electing candidates. The intraparty feud and the crescendo of charges had the unfortunate effect of making Utica look less attractive to outsiders who insisted upon a calm political climate before they would locate in the area.

Citizens of Greater Utica faced perils on the battlefields of World War II and the Korean War. Equally formidable were the problems on the home front, especially the decaying industrial base. Nevertheless a new generation of leaders and followers displayed remarkable enterprise,

daring, and hard work in bringing about a transformation of the economy from one based on textiles to one centering around services. Old voluntary associations took on new life; new ones sprang into being. Who in 1940 would have dared to predict that in the next quarter century the area of Greater Utica would have 30,000 new jobs, two new college campuses, a sparkling new Museum of Art, and scores of new enterprises. To be sure, the political scene had its scandals as well as its achievements, but reformers were challenging old-time leaders. In Utica and later in Oneida County professional "planning" was emerging. Clearly this period represented one of the most creative in the area's history.

Author's note:
I rely heavily upon the advice and works of Dr. Virgil C. Crisafulli. See his *An Economic Analysis of the Utica-Rome Area* (The Utica College Research Center, Utica, 1960); "Economic Development Efforts in the Utica-Rome, New York Area" in *Community Economic Development Efforts* (The Committee for Economic Development, New York, 1964); "Commerce and Industry," in *The History of Oneida County* (Utica, 1977), pp. 103-112.

Above
McConnell Field, built in 1937 just north of the Barge Canal and west of North Genesee Street, was home to two minor league professional baseball teams, the Utica Braves (1938-1942) and the old Utica Blue Sox (1943-1950). Fans tolerated the wooden bleachers ("Slivers Haven") and an outfield often shrouded by fog from the river and canal, especially when the Blue Sox won the league championship in 1945 and 1947. Several members of the 1947 team went on to become the Philadelphia Phillies' "Whiz Kids" of 1950. Most of the field was taken over for the Thruway entrance in 1953. Courtesy, Utica Newspapers.

CHAPTER NINE

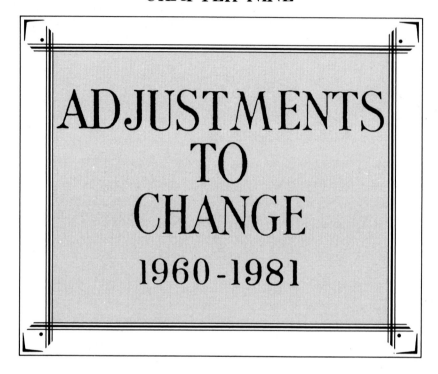

ADJUSTMENTS
TO
CHANGE
1960-1981

Uticans sought to consolidate the hard-won gains of the 1950s but were not able to escape the economic malaise so characteristic of many older industrial centers of the Northeast. The economic slowdown meant a declining population, which in turn fostered pessimism and forced the contraction of many services. Despite much bickering, political leaders and the business community did accomplish a good deal: a more efficient county government, a partial rebuilding of downtown Utica, a remarkable expansion in higher education, and the resurgence of Utica as a commercial center. Most significant of all was the emergence into leadership positions of many individuals from almost every ethnic and racial group.

The buoyant economy of the 1950s was followed by two decades of stagnation. New York State's overall job growth during the 1960s fell behind the national rate, and in the next decade it lagged far behind states in the Sunbelt and the West. Nonagricultural employment in the Utica-Rome area (Oneida-Herkimer counties) stood at 118,205 in 1960, easing off to 114,800 a decade later. When New York City and the state government stumbled near the abyss of bank-

ruptcy in 1975, the local economy faltered as well. Only 110,600 remained at work, but five years later this category had edged up to 115,800.

The Upper Mohawk region remained more wedded to manufacturing than the state as a whole. Manufacturing provided 26.6 percent of the jobs whereas it accounted for only 20.4 percent of the state total. During the 1960s the manufacturing sector employed about 40,000 persons, but by 1975 it included only 31,000, hovering at that level for the next five years. Weekly earnings in manufacturing in the Utica-Rome area in 1980 stood at $266.39, the lowest figure for all eight metropolitan districts upstate. The state average was $282.89.

If manufacturing jobs have shriveled, positions in the services have increased. Government employment skyrocketed during the 1950s especially because of the growth of employment at Griffiss Air Force Base. This category grew to 25,900 in 1970, with an additional 4,000 in the next decade. Government jobs thus constituted almost one-fourth of all nonagricultural workers, or roughly the same as those engaged in manufacturing. Although employment at Griffiss has slipped since 1960 to under

Above
Deerfield Corners in North Utica was a congested spot when Dante O.
Tranquille took this picture about 1955. Vacationers bound for the
Adirondacks, local travelers between Herkimer and Rome, and
commuters bound to and from downtown all had to pass through this one
intersection. A traffic circle and a connection between the Thruway exit at
North Genesee Street and the North-South Arterial, both completed in
1964, helped to relieve the situation but also removed numerous small
businesses in the area. Courtesy, Utica Newspapers.

5,000, local governments have grown to a total of about 17,000 while the state total has reached 8,000. The state hospitals at Utica and Marcy have over 1,000 workers each and the Rome Developmental Center and the Rome State School for the Deaf together employ more than 1,000 workers.

In 1960 a new generation of business and political leaders tackled the economic problems. Mayor Frank Dulan allocated $50,000 of city funds to cover the cost of an Industrial Development Corporation, which included representatives of unions on its board. Charles Lanigan, the first Oneida County Executive, pushed for the organization of an Oneida County Industrial Development Corporation. Robert Peach, president of Mohawk Airlines, aided him in this campaign by seeking funds to cover the expenses for the first three years of operation. The OCIDC hired Thomas Zappone as executive vice president, and he attracted several firms to the county. The OCIDC acquired over 500 acres near the airport for an industrial park. Among the firms that built or leased buildings in the park have been Metropolitan Life Insurance, GFM Machines, Inc., ARA Services, and Utica Fire Insurance Company. Mohawk Data Sciences built a fine new headquarters at the airport only to run into financial difficulties before it could occupy it. MDS moved its head offices to New Jersey although it kept its manufacturing plant in Herkimer. The Federal Reserve Board leased space at the airport for one of its operations. Dr. Virgil Crisafulli estimated that between 1963 and 1975 the OCIDC accounted for over 4,000 jobs, more than half of them new to the county. Well over $100 million in capital investment was stimulated by this agency.

During the 1960s the federal government began to provide funds for regional development. It set up the

Mohawk Valley Economic Development District serving five counties in the river basin. Under the able directorship of John M. Ladd, this agency funneled over $5 million into projects in Oneida County.

Changes have revolutionized the retail and service sectors during the past quarter century. Many stores and insurance companies have followed manufacturing plants to the outskirts, leaving behind vacant stores and buildings. The Boston Store, once the flagship of downtown retailing, ended operations when its parent company in 1977 passed into receivership. Other stores such as E. Tudor Williams closed their doors while Wicks & Greenman and Doyle-Knower headed for the New Hartford Shopping Center. Commercial Drive in Whitestown and New Hartford attracted many automobile dealers, stores such as Tehan's, restaurants, and even offices such as Prudential.

In the early 1970s the Riverside Mall in North Utica secured three department stores (Montgomery Ward, Howland, and J.M. Fields) as anchor stores, as well as attracting scores of specialty shops, eating places, and motion picture theaters. By 1980 Sangertown Square, an even larger mall, opened in New Hartford with Sears, Roebuck, J.C. Penney, Hess's, and later Bradlees as major stores. Meanwhile Charles Gaetano was converting the old Savage Arms building into CharlesTown, a center for outlet stores. Thousands of customers from all over the Northeast have come in automobiles and chartered buses in search of bargains in this complex.

Downtown Utica, however, witnessed the expansion of certain operations such as banking, government offices, and professional services. All the banks by 1960 had constructed new buildings or made extensive additions to old structures. The Savings Bank of Utica opened suburban branches and in the late 1970s built a large addition to its landmark building downtown. When the state lifted its ban on branch banking, several out-of-town institutions such as Albany Savings and Chase-Manhattan established branches in the Utica area. Meanwhile Oneida National Bank was acquiring many banks in a seven-county area as far north as Ogdensburg and as far west as Wayne County. Its deposits rose steadily, reaching $673 million in 1980. In 1981 it made an agreement with United Bank New York, headquartered in Albany, whereby it became a subsidiary of the latter institution which changed its name to Norstar Bank Corporation. Thus Utica's two major commercial banks, Oneida National and Marine Midland, have become subsidiaries of large banking groups.

Downtown revitalization made its greatest

Above
Riverside Mall opened in 1974 as the area's first enclosed shopping mall. Together with Sangertown Square—opened in 1980 after a long battle over environmental concerns—it provided stiff competition for both downtown and older, non-enclosed suburban shopping centers. Courtesy, Utica Newspapers.

breakthrough in 1979 when the doors of the Sheraton Inn swung open. This hotel with its large parking annex has hosted many conventions, since state and regional associations favor Utica's central location for their meetings. The increasing tourist and convention business has led to the modernization of the Quality Inn near the Stanley and has encouraged the owners of the Holiday Inn (formerly the Treadway, then Trailway) in New Hartford to improve its facilities.

Government officials on every level—city, county, state, and federal—acquired new quarters. The city abandoned its famous City Hall, a charming building designed by Richard Upjohn in Italianate style. In 1967 Mayor Frank M. Dulan and other officials moved into a new City Hall designed by Frank Delle Cese. Three years later Oneida County erected an office building on Park Avenue south of the Court House. During the expansive days of Governor Nelson A. Rockefeller, the State of New York built an office building on Genesee Street between Blandina and Devereux to house many state agencies. The federal government, however, decided to shift its postal operations from Broad Street to Pitcher Street near CharlesTown, but it opened in 1980 a new substation on Lafayette Street. Thus the enlarged government center downtown has added several thousand employees to the other thousands working in the banks, stores, and professional offices.

Certain buildings such as the State Office Building constructed parking spaces in their basements, while some stores, banks, and offices tore down old structures and created lots for customers.

Many Uticans became alarmed at the destruction of historic and architecturally significant structures, particularly the demolition of the old City Hall in 1968. Dr. Harry Jackson, president of the Oneida Historical Society, asked Dorothy W. Brown, Oneida County historian, to head a Landmark Preservation Committee. The new committee made an architectural survey and sponsored walking tours

of certain areas such as Rutger Park. One outgrowth was *Wood and Stone* (1972), an attractive book of photographs of historic and significant buildings in Oneida and Herkimer counties. Mr. William C. Murray, president of the Munson-Williams-Proctor Institute, encouraged the formation of the Central New York Community Arts Council, whose purpose was to foster the performing and fine arts. In 1974 the Council acquired the Stanley Theatre and renamed it the Stanley Performing Arts Center. The Council has encouraged concerts (Great Artists Series), plays (Broadway Theater League), operas (Utica Opera Guild), film showings, and ballets. It has collected upward of a million dollars to rehabilitate the Stanley and recruited dozens of volunteers to clean the old building.

An enthusiastic group formed in 1974 the Landmarks Society of Greater Utica, which has awarded prizes to firms and individuals who have restored old buildings. One can see on Rutger, John, and Genesee streets several houses and commercial establishments whose owners have restored

Above
The Barnaby Concrete Corporation, a New York City developer, unveiled its "Center City Mall" proposal for the Urban Renewal West site in October 1967, following the failure of another New York firm called Inter-County Development. Beginning at Columbia and Genesee streets, it included a department store, an enclosed shopping mall, a parking garage, a high-rise office building, and new apartment buildings. The plan became bogged down in financial and legal red tape and never came to pass in its original form. Courtesy, Utica Newspapers.

Above
The old City Hall was demolished in the fall of 1968 while steel for the new State Office Building was beginning to rise. A last-ditch effort to save the tower failed, but the clock was salvaged and installed in the Tower of Hope at the new City Hall in 1975. The loss of the old City Hall galvanized the historic preservation movement in Utica and broadened interest in the city's architectural heritage. Courtesy, Utica Newspapers.

them to their original form and charm. Frank E. Przybycien, a professor at Mohawk Valley Community College, published in 1976 *Utica: A City Worth Saving,* a book of illustrations accompanied by descriptions of the various styles of architecture still visible in Utica. The Landmarks Society has made a special effort to improve the area surrounding Bagg's Square. The centerpiece, Union Station, is a magnificent monument of the railroad age. In 1979 the Children's Museum of History, Natural History and Science acquired the John C. Hieber building where it has set up its permanent and rotating exhibits.

The builders of the Thruway in 1952 and 1953 had to relocate three quarters of a mile of the Barge Canal in order to accommodate the new superhighway. Over 50 men with several caterpillars and bulldozers dug a hole 150 feet wide and 16 feet deep. The green wood of the elm trees that were grubbed out were set on fire by burning large numbers of old rubber tires. The task was complicated by the need to leave half of the Barge Canal open for traffic.

West of Utica the contractors had to carry the highway across the main streets of Whitesboro, the railroad tracks, the Mohawk River, and then up the grade east of Oriskany bluff.

The Thomas E. Dewey Thruway, which opened in 1955, stimulated the growth of several motels, restaurants, and service stations around the Utica exit. The State built Route 49 from Utica to Rome linking more closely the two centers. It also constructed a four-lane Route 5S from Mohawk, thus making it easier for Herkimer County residents to work and shop in Utica. This arterial ran from the eastern limit of the city along the old Erie Canal bed and Oriskany Boulevard to Genesee Street. Within the city an arterial speeded traffic from north to south and permitted motorists using Routes 8 and 12 to pass through the city. Route 12 became a four-lane highway to Forestport, serving tourists traveling to Adirondack resorts. Route 8 in New Hartford became a four-lane highway advancing up the Sauquoit Valley. In the early 1980s the state began work on a major highway complex in North Utica intended to eliminate bottlenecks in that area.

Above
Donalty's, regarded by many as the city's last old-fashioned saloon, was one of the oldest and best-known of the businesses around Bagg's Square which were razed in 1971 for the new Genesee Street overpass. Located on the northeast corner of Broad and John streets in the cut-down remains of Washington Hall, a once-fashionable commercial block dating to 1822, Donalty's dispensed beer and sandwiches to a faithful following of retirees, railroad and newspaper workers, and others, until it closed in September 1970. Courtesy, Utica Newspapers.

Railroad lines merged to combat the effects of high costs, work rules, and the competition of trucks, buses, and airplanes. Locally, the Lackawanna joined the Erie in 1961 and the New York Central joined the Pennsylvania in 1968. Neither merger prevented bankruptcy and in 1976 the government pushed the Penn-Central and the Erie-Lackawanna into Conrail, whose existence was dependent upon federal subsidies. Passenger service to New York City and to the west has improved since Amtrak took over in 1971.

In 1947 the county board of supervisors authorized construction of the airport to serve both Utica and Rome. Ten years later Mohawk Airlines selected the Oneida County Airport as its headquarters. Mohawk grew rapidly and became one of the largest feeder lines in the nation. Unfortunately, recession and heavy debt charges drove it into insolvency and Allegheny Airlines in 1972 took over its operations. Allegheny, however, cut costs by moving maintenance and headquarter operations to Pittsburgh and

other cities, which automatically reduced service to Oneida County Airport. Later Allegheny withdrew all its service and under its new name of U.S.Air concentrated on new routes to the South and West. In 1974 Paul Quackenbush founded Empire Airlines to meet local needs. This company expanded rapidly by buying jet planes and by adding routes to Boston, Washington, and many other points.

The sluggish economy of the 1960s was accompanied by a drop of 9,000 residents in Utica proper. The black contingent, however, soared from 3,092 to 5,207. Although blacks lagged behind whites in income and employment, they were also making striking gains, especially in education. A black professional class—engineers, physicians, teachers, social workers, army officers—was emerging. Compared with the Irish in the 19th century and the Italians in the first third of this century, blacks made educational and economic gains at a faster rate.

The 1980 census shocked New Yorkers when results revealed that the Empire State had lost almost 700,000

Above
Helen Hoffman, with her ramshackle newsstand huddled against the Columbia Street flank of the old Marine Midland Bank, was an institution of downtown Utica for half a century. Construction of a new bank forced her to the south side of the street in 1969. Helen and her stand were condemned by the Observer-Dispatch *and city officials as a nuisance and an eyesore and defended by the* Daily Press *and others as "a testimonial to the indomitable spirit of man." But support eroded and the city demolished the stand on January 3, 1973. Courtesy, Wolfe News Service, Inc.*

Above
The Stanley Theatre, its original grandeur still evident despite a half century of service, presented both a formidable challenge and a great opportunity when the Central New York Community Arts Council purchased it in 1974. Courtesy, Utica Newspapers.

people. Oneida County slipped to 253,466, a percentage drop of 7.2. Only Erie County (Buffalo) in the upstate region showed a greater decline. Utica's total fell to 75,632, a loss of one sixth within 10 years. Even suburban Whitestown and New Hartford showed losses.

The black total was 5,304, approximately the same as that of 1970. Those whose mother tongue was Spanish (mainly Puerto Rican) rose to 1,230 and other nonwhites (Asians, Indians) exceeded 1,000. A few refugees from Vietnam and Cambodia made their way to wintry Oneida County. A score or more Amish farm families have recently settled in Herkimer County, renewing a Germanic touch to the countryside which was first settled by Palatine Germans well before the Revolution.

Most Uticans in this century have belonged to the Roman Catholic faith. A religious census undertaken by the Interfaith group in 1963 recorded 58,969 Catholics, roughly 73 percent of those who expressed any religious preference. Members of the Eastern Orthodox churches were few: Ukrainian, 270; Greek, 194; Russian, 134. The Polish National Catholics had 409 members in their Utica Church and another parish in New York Mills.

Jews, if we adjust for those who did not affiliate with a synagogue, totaled about 3,600. Most Jews by the 1960s had moved to South Utica or New Hartford from Corn Hill or from the old quarter around Whitesboro Street. Indicative of this southward shift was the opening of the new Jewish Community Center in 1971 on upper Oneida Street. This center offered a wide variety of services to its members and to the community at large. Charles T. Sitrin Nursing Home, which received generous support from the Jewish community, took care of persons of all faiths.

About 11 percent of Uticans belonged to Protestant churches and a similar number expressed a preference for Protestantism. Main line Protestants such as Presbyterians, Episcopalians, and Lutherans had lost adherents both

absolutely and relatively since 1920. In contrast, denominations, which might loosely and perhaps inaccurately be called fundamentalist, evangelical, or conservative, have enjoyed considerable success. For example, the survey counted 333 members of Jehovah's Witnesses. The Witnesses meet two weekends each year in a regional conference and have filled the Utica Memorial Auditorium. The Church of Jesus Christ of Latter-Day Saints (Mormons) established a stake in the Hart's Hill area of Whitesboro.

Conservative Protestants demonstrated their vitality by establishing churches on Genesee Street, once the showcase of main line Protestants. The Christian and Missionary Alliance moved from Seymour Avenue and erected a church close to St. Elizabeth Hospital. The Assembly of God attracted a large and active membership and the Church of the Nazarene bought the building vacated by South Congregational. Trinity Lutheran, which belonged to the conservative Lutheran Church-Missouri Synod, constructed a church of modern design set in beautifully landscaped grounds. The Church of the Living God, a black congregation, took over the building of the Church of the Reconciliation (Unitarian-Universalist) on Oneida Square. St. George's Episcopal, with its Anglo-Catholic emphasis, moved from State Street and became a neighbor of Trinity Lutheran.

Above
Some 4,000 Uticans rallied at Oneida Square on March 14, 1965, in a demonstration of sympathy and support for the civil rights activists led by Dr. Martin Luther King, Jr., who were marching on Selma, Alabama. Courtesy, Utica Newspapers.

Paul's Baptist opened an elaborate church house on Leah Street.

Since 1960 the sharp decline in population has led to the dissolution of some congregations and combinations among others. The Congregationalists, who after 1959 became part of the United Church of Christ, consolidated three churches into Plymouth-Bethesda on Oneida Square. Urban renewal demolished Bethesda's building on Washington Street and its members merged with Plymouth, its daughter church. Most members of South Congregational also joined, but others attended Messiah in nearby Washington Mills. Christ Reformed disbanded and sold its building on the corner of Cornelia and Genesee. A few years later a group of persons belonging to the "Reformed" tradition built a new sanctuary on Herkimer Road in Deerfield. Sayre Presbyterian was disbanded by 1979 but a gospel group leased the building. In 1981 Moriah and Olivet Presbyterian churches voted for a shared ministry with C. Davis Robinson as minister. Central Methodist, which had already absorbed several small congregations, brought in Dryer Memorial on Court Street and it also assisted Asbury Church in the east end of Utica.

Five Lutheran churches became three, all in South Utica. St. Paul's on South Street combined with the Church of the Redeemer to become Our Saviour, while Holy Communion on Sunset Avenue joined with Zion, which had already moved in the early 1960s from the old German neighborhood in West Utica to its site near Utica College. The Moravians, who at one time had three churches including one in New Hartford, consolidated into the Church of the Good Shepherd on Higby Road. The Episcopalians gave up Holy Cross on Bleecker Street but an Ukrainian Orthodox parish bought the building and retained the name. St. Luke's, a small congregation in the

The black influx led to the establishment of several churches chiefly of Baptist, Methodist, and Pentecostal background. Black congregations have taken over older churches or synagogues in the area of Washington and Liberty streets. The Metropolitan Baptist Church acquired the building formerly used by Dryer Memorial, and St. Matthew Temple Church of God in Christ erected a new church on Washington Street in the mid-1960s. In 1977 St.

Above
The Reverend Franklin Upthegrove became pastor of St. Paul's Baptist Church in 1966, has served the city as human relations commissioner, and has been active in many groups dedicated to improving conditions in Corn Hill and other inner city areas. In 1976 he surveyed a model of the church's new Leah Street complex while standing in front of the former Zion Lutheran Church on Fay Street, one of several secondhand homes used by St. Paul's since its founding in 1922. The new building was completed in 1977. Courtesy, Utica Newspapers.

Above
The projected route of the East-West Arterial along Oriskany Boulevard is outlined in this photo published in 1964. Whole blocks of old commercial buildings were torn down and the statue of Columbus opposite the Utica Newspapers' office was moved to the Parkway to make way for this road, opened in stages between 1966 and 1968. Many of the buildings at left were also torn down for the new Genesee Street bridge, built in the early 1970s. Courtesy, Utica Newspapers.

Highland area of West Utica, combined with Trinity
Church to become All Saints. St. Paul's in North Utica and
St. Stephen's in New Hartford benefited by the movement
of Episcopalians to the outskirts.

The Roman Catholic Bishop of Syracuse decided to
combine two famous parishes into St. Joseph's and St.
Patrick's Church, using the beautiful Baroque sanctuary
formerly used by St. Joseph's. The decline in Jewish
population led to the merger of two Orthodox congregations
into Congregation Zvi-Jacob, which constructed its
synagogue on the Memorial Parkway. Meanwhile the
Salvation Army, which for decades had operated out of its
citadel on Blandina Street, purchased the House of Jacob
on Clinton Place as the site of its new headquarters.

Each church that closed its doors meant heartache for
members who loved the institution in which they attended
Sunday School, exchanged marriage vows, or held services
for their beloved dead. More significant, however, than the
decline in the number of churches is the abundant evidence
of religious vitality in the last quarter century.

Several denominations saw opportunities for service in
building and operating nursing homes. The Lutherans
greatly enlarged their home in Clinton in the 1970s and in
1981 opened a large housing complex for older persons in
Clinton. The Roman Catholics in 1971 opened St. Joseph's
Home on Genesee Street. The Charles T. Sitrin Home
expanded and made many improvements to its facility on
upper Tilden Avenue. The Presbyterians founded the
Presbyterian Home of Central New York in New Hartford
and offered nursing care on two levels. In addition it rented
145 apartments to older individuals and couples.

Catholics continued their ministry of healing by adding
to the facilities of St. Elizabeth Hospital. Notre Dame High
School gathered in the students of older academies, and its
students won distinction in scholarship as well as on the

playing fields. The southward movement greatly increased
the membership in Catholic parishes in South Utica and
New Hartford. Our Lady of Lourdes Church constructed its
beautiful sanctuary on Genesee Street in 1968. The Church
of Our Lady of the Rosary on Burrstone Road, once a
mission, attracted many new members moving into its
neighborhood. In New Hartford St. John the Evangelist
parish built a new sanctuary for its growing membership in
1965. When more people moved into the Perry Manor area
south of the Utica Mutual building in New Hartford, the
Catholic bishop of Syracuse authorized the formation of St.
Thomas parish on Clinton Road. Ukrainian Catholics,
however, built a new church in downtown Utica. The

Above and right
*Although the higher elevations of Oneida County such as Boonville are
more famous for snow, Utica sometimes receives more than its share, and
the efficiency of the Department of Public Works in removing it is an
annual topic of conversation. One of the worst storms of recent memory
was the Blizzard of '66 (January 31-February 3). Thirty inches of snow fell
on Utica, the Thruway was closed, city buses stopped running, bread and*

*milk were in short supply, and many area residents were stranded at
home or on the job. Things were beginning to return to normal when these
snapshots were taken. Courtesy, Rear Admiral William R. Cox, U.S.N.
(Ret.)*

striking new sanctuary of St. Volodymyr the Great on Cottage Place manifests the traditional style of eastern Europe, a sharp contrast with the modern design of the Museum of Art.

The movement of Protestants and Jews to the outskirts led to the construction of new institutions to serve them. Jews who followed the Reform movement erected Temple Emanu-El on Genesee Street near the New Hartford line. The rapidly growing Deerfield area saw the formation of new churches such as Christ Reformed and the revitalization of old ones such as the Deerfield Baptist, whose first building was erected in 1812. After a brief interlude of nonuse, members began the process of

Above
Bishop Walter A. Foery presided at a special Mass in honor of the centennial of St. Patrick's Roman Catholic Church in 1950. Sixteen years later, St. Patrick's merged with St. Joseph's Church, located just across Columbia Street, and this edifice was torn down. Courtesy, Utica Newspapers.

restoration and adopted the name of First Baptist Church of Utica. After World War II Episcopalians built a new church for St. Paul's on Riverside Drive and the Roman Catholics founded St. Mark's on Keyes Road. St. Peter's, founded in 1872, greatly expanded after World War II. In 1953 it constructed a new building which was soon outgrown, and in 1969 completed the present structure.

Whitesboro Presbyterian, the third oldest church in Oneida County, suffered a disastrous fire on July 18, 1979. Its historic building dating back to 1834 was heavily damaged. Undaunted, its members set to work—literally—contributing hundreds of hours of work as well as funds toward the quarter-million dollar cost of reconstruction.

Most downtown churches decided to remain in their old locations and to minister not only to their membership but also to the changing neighborhood. They continued to improve their plants. Grace Episcopal installed an elaborate new organ to maintain its tradition of excellent music. Central Methodist replaced its steeple and sandblasted its exterior. Westminster Presbyterian refurbished its interior, while Tabernacle Baptist in 1980 spent over $300,000 in reconstructing Thorn Chapel behind its sanctuary.

Individual churches showed an increasing concern for social needs. St. John's served the Puerto Rican community with special services in Spanish. Calvary Episcopal on South Street became headquarters for many agencies serving the troubled Corn Hill area. Other churches aided the elderly and the mental patients who have been discharged to live outside the mental hospitals. During the Vietnam War some clergymen took the lead in organizing antiwar protests and in giving counsel to young men facing the draft.

The Utica Council of Churches under the leadership of Dr. Alan Peabody has broadened its jurisdiction by becoming the Council of Churches of the Mohawk Valley Area. It has encouraged a wide variety of community activities ranging from Holy Week services to weekly commentaries on the radio and television. Cooperation between Protestants and Roman Catholics has become much closer since Pope John XXIII urged Vatican II to foster the ecumenical spirit. Relations among the various faiths and between individual churches have never been more cordial than during the past two decades. Perhaps the most striking symbol of such interfaith respect is the traditional Thanksgiving service in which First Presbyterian and Temple Beth El join in alternate years to praise God for His blessings, and which in recent years has become a community interfaith service.

Of the 23,000 persons employed in the Utica area in 1963, some 6,600 were women. Although most women, like

most men, engaged in routine occupations, a considerable number became managers and professionals. Sister Rose Vincent, executive administrator of St. Elizabeth Hospital, managed this large and complex institution with great success. Pearle Nathan, a member of the Utica College Foundation, took a leading role in acquiring and preserving the Stanley Theatre for artistic use. In these endeavors she was allied with Bettie Nusbaum. Elizabeth Hubbard guided the YWCA into fields of greater service and also served as chairman of the Board of Trustees of Mohawk Valley Community College. Equally prominent in education was Margaret Quackenbush of Herkimer, who served as a trustee of the State University of New York and who also provided much of the energy behind the founding of Herkimer County Community College in 1966. The Utica Public Library has been managed by Alice Dodge and Helen Dirtadian during trying times of reduced budgets. The Oneida Historical Society flourished under the

---

Above
The first buildings on Utica College's Burrstone Road campus—shown in a 1964 photo—were (left to right) South Hall dormitory, Strebel Student Center, and the Gordon Science Center/Administrative Building/Hubbard Hall complex. The new Zion Lutheran Church, completed in 1959, is at lower left at the corner of Burrstone and French roads. Courtesy, Utica Newspapers.

presidencies of Alice Dodge, Ruth Auert, and Martha Shepard.

In politics Mrs. Moses G. Goldbas was a power in the Second Ward and the Goldbas Apartments were named in her honor. In East Utica Mrs. Beatrice De Santis took a leadership role in Democratic party and ethnic organizations. Lucille Keefe was a founder and longtime director of the Utica Senior Day Center. In 1974 Mary Lou Bartlett became the first woman to be elected as County Clerk.

The winds of change even penetrated the paneled parlors of the Fort Schuyler Club, a bastion of male supremacy for almost a century. Late in 1981 this club elected as members Donna Hagemann, executive editor of the Utica newspapers, and Be Denemark, president of the Downtown Utica Association.

Enrollment in public schools in Oneida County fell from 58,000 in 1968 to 45,389 in 1980, a decline of more than one fifth. Utica's total of about 15,000 in 1960 fell to about

10,000 in 1980. Nevertheless the number of high-school graduates increased steadily because the dropout rate for schools in Utica and the county was less than the state average. In 1965 Utica opened its third high school, John F. Kennedy, in North Utica. Enrollments in parochial schools also registered similar trends. By 1980 Utica Catholic Academy and St. Francis de Sales high schools were consolidated with Notre Dame High School. The Board of Cooperative Educational Services opened a new facility on Middle Settlement Road in new Hartford in 1976 to provide specialized vocational training as well as facilities for handicapped students.

Higher education experienced a tremendous expansion in enrollments, number of faculty, and facilities. Over 90 percent of all the buildings used in higher education in the Utica-Rome area were constructed in the past quarter century. In 1976 over 17,000 students, almost half of them part-time students, attended the various colleges, and since that date the number has increased.

Hamilton College, which before World War II had only 450 students, grew steadily, and in 1968 its trustees sponsored the formation of Kirkland College, which soon attracted over 600 women. The buildings on the Kirkland campus were designed in bold modern style. Unfortunately Kirkland's trustees and administration were unable to raise enough money to pay the carrying charges on the large debt borrowed from the New York State Dormitory Authority. In 1978 Hamilton took over the students, plant,

Above
Mohawk Valley Community College is shown in a 1978 aerial view looking southeast. Payne Hall (library, classroom, laboratory, and administration) is at lower right and Penfield, Dougherty, Butterfield, and Huntington halls (dormitories) are at upper left, with the Academic Building (lower left) and College Center in between. The Gymnasium is at upper right near Culver Avenue. Courtesy, Utica Newspapers and MVCC.

faculty, and debt and became a coeducational institution with approximately 1,600 students. Since 1960 Hamilton itself has built an elegant library and a fieldhouse, and has reconstructed its chemistry building and the former library building.

Utica College opened its Burrstone Road campus in 1961 and attracted over 2,000 full-time students as well as an even greater number of part-time students. Deans Ralph Strebel and Kenneth Donahue secured funds from private and public sources for a fine library, a student center, a gymnasium, and several dormitories. During the 1970s Utica College shifted its offerings toward more vocational majors such as accounting, nursing, and the like.

Units of the State University of New York accounted for at least two-thirds of all enrollments. Mohawk Valley Community College moved to Sherman Drive in 1960 where a new campus designed by Edward Durrell Stone was developed. Unlike most community colleges MVCC has four dormitories and also has a branch in Rome, the latter with its own building in 1980. Ten miles to the east Herkimer County Community College took form in 1966 and soon enrolled 1,400 full-time students.

In 1966 the trustees of SUNY established an upper division college to meet the needs of the state's community college graduates. Known today as the State University College of Technology at Utica-Rome, it emphasizes scientific and technological studies. Over 1,000 students have found a temporary campus in the old Globe Woolen Mill on Court Street. After much debate the trustees of SUNY in 1981 fixed upon a site for a permanent campus near the Riverside Mall in the town of Marcy.

The respected proprietary Utica School of Commerce, founded in 1896, continued to provide vocational education for the increasingly complex world of business. Following a fire in its long-time quarters in the Mayro Building in 1978, USC moved to the former Boston Store Annex on Bleecker Street.

The area continued to receive attention from novelists and historians. No doubt the most significant work was *Upstate* (1971) by Edmund Wilson, the outstanding man of letters in America. Richard Costa wrote a charming book, *Edmund Wilson: Our Neighbor from Talcottville* (1980). Walter Edmonds, a neighbor of Wilson in northern Oneida County, began his literary career in 1929 with *Rome Haul,* a fictional treatment of life on the Black River Canal. His most famous novel, *Drums Along the Mohawk* (1936) depicted the life of frontier families during the Revolution. Charles L. Todd recaptured the career of Alexander Bryan Johnson (1977), and Dr. Harry Jackson wrote *Scholar in the Wilderness* (1963), a biography of Francis Adrian Van der Kemp, an early Dutch pioneer. Thomas F. O'Donnell wrote a biography of Harold Frederic and many other essays on writers of New York literature. The Bicentennial stimulated many towns to write their histories and the county government to sponsor *The History of Oneida County* (1977), which combined the work of academic and

Above
Governor Hugh L. Carey signed a bill allocating $34.9 million for construction of a permanent campus for the State University College of Technology in a ceremony at Utica's State Office Building on July 24, 1981. Seated, from left to right, were Oneida County Executive Sherwood Boehlert, Utica Mayor Stephen Pawlinga, Assemblyman Richard Ruggiero, Governor Carey, and State Senator James Donovan. Among those standing were Chamber of Commerce President E. Porter Felt (left) and Regent Emlyn Griffith (third from left). Courtesy, Utica Newspapers.

amateur historians so successfully that it required a second printing. Judge John Walsh has written charming vignettes of personalities, episodes, and institutions of Utica.

Munson-Williams-Proctor Institute attracted an increasing number of visitors to its exhibits and permanent collection. It received worldwide attention for its show celebrating the 50th anniversary of the famous Armory Show in New York City, with Arthur Davies of Utica as one of its promoters. Joseph F. Trovato organized this exhibit of pictures from scores of museums, which brought distinction to the Institute.

The jockeying for political power and a succession of petty quarrels have obscured the solid achievements of most government units. After the new charter took effect, the county administration became more professional and gradually assumed more responsibility for such matters as welfare, sewage, public health, library services, and even the Stanley Theatre. Utica officials, however, have complained that the city provides many services involving streets, traffic control, the library, and public safety, all

used by suburban dwellers. Furthermore the declining population and the removal of thousands of buildings from the tax rolls have reduced the city's income.

Utica's uniformed services have maintained high standards in difficult times. In their joint centennial year of 1974, the Police Department received a commendation from the state legislature for making Utica the "fourth safest" city in the nation, and the Fire Department gained wide support for a huge parade, publication of a history, and other activities. In 1977 the Fire Department opened a new Central Station on Bleecker Street and in 1980 added an emergency medical services unit.

In 1973 Edward Hanna began his colorful and controversial administration as mayor. Hanna attracted national attention by denouncing the business "establishment," labor unions, the media, and local politicians. Denied renomination by the Democratic party, in 1975 Hanna won as an independent in a three-way race. An urban renewal site at Genesee and Columbia streets was cleared but soon became bogged down in a bitter debate over whether to build La Promenade, a complex of plazas, small shops, and apartments, as proposed by Hanna, or to secure a major hotel. Hanna's most visible accomplishment was the creation of Terrace Park adjacent to City Hall, where free entertainment and cheap snacks won him many supporters.

Stephen J. Pawlinga became mayor in 1977, and his administration has proven successful in combining public and private investment in such projects as the construction of the Sheraton Inn on La Promenade site, the renovations

Above
Few Uticans were neutral about Mayor Ed Hanna; they either loved him or hated him. A crowd of well-wishers joined the quixotic mayor in celebrating his 1975 reelection in front of the Genesee Street headquarters of his independent Rainbow Party. Although Hanna received barely 50 percent of the vote in a three-way race with Republican Councilwoman Sue Baum and Democrat-Liberal Frank Scalise, he took the increase of 6,000 votes over his original election in 1973 as a mandate from "the people." Courtesy, Utica Newspapers.

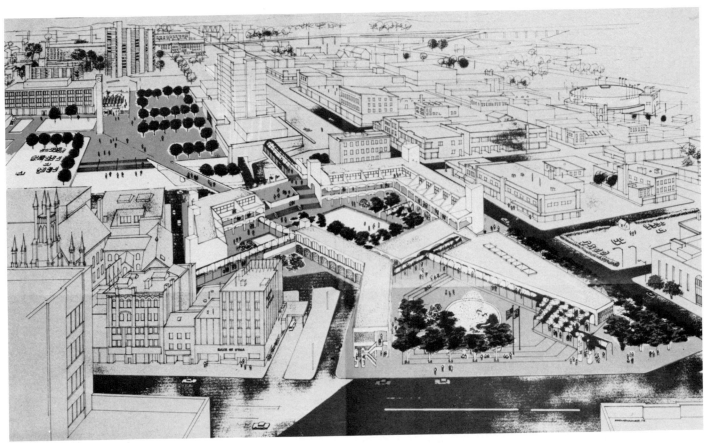

of Mill Square and Genesee Towers, and the sprucing up of Genesee Street, Oneida Square, and Varick Street. When Pawlinga lost the Democratic primary in 1979, he ran as an independent and won reelection. Two years later he easily won a third term marked by deficits.

Each spring since 1974 the Central New York Community Arts Council has sponsored a Celebration of Nations in the Utica Memorial Auditorium. A score of ethnic and racial groups participate, some dressed in the costume of their homeland. Tens of thousands attend this festival in order to sample ethnic food, observe colorful dances, and hear singers and musicians.

From its inception as a tiny settlement, Uticans have prided themselves on their diversity, and people of all backgrounds have worked together in a spirit of goodwill. Each group of newcomers had to make adjustments and some met discrimination in employment, social life, and politics. Nevertheless most secured a comfortable livelihood considerably better than that in their home countries. Furthermore the talented and enterprising won recognition and wealth, if not for themselves, at least for their children.

Each group can point to individuals who have achieved recognition in politics, success in business, and distinction in the professions. The Irish, for example, provided Utica with a large number of priests, mayors, police and fire chiefs, and other officials. The Welsh can lay claim to the Honorable Hugh R. Jones of the New York State Court of Appeals as well as Emlyn Griffith, member of the Board of Regents of the University of the State of New York. Persons of German descent have excelled in manufacturing and retailing. The most famous family is the Matt clan, which has operated the West End Brewing Company for nearly a century. An unusual number of Jews have enjoyed

distinguished careers in the professions and in business. One can trace their careers in S. Joshua Kohn's *The Jewish Community of Utica, New York, 1847-1948*.

By 1950 Italians, Poles, Lebanese, Syrians, and smaller groups had made their mark in business and the second generation was climbing into the professions and management positions. For example, Stephen Pawlinga became the first mayor of Polish stock following Edward Hanna, the first mayor of Lebanese extraction. In the 1960s Dominic Assaro had won election to this position and he was the first mayor of Italian origin.

Italian-Americans, the largest single ethnic group in Utica, have achieved prominent positions in most aspects of business and professional life. In 1981, for example, Martin Carovano was guiding Hamilton College, Paul Farinella the Munson-Williams-Proctor Institute, and Sal DeVivo the Gannett newspapers in Utica. Rocco F. DePerno of the Teamsters and Samuel Talarico of the meatcutters' union have become nationally known labor leaders. Charles Gaetano has acquired and managed a remarkable range of enterprises in retailing, real estate, and construction. This list could be extended to include hundreds of physicians, lawyers, judges, school teachers, retailers, and civil

Above
Unveiled in 1974, Mayor Hanna's La Promenade proposal became the topic of fierce public controversy between its supporters and those who contended that a hotel should be built on the Urban Renewal site. The area stood vacant and windswept while the battle raged, until the Sheraton Inn was opened in 1979. The only elements of La Promenade actually built were Terrace Park (briefly christened Hanna Park), the clock tower, and the "Spanish steps," all located near the new City Hall. Courtesy, Utica Newspapers.

servants.

The Polish community has provided scores of priests and nuns as well as a good number of physicians, lawyers, and teachers. George Dastyck became in the late 1970s the publisher of the local Gannett papers. In addition to Mayor Hanna, the relatively small Lebanese and Syrian community has a large number of professional people as well as retailers. Professor Eugene Nassar of Utica College wrote *East Utica,* a prose poem of life on Bleecker Street and in the Broad Street mills.

Black historian Alex Haley lived for several years in Rome and taught at Hamilton College for three years. There he began his famous work, *Roots,* which spurred new interest in local history and genealogy and stirred the conscience of Americans in both its written and television versions. Representing sports is Dave Cash of Utica who has played second base for many big league teams. In boxing, Bushy Graham (Angelo Geraci) was a contender for the bantamweight title in the 1920s and 1930s.

Uticans of old Yankee or Yorker stock, although a

small minority, continue to make their mark in many occupations—especially the professions, business, and philanthropy. For example, Addison White, a descendant of the original Hugh White of Utica in the 1970s, was president of the Savings Bank of Utica in the 1970s. Immigrants from Great Britain have continued to provide leadership, as exemplified by Albert Payne, president of Mohawk Valley Community College during the 1950s and 1960s and replaced by George H. Robertson, a Scot.

It is not surprising that Utica, a gateway between east and west, should have attracted tens of thousands of individuals from a great number of nations. Each generation of newcomers has had to make thousands of adjustments, formal and informal. Men and women of all races, creeds, and nationalities have created a pluralistic society tolerating significant differences in social institutions and economic status. If Uticans have been a diverse people, they have also been an accommodating people. Proud of their individual traditions which they preserve in part, they are prouder still to be Americans.

Above
Annette Funicello was born in Utica in 1942 and moved to California with her family when she was four. Discovered by Walt Disney at age 12, she gained overnight fame as probably the most popular Mouseketeer of the Mickey Mouse Club television show. She was featured in many Disney productions and in the early 1960s starred with Frankie Avalon in a series of popular ''beach party'' movies. Married, with three children, she has remained active in television guest appearances and commercials. Courtesy, Utica Newspapers.

Above
Dave Cash began his baseball career at Proctor High School (where he also played football and basketball). He was drafted by the Pittsburgh Pirates upon graduation in 1966 and helped them to a World Series victory over Baltimore in 1971. Traded to the Philadelphia Phillies in 1973, he was named to the 1974 National League All-Star Team. As a free agent, Cash joined the Montreal Expos in 1977 and moved on to San Diego for his last active season in 1980. Courtesy, Utica Newspapers.

CHAPTER TEN

COLORFUL
UTICA
PAST
AND PRESENT

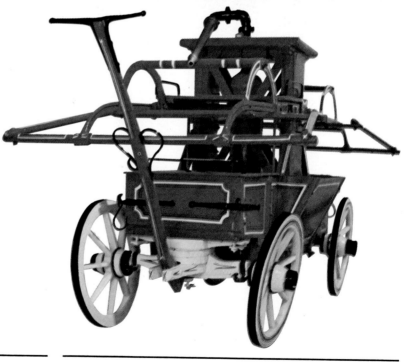

Top
Frederic C. Yohn (1875-1933) painted this popular and vivid rendering of General Herkimer at the Battle of Oriskany. It was featured on a Bicentennial commemorative postage stamp in 1977. Courtesy, Utica Public Library.

Above
The Drums and Fifes of Gansevoort's Third New York Regiment bring history to life at Fort Stanwix National Monument and other historic sites of the upper Mohawk country. Photo by Douglas M. Preston.

Above
Utica's third fire engine was purchased secondhand from New York City in 1823, served Utica until 1834, and then was used in Sauquoit until 1876. Preserved first by the Veteran Fireman's Association and now owned by the Oneida Historical Society, it is displayed in the lobby of the Utica Mutual Insurance Company. Photo by Douglas M. Preston.

Top left
English Staffordshire pottery decorated with American scenes or inscriptions was very popular in the early 19th century. This pitcher describes Utica on one side and the Erie Canal on the other. Courtesy, Munson-Williams-Proctor Institute. Photo by P.A. Romanelli.

Top right
This tiger maple secretary bookcase belonged to Dr. Alexander Coventry (1766-1831), pioneer physician, farmer, and diarist. His little brick house

still stands on Coventry Avenue (Walker Road) near Cosby Manor Road. Courtesy, Munson-Williams-Proctor Institute. Photo by P.A. Romanelli.

Bottom
Elizabeth Wilcox painted this charming oil sketch of Utica as it appeared when first incorporated as a village in 1798. The Mohawk River ran close to Bagg's Square and the Holland Land Company's hotel was under construction. The site of Old Fort Schuyler was marked by a large apple tree. Courtesy, Elizabeth A. Wilcox. Photo by P.A. Romanelli.

Top
The first section of the Erie Canal was opened between Utica and Rome on October 22, 1819. The Chief Engineer of Rome, *named in honor of Benjamin Wright, made the first trip. Dr. Robert Hager's painting shows it crossing the Sauquoit Creek aqueduct near Whitesboro. Courtesy, Canal Society of New York State and Erie Canal Village. Photo by P.A. Romanelli.*

Above
Carved and painted wooden emblem of the Utica Grand Army of the Republic post named in honor of Colonel James McQuade. Photo by P.A. Romanelli. (OHS)

(OHS)

Top
Full-color cartoons and illustrations were a distinctive and popular feature of the Utica Saturday Globe. *The Globe's artists gave especially vivid treatment to disasters such as the burning of the steamboat* General Slocum *on the East River, a 1904 tragedy that claimed over 1,000 lives. Photo by Douglas M. Preston. (OHS)*

Above
The Richelieu Knitting Mills promoted their wares about 1920 with this fanciful boxtop illustration. Photo by P.A. Romanelli. (OHS)

Above
William Howard Taft and Utica's own James Schoolcraft Sherman won the White House for the Republican Party in 1908. Their portraits appeared on a lithographed metal campaign plate along with those of all of the G.O.P.'s standard-bearers back to John C. Fremont and Abraham Lincoln. Photo by P.A. Romanelli. (OHS)

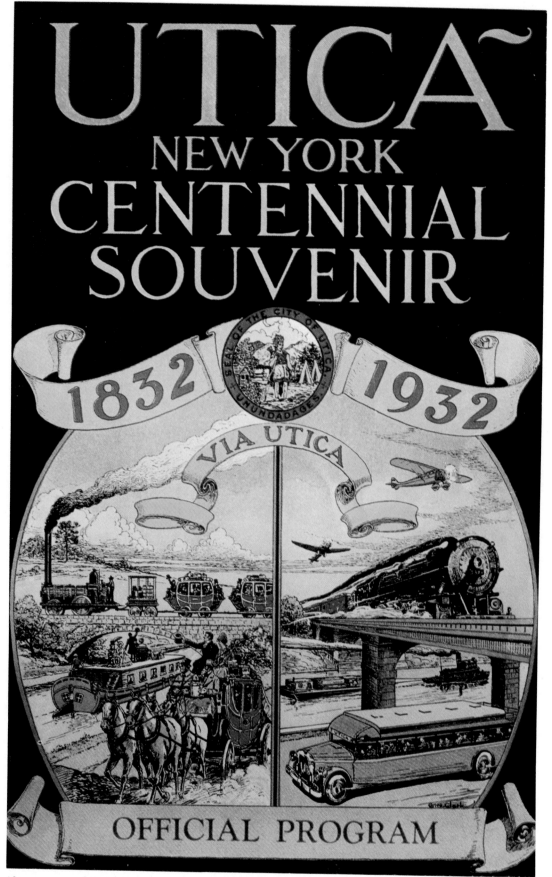

Above
E.N. Clark's cover illustration on the program booklet for Utica's 1932
centennial depicted the tremendous advances made in transportation
during the city's first century. Photo by Douglas M. Preston. (OHS)

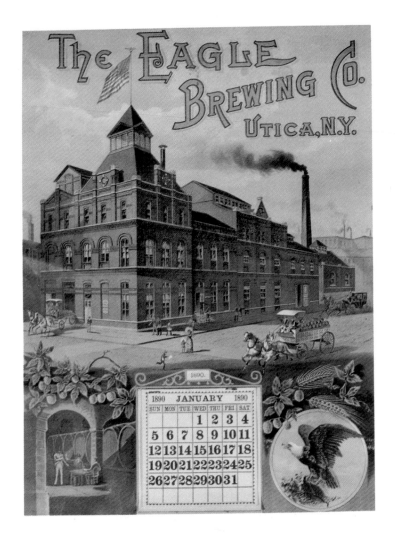

Ever since William Inman began making English ale on Whitesboro Street in 1804, Utica has been home to many local breweries. Most eventually fell victim to Prohibition or competition from larger firms, but their names live on in colorful signs, trays, and other advertising pieces which are avidly sought by collectors of "breweriana." Talking steins

Schultz and Dooley (above, far right) have been symbols of the West End (later F.X. Matt) Brewing Company since 1959 and starred in a series of popular television commercials. Photos by P.A. Romanelli. Breweriana from the collection of Lowell Owens.

Top left
Mrs. Thomas R. Proctor placed this bronze eagle at the overlook above Roscoe Conkling Park as a memorial to her husband, the donor of most of the city's parks, who died July 4, 1920. Photo by P.A. Romanelli.

Top center
Erected on Oneida Square in 1891, the Soldiers and Sailors Monument was dedicated to "the men of Utica who risked their lives to save the Union" during the Civil War. It has since come to stand for all of the city's men and women who have served in America's armed forces. Photo by Douglas M. Preston.

Top right
The slender stone spire of Grace Episcopal Church, a memorial to Alfred Munson and James Watson Williams, has been a Utica landmark since its completion in 1875. Seen from the State Office Building, it stands in counterpoint to the Bankers Trust Building (the former First National Bank,) and the Hunter House (the former Hotel Utica, left). Photo by Douglas M. Preston.

Facing page

Bottom left

The distinctive architecture and beautiful workmanship of the little stone building constructed in 1933 by Mrs. Thomas R. Proctor to mark the site of Bagg's Hotel have made it a local landmark in its own right. Mrs. Proctor selected the scriptural passage above the door, "Except the Lord keep the city, the watchman waketh but in vain." Photo by Douglas M. Preston.

Bottom right

Forest Hill Cemetery is the resting place of many noted Uticans such as John Butterfield, Vice President Sherman, Colonel Benjamin Walker, and Thomas R. Proctor. Photo by Douglas M. Preston.

Preceding page

Top left
The restored marquee of the Stanley Performing Arts Center advertises a rich variety of events and, as a fund-raiser between shows, displays personal messages and advertisements for people and organizations who pay to see their ''name in lights.'' Photo by Douglas M. Preston.

Top right
The Bagg's Square bridge was completed in 1974. Most of the old buildings that formed the perimeter of the original square were removed to make way for this new gateway to the city. Photo by Douglas Preston.

Bottom
Steam and flavorful smells billow from the brewhouse of the F.X. Matt Brewing Company on a cold winter's day. A hard-fighting David among the Goliaths in its field, ''the brewery'' is an important local industry and its Tour Center (left) and new Brewery Shop (right) are popular attractions for local residents as well as visitors. Photo by Douglas M. Preston.

This page

Above
The Utica Curling Club was organized in 1868 and preserved an ancient Scottish winter sport, played on ice with brooms and round granite stones. Among the many tournaments hosted by the club, the most prestigious was the 1970s Men's World Championship (the Silver Broom), the first time it was held in the United States. Photo by Edward Michael.

Left
The weekly farmers' market is a popular downtown attraction during the summer and fall. Photo by Douglas M. Preston.

Top
No parade within 50 miles of Utica is complete without one or more of the
units of Shriners from Ziyara Temple such as the motor patrol or the
Ziyara Zanies. Freemasonry in Utica dates back to 1805, when John Post
served as master of Oneida Lodge No. 123. Photo by Douglas M. Preston.

Above
The Celebration of Nations features ethnic history, food, crafts, and
performing arts. It is not unusual to see a bagpiper quaffing a glass of
German beer or a Cambodian youngster munching a slice of pizza.
Sponsored by the Central New York Community Arts Council, the
Celebration of Nations is one of the area's most popular annual events.
Photo by Douglas M. Preston.

Facing page
A Torah scroll in a stained-glass window at Temple Beth-El is but one
artistic symbol of Utica's Jewish community. Photo by P.A. Romanelli.

Above
Among the most magnificent stained-glass windows in Utica are those of
Tiffany "drapery glass" at the Masonic Home's Tompkins Memorial
Chapel. Photo by P.A. Romanelli.

Above
The polished "onion" domes of St. John of Kronstadt Russian Orthodox
Church on Conkling Avenue, completed in 1979, are distinctive reminders
of Utica's richly divergent religious and ethnic heritage. Photo by Douglas
M. Preston.

Top
The observation floor of the New York State Office Building—at 16 stories, the tallest building in Utica—provides interesting vistas of the city and surrounding country. This view looks southwest over the Savings Bank's famous gold dome and the corner of Genesee and Washington streets. Photo by John Caruso.

Above
Diesel tugboats still push barges, most loaded with fuel oil, to Utica on the 20th-century successor of "Clinton's Ditch," the New York State Barge Canal. Canal tonnage has been declining for years, and despite the waterway's popularity for pleasure boating, its future remains a subject for debate. Photo by John Caruso.

Top
The Val Bialas Ski Center is named for a Utican who competed in the Winter Olympics of 1924, 1928, and 1932. Complete with lifts and lights for night skiing, it provides winter recreation within the city limits and is but one of the sports facilities at Roscoe Conkling Park. Photo by John Caruso.

Above
The city reservoirs on the hillside above the Parkway provide a pleasant backdrop for the municipal Valley View Golf Course. The links were first laid out in 1916 by Walter Travis and improved in the late 1930s by Robert Trent Jones. Both men were nationally prominent course designers. Photo by P.A. Romanelli.

Above
The drive above the Parkway reveals a beautiful panorama of downtown Utica and the hills of Deerfield to the north. Bright leaves and clear air make fall one of the most beautiful seasons in the Mohawk Valley. Photo by P.A. Romanelli.

CHAPTER ELEVEN

PARTNERS IN PROGRESS

Timothy Dwight, president of Yale College, rode through Oneida County on horseback soon after 1800 and praised the citizens of New Hartford and Whitesboro for reproducing in the wilderness the church, schools, and "sprightliness, thrift, and beauty" of New England. Each subsequent generation of newcomers has emulated these Yankees not only in their enterprise but also in their concern for things of the spirit. And necessarily so. Few regions have been more exposed than the Upper Mohawk country to the full brunt of competition, the influx of immigrants, and the impact of new ideas.

Transportation has been the key to development from the earliest days when Iroquois braves and white traders paddled their canoes up the Mohawk River and the network of lakes and streams. In 1792 the legislature responded to demands for better transportation by incorporating a company to build a canal at Little Falls and also by authorizing the Genesee Road, the latter hardly more than a trace through the wilderness to the west of Old Fort Schuyler, Utica, after 1798. These improvements did not satisfy frontier demands so merchants, landholders, and settlers promoted private turnpike companies which after 1800 built toll roads in all directions from Utica. Turnpikes, however, could not

provide cheap carriage of freight but Governor DeWitt Clinton, responding to frontier demands, promoted the construction of the Erie Canal.

Even though the Erie Canal caused Utica's population and trade to soar, it also threatened the local economy. Cheap western wheat undercut local farmers, who swung over to dairying. Buffalo and Detroit seized the profits of provisioning westering frontier families. Taking stock of this loss, Utica's businessmen erected textile factories in the late 1840s using Pennsylvania coal passing northward over the Chenango Canal, completed in 1836. Utica sheets and underwear were to become household words for the next century.

The thickening web of railroads enmeshed the region into the national economy, but not always to Utica's advantage. Only the hardiest could survive the competition from goods made in New England or Europe and also goods made in the Midwest and the South closer to raw materials and markets. Uticans for several decades found knit goods their most profitable enterprise, but after World War I low-cost producers in the Carolinas undermined Utica's hold on this manufacture.

Local entrepreneurs founded scores of businesses—clothing, shoes, foundries,

food processing—in their search for a livelihood. German brewmasters, Italian contractors, Jewish retailers, and Lebanese grocers emerged from the ranks of the highly diverse population and displayed an enterprising spirit worthy of the Yankee founders.

When the textile industry collapsed after World War II, business and civic leaders carried out a successful campaign to revitalize the economic base. Such names as General Electric, Bendix, and Chicago Pneumatic Tool underline the shift from light consumer goods to heavy goods and electronics. Furthermore, a host of service industries sprang up. Since 1946 Utica has witnessed the births of three colleges, extensive enlargement of its hospitals, and expansion of government services—notably the growth of Griffiss Air Force Base in nearby Rome.

The gateway to the West and the major thoroughfare for trade and travel to and from the interior, the Upper Mohawk country has, like a barometer, registered every change in the economic climate of the nation. Its residents have survived and generally prospered by dint of hard work, thrift, and enterprise, flavored with a touch of "sprightliness."

AUTOMOBILE CLUB OF UTICA AND CENTRAL NEW YORK

When a small but enthusiastic group of Uticans, all owners of the then-new "horse-less carriages," gathered together in 1898 to form a socially oriented motoring club, little did they envision that their early efforts would, at a later date, contribute so substantially to the founding and growth of the world's largest and most effective motoring organization, the American Automobile Association.

Naming their group the Automobile Club of Utica, they sought, and obtained, their corporate charter in 1901. Elected to the club's presidency that same year was Charles S. Mott, a local industrialist and owner of Weston-Mott Wheel Works, a supplier of wheels and axles to the fledgling American automobile industry.

Invited to Chicago in 1902, Mott joined with the representatives of eight other regional motoring associations in a meeting following which the now universally recognized American Automobile Association (AAA), was founded.

While Mott was to later relocate his business, moving to Flint, Michigan, in 1907, his interest in the Automobile Club of Utica, and the national AAA, never waned. Until his passing in 1973, Mott continued to serve the local club as an honorary director.

In the years between 1909 and 1943, the local club established its headquarters at the Hotel Martin. Under the able management of Edward O'Mally, the club joined with the Automobile Club of Central New York in 1924, thereby expanding its area of services to include the already-growing number of motorists residing within the greater Mohawk Valley.

Charles L. Hughes assumed club management responsibilities in 1943; and under his guidance, membership in the local organization continued its growth as motorists came to rely upon the AAA for such services as accurate road maps, tour routings, and emergency road services for disabled vehicles.

Out for a "spin" on the muddy roads of the historic Mohawk Valley in 1904.

The late Charles S. Mott at the wheel of his Utica-built Remington automobile, circa 1901.

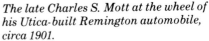

In 1959, at a time when the club's membership numbered 6,000 and full-time employees numbered 3, club leadership passed to Richard W. Richards. Elected to the presidency, a position he continues to hold, Richards further expanded membership services to include airline and steamship ticketing, traveler's checks, radio-dispatched emergency road service vehicles, and many other allied traveling services.

In 1965 the club moved to its current offices on Court Street, where by 1982 its full-time staff had grown to 38 employees serving a club membership in excess of 31,000.

BLUE CROSS AND BLUE SHIELD OF UTICA

On February 5, 1937, four Utica health care facilities—St. Luke's Home and Hospital, Faxton, St. Elizabeth, and Utica Memorial—banded together for the first time and formed the Hospital Plan Incorporated (Blue Cross). At that meeting Walter Roberts, a local merchant, became the Plan's first president. Also elected to offices were banker Roy Van Denbergh, vice-president; industrialist A.O. Foster, treasurer; and newspaperman Paul B. Williams, secretary.

The original offices were on Genesee Street, and only four people were employed as the Plan began signing up subscribers in the Utica area. Growth was slow until World War II. During the war many companies froze wages but not fringe benefits. This allowed the Plan to establish a strong foothold in Utica and the firm began to expand in all geographical directions.

Today close to 50 percent of the population of the Utica district subscribes to either Blue Cross or Blue Shield, a sister plan begun in 1939. The Utica office covers 15 counties for Blue Cross and 16 counties for Blue Shield. The office, now located at 245 Genesee Street, has a jurisdiction as far-reaching as Lake Placid, Potsdam, Oswego, Oneonta, and Norwich. Thirty hospitals now participate, up from the original four. The Plans also represent 800 doctors, 100 pharmacies, 50 skilled nursing facilities, and 10 home health agencies. The Utica office currently employs 165 people in data processing, claims, research, finance, and actuarial.

The Plans still retain their uniqueness because they pay the full cost of a hospital room (a cost that has risen from about five dollars a day in the '30s to more than $200 a day in the '80s). The Plans offer dental, major medical, and prescription drug coverage now as well.

Pilot programs the Utica office has helped initiate include the detoxification program at Faxton Hospital and the outpatient diabetes program at St. Luke's Memorial. Current director John Porn says Hospital Plan Incorporated will actively push for more such programs in the future.

In the 45 years' existence of the Blue Cross Plan, several prominent Uticans have served as president of the board. They include William C. Murray, an industrialist; Alvin F. Roepneck, an industrialist; H. Russell Johnson, a prominent banker; V. Boyle, an officer of a utility corporation; and Peter Carparelli, a prominent businessman.

The first presidents of the Blue Shield Plan were Dr. F.M. Miller, Jr., a local physician; Dr. H. Dan Vickers, a prominent surgeon; V. Lally, a local industrialist; Dr. James Bordley, a staff member of the Presbyterian Medical School in New York City and an administrator of Mary Imogene Bassett Hospital; and Dr. Joseph Chanatry, a local physician.

H.J. BRANDELES CORPORATION

Before the turn of the century, Herman J. Brandeles was installing sprinklers in the Utica area. The firm that bears his name still does so over 80 years later. Emigrating to the United States from Sweden, Mr. Brandeles' first job was as a foreman of the Grinnell Corporation of Providence, Rhode Island, pioneers in automatic sprinklers. Mr. Brandeles supervised their installation here and eventually moved to Utica where he met and married his wife, Ellen.

Seeing a growing need for automatic sprinklers in such firms as the Oneida Bleachery, the New York Mills Corporation, and the Hind Harrison Plush Mills, Mr. Brandeles established the corporation about 1897. The first office was in their home at 435 Lafayette Street. There the family and business flourished. A flower garden thrived behind wrought-iron gates; the two Brandeles children, Clifford and Christine, were born in that house; and there Mr. Brandeles hung his tin plumber's license on a chain.

In the 1900s, one might have seen the "basket plumbers" riding to work at H.J. Brandeles Corporation on their bicycles, the tools of their trade in a wire basket in front. A ledger from 1901 records the installation of plumbing and heating at the old House of the Good Shepherd for $14,611 and also notes the sprinklers put into Savage Arms (now CharlesTown). Payrolls from 1911 indicate plumbers made one dollar a day while sprinkler fitters earned three dollars; both worked six days a week.

Herman J. Brandeles remained president until his death in 1957, when his son, Clifford, assumed the post. Clifford Brandeles had been in heavy construction, and had also operated a bottled gas company until he joined his father's firm in 1948.

Herman J. Brandeles, founder of the firm that bears his name.

Two years after assuming the presidency, Clifford died; there is no longer any Brandeles family member involved. The current president, Louis A. Falvo, Sr., came to work for the firm in 1938 with a mechanical background. His son, Louis A. Falvo, Jr., joined the firm in 1959 after receiving his degree in mechanical engineering from Syracuse University. He is secretary of the corporation. After graduation from the Utica School of Commerce, Lee F. Warchol came to the firm in 1948

and currently serves as vice-president and treasurer.

At first formed to install automatic sprinklers, the H.J. Brandeles Corporation now installs and maintains industrial heating and piping, including boilers, oil burners, and automatic sprinkler systems. Work is performed in Utica and a 150-mile radius for industrial, commercial, and public utility accounts. A Brandeles specialty is process piping, used in chemical plants and dairies.

One of the original members of the Mechanical Contractors Association of America, Inc., the H.J. Brandeles Corporation is the oldest surviving mechanical contractor in the area. In 1978 the firm purchased its present building at 300 Lafayette Street. Built in 1907 on the site of the historic Theodore Faxton home, the structure was originally a trolley freight and express depot.

Changes have occurred in the business. Now most plumbing and heating work can be done through winter, as buildings are closed up more rapidly. Fittings and connections have been improved. Plastic and fiberglass are used in some installations. There is now great emphasis on retrofitting existing buildings for energy conservation.

However, the quality of the corporation's mechanical work has not changed. From the Frederick Rutter Memorial Building, a classic designed by Egbert Bagg, to the new Utica City Hall, to whatever industrial plant may be built in years to come, one is sure to see piping and sprinkler systems installed by the H.J. Brandeles Corporation.

The H.J. Brandeles Corporation clambake, August 2, 1941.

RICHARD M. BUCK CONSTRUCTION CORPORATION

The company continues its 20-year association with Griffiss Air Force Base through construction projects such as this flight simulator.

The approaching birth of one of Kathryn and Richard Buck's children was a deciding factor in keeping the family from accepting a job in Rochester and resulted in the formation of Buck Construction Company in 1962.

After graduation from Utica College, Richard Buck had worked as an estimator, field engineer, and superintendent for the John J. Harvey Company, at that time the largest contractor in the area. This background gave him the experience to go into business for himself, encouraged by his wife and parents.

The first office was in their home. From the start, Buck Construction Corporation was a joint effort: Kathryn Buck answered the telephone while Richard Buck performed construction work during the day and did paperwork and estimating for new jobs at night. At that time there were only 3 or 4 workers; current employment fluctuates between 20 to as many as 100 during peak seasons.

Griffiss Air Force Base was the site of the firm's first job: a two-stall ambulance garage built in 1962 by Buck and one other man. Twenty years later Buck Construction continues to perform substantial work for the base—including the gym, a 500-seat theater, and a flight simulator.

The cyclical nature of the industry and a seminar in Washington involved Buck Construction in building federally subsidized housing under various Housing and Urban Development grants. Seeing a need for residential units for the elderly,

Richard Buck erected an eight-story highrise in Whitesboro, named the Mary D. Buck Memorial Apartments for his mother. Another project under HUD was Historical Park Apartments on Rutger Street.

Scrapbooks overflow with pictures of completed contracts: the Presbyterian Home, schools, office buildings, churches, factories, nursing homes, banks, hospitals, "turnkey" family housing—but probably the work closest to the Bucks' hearts is the renovation and rehabilitation of historic structures. Kathryn Buck's fondness for old buildings is contagious.

A visit to 110 Genesee Street rewards the

visitor with the sight of a lovely old lobby lighted by rewired and burnished brass fixtures. By combining the Bucks' vital interest in preservation with a recognition of housing needs, this renovation is a true "neighborhood strategy job." An existing structure of historical significance was rehabilitated for new use.

The renovation of old buildings can be costly and difficult. "You never know what you will run into," says Richard Buck, adding, "The challenge is to design around the existing structure, adding insulation and other energy conservation features." This is well illustrated by the company's new location at 105 Main Street, Whitesboro, where 16-inch-thick brick walls once housed a bakery and now contain the Richard M. Buck Construction Corporation and other offices.

Having started the organization for family reasons it is very appropriate that 6 of the 11 children already work for Buck Construction Corporation. Two generations of Bucks can arrive in the nick of time to save a wonderful old building from the demolition ball. Such architectural delights as Gothic arches in the Sherburne and Norwich schools can be enjoyed instead of destroyed. Inspired by Kathryn Buck, the Richard M. Buck Construction Corporation is committed to saving and reusing historical buildings. Uticans can look forward to the preservation of cherished landmarks for generations to come.

The Mary D. Buck Memorial Apartments in Whitesboro are housing units for the elderly constructed by the Richard M. Buck Construction Corporation.

CASATELLI ELECTRIC, INC.

Few men can complete two careers in one lifetime, yet that is exactly what Dewey Casatelli has managed to do. With the support, encouragement, and help of his wife, Helen, and his three daughters, Angela, Alberta, and Jane, Mr. Casatelli went from serving for over two decades on the police force to founding his own electric company.

A native Utican (his Italian-born parents owned the Acme Floral Shop on Bleecker Street), Dewey Casatelli had learned the electrical trade in high school. However, the necessity of providing security for his family meant delaying that career. In 1964 he retired at the rank of captain from the Utica Police Department with 25 years of distinguished public service behind him.

Retirement from the force meant that Dewey Casatelli would enter his second career, that of an electrician, a field in which he had always had an interest and natural ability. Again, Helen and "Dewey's daughters" stood behind him and Mr. Casatelli entered his new career with motivation, training, and the willingness to put in the many long hours required.

The first office of Casatelli Electric Company was in his home at 1339 Mary Street. Mrs. Casatelli took phone calls, Jane typed and kept the books, a part-time estimator was employed, and the electrical wiring was performed by Dewey Casatelli and two to four men from Local 181 of the International Brotherhood of Electrical Workers. Most of the early jobs were small residential projects. Friendships made during a lifetime of living in Utica provided the necessary contacts and invaluable recommendations during the first two years.

Dewey Casatelli earned respect as both a policeman and as a tough competitor in the electrical contracting field.

In earlier years electrical codes and standards had been less rigid, often resulting in fires from faulty old wiring. Recognizing this, an early advertisement for Casatelli Electric Company showed Dewey in a policeman's uniform, ready to "troubleshoot" electrical problems.

In 1966 the business began to expand. William J. Brittelli, Mr. Casatelli's son-in-law, began working nights and weekends.

One of the most important contracts Casatelli Electric, Inc., was awarded during the 1970s was the St. Elizabeth Ambulatory Care Center, a facility for which Dewey Casatelli sits on the fund-raising board.

Union hiring was increased to six men, the office moved to 204 Park Avenue, and his daughter, Alberta (Mrs. William Brittelli), took over as full-time secretary. This move paralleled a shift into bidding on large electrical construction.

A major project which firmly established Casatelli Electric Company was the construction of Mohawk Data Sciences in Herkimer during 1967 and 1968. Up to 20 union electricians were utilized in various phases of this project, and from then on Casatelli never looked back. Federally supported housing developments carried the company in the '70s. Two estimators and 25 to 50 electricians were kept busy with work on Six Nations Square, Kennedy Plaza, and Twin Towers apartments.

By 1976 Casatelli Electric had become a leading local electrical subcontractor and was involved in two important health care projects, the Faxton-Sunset-St. Luke's Nursing Home and the St. Elizabeth Ambulatory Care Center, both of which took several years to complete. William J. Brittelli came to work on a full-time basis and the growing organization moved to the CAG Building at 1506 Whitesboro Street, the former St. Luke's Hospital. Incorporation followed in 1977 as Dewey Casatelli assumed the presidency and Helen Casatelli and William J. Brittelli became vice-presidents. In 1979 Dewey Casatelli entered his second, but first true, retirement, his son-in-law succeeding him as president and his daughter, Alberta, becoming secretary/treasurer. Mrs. Casatelli continues as vice-president and a third generation is beginning to take interest in the firm.

This family-run business entered the '80s with a staff of four estimators, two truck drivers, and from 30 to 60 electricians. Recent projects include the Sheraton Inn, the Teamsters Fund Building, Genesee Towers, the Olin II Science Building at Colgate University, and Bleecker Street housing for the elderly.

To have come so far from so little is a tribute to the dedication and devotion of Dewey Casatelli. Beginning a second career when one is 50 years old is no mean feat. Whatever he attempted, Dewey Casatelli succeeded and although he is "retired," he continues his interest in the St. Elizabeth's Development Council and Casatelli Electric still relies on him for advice.

CENTRAL NEW YORK COACH LINES, INC.

Now licensed to operate in 48 states and the District of Columbia, Central New York Coach Lines has come a long way since 1930. Harrison Sweet and four other men formed the company that year to take over the Utica-Oneida portion of the route, which had formerly been served by the New York State Railways. With a fleet of three buses purchased from the American Car and Foundry Company (ACF), service was inaugurated in July 1931.

Originally based in Oneida, CNY moved to Utica in 1933. That same year the New York State Railways also abandoned its Utica-Little Falls trolley line—CNY took over this route in 1934. Together with the Utica-Syracuse line, it remains the backbone of the company's local intercity operation today.

Highways began to improve dramatically during the New Deal, and during the '40s and '50s Central New York Coach Lines saw regular route service and passenger miles grow steadily. Vernon Downs, the harness racing track opened in 1953, became a popular on-line destination.

CNY moved into the important new area of "touring" in the early 1960s, prompted by a sudden, marked demand from groups of people bound for common destinations and facilitated by the completion of the Interstate highway system. In late 1965 the company purchased its first bus designed especially for long-distance charters and tours. On May 20, 1966, the Interstate Commerce Commission granted the firm charter rights and "special operations" authority to operate from Utica and Rome

Harrison Sweet, founder of Central New York Coach Lines, Inc.

throughout New York State, as well as to a number of other eastern states.

Harrison Sweet's son, Wallace, had "taken the wheel" at CNY in 1957, and it was he who steered the organization into the growing tour field. Business boomed in

One of the new MC-9 tour coaches.

Schuyler Sweet, president of Central New York Coach Lines, Inc.

1967 with tours to the Montreal Expo, and Sweet purchased a travel agency to promote the Expo and other tours. In 1968 the company moved to its present headquarters in Yorkville.

Wallace Sweet met an untimely death in 1970, but the family tradition has been carried on by his sons, Schuyler and Stephen. Schuyler joined the firm in 1964 and took over the presidency in 1980; Stephen became vice-president in 1981.

Central New York's tour business, bus fleet, and operating rights all continued to grow during the 1970s. In 1979 the company hired L.B. "Spike" Herzig, an experienced motor coach tour operator and former president of the National Tour Brokers Association, to head up a new Central Coach Tours division (CCT). He initiated the design of new logos and paint schemes for both CCT and Central Coach Lines buses, increased the frequency of sports tours, and expanded the operation of shopping tours as well as holiday tours.

In 1981 Central New York received two new MC-9 deluxe coaches for its tour fleet. These air conditioned diesels, a far cry from the gas-powered, standard-shift ACFs of 1930, speak eloquently of the company's forward-looking policies.

CHICAGO PNEUMATIC TOOL COMPANY

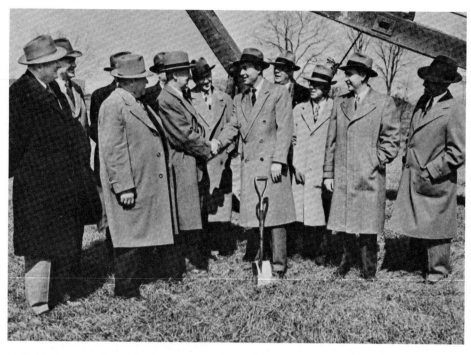

Chicago Pneumatic Tool Company is a worldwide leader in the production of industrial air tools. It is also a company with a large investment in the Utica area. In the depressed economy of the early 1890s, J.W. Duntley, a foundry foreman from Milwaukee, recognized the promising market potential for small, air-powered hammers. Working with inventor Joseph Boyer, Duntley successfully introduced the Boyer hammer to foundries throughout the United States. The hammer's immediate acceptance led to the development of a number of other types of air-powered tools, and to the founding of the Chicago Pneumatic Tool Company in 1894. The firm was incorporated in New Jersey in 1901 with the financial backing of Charles M. Schwab, president of U.S. Steel. Within a few years Chicago Pneumatic was operating manufacturing plants in Detroit, Cleveland, and Chicago.

As the nation's industrial base (particularly the automobile business) grew over the years, so did Chicago Pneumatic, into an international corporation. Add to this the increased demand for its product in the post-World War II years and the company was ripe for a major expansion and relocation. In 1947 Vincent R. Corrou, then head of the local chamber of commerce, met with Chicago Pneumatic president W.L. Lewis and presented his pitch for Utica. Corrou

---

Chicago Pneumatic's Utica plant, when it opened, was the largest in the world built especially for the production of air tools.

---

touted Utica as a city with plenty of available labor (the textile mills were all moving to the South), centrally located among major population centers, and with an enthusiastic and supportive government and chamber of commerce.

Apparently Lewis liked what he heard, for in 1948 construction of a new half-million-square-foot plant was begun on a site just east of the Utica city line. With the transfer of workers from Cleveland, the

Groundbreaking ceremonies for the Chicago Pneumatic Utica plant took place on March 24, 1948, with officials of the company and community present.

---

new plant started production in 1949. The next year Detroit's operations were moved to Utica, and an additional 2,000 local residents hired. The first Utican hired was George Harrer, as personnel manager. Mr. Harrer recalls those days: "I set up an office in downtown Utica on Blandina Street and the line of people waiting to apply would sometimes stretch a block around the corner of Genesee Street. I went out, hired the first person in line, and put him to work taking applications."

The Chicago Pneumatic plant was a boon to the local economy and Utica was good to the company. In the years following the move to Utica, Chicago Pneumatic concentrated on expansion and diversification. The Jacobs Manufacturing Company, the world's largest manufacturer of drill chucks, was acquired in 1953. Allen Manufacturing Company was added in 1956, Qualitrol Corporation in 1965, and Partlow Corporation in 1972, among others. Today, with 23 plants throughout the world, Chicago Pneumatic is a pacesetter in the manufacture of air-powered tools, instruments and controls, portable drill and machine tool chucks, and threaded fasteners. It remains the world's leading supplier of air tools to gasoline stations, car dealers, automotive repair shops, and truck and bus operators. It also remains one of the chief employers in the Utica area.

FERRARO LANDSCAPE CO., INC.

Going from mowing grass to designing and landscaping a large park represents major changes which would surely amaze and please Carl Ferraro, the founder of Ferraro Landscape. For 42 years, Carl was in the landscape maintenance business, tending lawns and gardens until his death in 1964. His son, Frank, often worked with him after school, since his mother had died when he was five. Frank spent a great deal of time with his father, absorbing his knowledge and learning his techniques.

For four and a half years Frank served in the Air Force as a radar technician and aircraft controller. In the spring of 1962 he received an honorable discharge and decided to remain in the area to help his father, who was ill. Carl turned over all the maintenance accounts, some of which had been with him for over 40 years, to his son.

The business was run out of the Ferraro's apartment. Gerry (Frank's wife) answered the phone and kept books while Frank and two employees performed maintenance work for 40 homeowners.

Soon the family and the firm began to grow. Three children—Frank Jr., Christina, and Michael—were born and the maintenance business changed to resi-

dential and light commercial planning and design. Often nursery stock was kept in the backyard, so Gerry saw her landscaping trees and shrubs come and go, depending on customer needs.

The first municipal contract was completed by Frank in 1969. Subsequent joint ventures with Anthony Bianco resulted in a partnership in 1971. First located on Kellogg Road, Bianco and Ferraro Nurseries, Inc., moved to Oneida Street in 1976. The partnership was dissolved three years later and Ferraro Landscape Company was born. A second story was added to the building, most maintenance work was discontinued, and the firm concentrated on contract and design work.

The size of job performed by Ferraro Landscape Company ranges from a large state park to a small memorial planting at a cemetery. The Ferraros have laid sod along state highways and planted grass in large areas with a hydroseeder, which sprays fertilizer, mulch, and seed in one operation. More of Ferraro's fine design work and planting may be found at the Amalgamated Meat Cutters building on the Parkway, in a rooftop garden at Genesee Towers, or in Chancellor Park.

Ferraro Landscape has put in irrigation systems and installed and landscaped pools and a Japanese garden. The firm landscaped a complete athletic complex in Ilion, including football, softball, and baseball fields, and in the dead of winter planted a 40-foot sugar maple weighing nine tons. The trees and shrubs used by the Ferraros are varied and include unusual plant material like dwarf specimens or topiaries. Hardy new strains of trees, shrubs, and ornamentals and strict inspection assure lasting plantings.

Carl Ferraro would be proud to know that a third generation will be entering the business. Frank Jr. is completing a degree in landscape contracting at the University of Mississippi. The growth of Ferraro Landscape from a maintenance operation to large-scale contract landscaping has meant long hours, hard work, and commitment. The business that Carl Ferraro started will continue to beautify highways, parks, and building sites in the Mohawk Valley in coming decades.

Ferraro Landscape Co., Inc., on Oneida Street in 1982.

FIRSCHING KNITTING MILLS
J.A. FIRSCHING & SON, INC.

From canal towpath to president of the Firsching Knitting Mills: quite a story lies there. Joseph A. Firsching was born in Bavaria, Germany, in 1879 and came to Utica at the age of six. His first job, at 12, was riding the mules that dragged barges on the Erie Canal. By 14, however, he had begun his career in textiles, holding positions with Globe Woolen Mills, Utica Knitting Company, Capron Knitting Company, and Fort Schuyler Knitting Company. He developed a machine for cutting and folding a double cuff used on fleece-lined underwear and canvas gloves, and it is believed that he invented the union suit while with Fort Schuyler.

In 1905 he was a consulting expert on textile sewing machines with offices in the Devereux Block. He then became a partner in the Utica Novelty and Mill Specialty Company, where he introduced some new machines. He later sold his interest and purchased the Coleman & Dowd repair shop, where he manufactured textile machinery. After buying the Holdring Shops and Foundry and increasing its business, Firsching erected a large mill at 614 Broad Street.

Firsching began producing cotton underwear, as the K.F. Knitted Waist Mills, in 1915. The name was changed in 1920 to Firsching Knitting Mills, with Joseph A. Firsching as president and treasurer. Large contracts for underwear for the U.S. government during World War I resulted in additions to the plant.

After the war, the mills began the manufacture of artificial silk, and in 1920 a larger building was erected especially for the manufacture of this fabric. By 1923 the Firsching Knitting Mills had created numerous individual fabrics (including Velete and Firsheen). From these materials they made up coats, capes, wraps, dresses, blouses, skirts, turbans, scarfs, tuxedos, slips, petticoats, nightgowns, pajamas, negligees, vests, netherbockers, bloomers, envelopes, union suits, and step-ins—each one cut and sewn to the individual measurement of the customer.

The firm had the distinction of being the only manufacturer that sold made-to-order garments directly from factory to consumer. To accomplish this, Firsching Knitting Mills employed over 1,200 representatives with offices in principal cities from coast to coast, enlarged the plant again, and published the *Firsching Knitter* for sales representatives.

Joseph Firsching's younger son, Robert A., bought the business in 1950. The senior Firsching retired the following year and his son conducted the business until his death in 1969. Robert's wife, the former Helen Roehrig, has run the business ever since, completing a 47-year connection with the company in 1982. Her father was the respected owner/operator of Utica's original Ford Repair Shop, having been trained in Detroit under Henry Ford, Sr. Many years after coming to work for the man who was eventually to become her father-in-law, Mrs. Firsching discovered that she had been born and raised in the house built by her husband's grandparents when they came to this country from Germany.

Today J.A. Firsching & Son, Inc., manufactures textile machinery sold all over the world. There are 25 employees at 421 Broad Street, and the Diamond Jubilee of the company was celebrated in 1981. Just as the original organization made garments to exact dimensions, today custom-made machines are produced for each customer. Electronic control boxes have replaced mechanical levers and pulleys, but the attention to special customer needs remains the same.

The J.A. Firsching & Son, Inc., letterhead is recognized around the world.

The Original

J·A· FIRSCHING & SON, INC.
MANUFACTURERS OF
Textile Machinery — OUR DIAMOND JUBILEE

Seventy-Five Years

1906   1981

FLORENTINE PASTRY SHOP

Buon giorno! How about a cup of cappuccino and some "artistically different" Italian pastries? Since 1928 Uticans have enjoyed this Old World treat. More than a bakery, the Florentine Pastry Shop has been a meeting place where one can discuss politics over an espresso and a fresh pastry.

In 1928 Joseph Borgovini and Vincent Gennaro, from Italy, formed a partnership to open the new Florentine Pastry Shop at 605 Bleecker Street. When the partnership ended, Gennaro ran the shop until his death. His wife, Louise Gennaro, continued to manage it until the early 1960s, when Gabriele B. Alessandroni and Rocco Vitullo took over.

At first there were two bakers and five or six sales clerks in front. Today there are four bakers, plus Gabriele Alessandroni and 10 or 12 in front. Early employees worked six days for about $20 a week; the bakers received $70. Alessandroni both bakes and runs the Florentine Pastry Shop, and his sister, Iole Vitullo, manages the front. The Florentine moved to 667 Bleecker Street in 1942, and with expansion has remained there since.

Gabriele Alessandroni's day begins at 6 a.m. since every pastry is made from scratch—dough, filling, and decoration. At this early hour he makes sfogliatelle (a pastry that "unfolds" as it bakes), the most time-consuming product. Perhaps he is baking pasti, small vanilla or chocolate pies, or Italian cheesecake. Maybe the cannoli are being filled with a cream made of

Specialty cakes for any occasion from the Florentine Pastry Shop. Photo circa 1942.

Italian ricotta and chocolate chips. Often a grandmother whose own wedding cake came from the Florentine Pastry Shop will send in her granddaughter to order one of their special rum cakes covered with heavy cream or buttercream and nuts.

Holidays are special at the Florentine Pastry Shop. At Christmas, they make pignolata; which are tiny cream puffs mounded with honey; and marzipan, made

A window full of tempting baked goods at the Florentine Pastry Shop, soon after it opened in 1928.

from their own ground almond dough and molded entirely by hand into strawberries, apples, peaches, and bananas. In 1981 the Florentine baked 500 Christmas cakes, using 1,500 eggs one day and 1,500 the next. Easter brings cassata, an Italian cheese pie using ricotta and cooked cream wheat, and egg bread, a sweet bread with whole eggs on top. The last Sunday of September is the feast day of St. Cosimo et Damiano, celebrated at St. Anthony's church. Buses come from as far as Canada and New Jersey, and stop at the pastry shop discharging 70 people at a time. The Florentine Pastry Shop supplies as many as 1,000 dozen pastries to the church.

Pastries are not the only delight of the Florentine. Gelati, a rich cream and egg ice cream, is available all year, and in summer, lemon ice, made with fresh lemons, cools off many Uticans. A customer of 36 years walks in: "I remember when my father brought me in every Sunday for gelati!"

Customers order from as far away as New York City, New Orleans, and Los Angeles. Some patrons even fly Florentine pastries to Florida in the airplane refrigerator. Alessandroni has installed a new oven and a new mixer, but still prefers working by hand. "You get a better pastry when you feel the dough." Three generations of Uticans would agree.

GAETANO ASSOCIATES

Early in life, Charles A. Gaetano knew that he enjoyed building. Starting as a mason's helper, he progressed up the ladder to the developer he is today. In 1955 he founded Gaetano Construction Company, considered one of the largest in New York State.

The first office was in the Gaetanos' home, but growth in the business required additional room. In 1968 the former St. Luke's Hospital on Whitesboro Street was scheduled for the wrecking ball. Charles Gaetano purchased this historic structure—built in 1905—pigeons, leaky roof, and all. Now known as the CAG Building, it has been completely renovated and contains 70 apartments and 15 offices, including Gaetano Construction Corporation headquarters.

This structure has special meaning, since four Gaetano children were born there when it was St. Luke's. During its reconstruction, a workman found in the debris the hospital birth record of the Gaetanos' second son. Scrawled in the space for father's occupation was one word, "unemployed." Little did Charles then dream that one day the entire building would belong to Gaetano Realty.

Six children to feed, a depressed economy with uncertain income in the construction industry, and a love of old structures led Charles Gaetano into the real estate development business and the renovation of older area buildings, an excellent alternative to new construction. Gaetano Realty was formed in 1970 and by 1981 owned and

The New York State Teamsters Fund Building, 1976, is an example of Gaetano's modern construction.

operated over 30 pieces of property, many of which are prestigious Utica landmarks of historical value.

The first purchase was the vacant, run-

The Paul Building, located on Elizabeth Street, is the home of the Utica Chamber of Commerce.

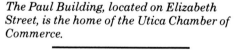

down nurses' building next to the former St. Luke's Hospital. Every cent and every Gaetano workman was thrown into the renovation of the dilapidated structure. The apartments rented so quickly that the hospital was tackled next. In 1974 the Paul Building was acquired and currently houses some of Utica's major legal firms and the Chamber of Commerce. Utica Catholic Academy, purchased in 1976, is being converted into luxury condominiums, and the former convent now houses several family medical practitioners.

One of Utica's finest landmark homes, the Wheeler mansion, was acquired in 1979. Retaining its beauty and handsome structure, it will house offices for mental health services. Gaetano's latest venture is the purchase of the Niagara Mohawk (or 258 Genesee Street) building, another Utica landmark.

Restoring any old structure requires vision, but perhaps the greatest challenge to Charles Gaetano was the purchase of the Savage Arms plant, a building whose potential he knew, having worked there after high school.

Built between 1902 and 1915, the plant had manufactured guns during world wars I and II and later Sperry Univac computers. Charles Gaetano purchased the 33-acre site in 1977 and achieved his dream of converting 750,000 square feet into the world's largest factory outlet center. Named after the developer, CharlesTown in 1982 houses restaurants, specialty stores, and 39 outlets, including Utica industries like Duxbak, Utica Cutlery, Mele Manufacturing, and Dandee Donuts.

At CharlesTown, discounted top-brand merchandise is available in a European marketplace setting. A visitor can enjoy courtyards landscaped with trees and flowers, sandblasted mellow old bricks, cobblestone walks, wide-plank wood floors, park benches, and arched windows and doorways. The former Savage Arms fire pond, visible from many windows, serves as a focal point, with ducks in summer and a skating rink in winter. Visitors can stroll the boardwalk, listen to a band in the gazebo, eat in an outdoor cafe. Called "a bold and imaginative step in factory outlet retailing," CharlesTown is also a tourist attraction, drawing busloads of out-of-town visitors who bring business to the entire area.

Many antique items from renovated area buildings enhance Charlie G's, the newest restaurant at CharlesTown. One may eat at the long St. Agnes convent table, or the white marble ones from St. Luke's Hospital, or on pink marble from Utica Catholic Academy. Lighting fixtures and stools from Savage Arms, the barber chair from the Paul Building, pews and the gym floor from UCA—all create a fascinating historical atmosphere.

Charles A. Gaetano was the featured speaker at the dinner where Cornelia Gaetano received the Business and Professional Women's Club Woman of the Year Award in 1977.

Both Cornelia and Charles Gaetano have been very active in the community and both have received awards for their efforts. President of the Senior Day Center of Utica in 1982, "Connie" Gaetano has served on a number of civic boards.

Named Industrial Man of the Year in 1978, "Chuck" Gaetano has been active with the St. Elizabeth Hospital Development Council and the Central Association for the Blind. Concerned about small quarters on Court Street, he was instrumental in obtaining the former G.E. Kent Street location. Renovated and designed to permit easy access for the handicapped, the building now houses two agencies, the Mohawk Valley Workshop and the Central Association for the Blind. Neighboring Chancellor Park has also been redesigned for better access. An entire area has thus

been revitalized and made productive, with dignity for the handicapped.

New construction is as important as recycled old buildings to the Gaetanos. Looking at the gallery of photographs in the CAG building, one is struck by the diversity—from banks to churches, from parking garages to nursing homes, factories, schools, a synagogue, and a rectory. Among the contracts are the New York State Teamsters Fund Building, the Hamilton College athletic complex, Six Nations housing, and the Central Fire Station.

A native Utican, Charles Gaetano feels passionately about the area and believes in reinvesting in Utica. His family agrees. The four oldest children returned after college and joined their parents in Gaetano Associates. Bill is president of Gaetano Construction, Brian is in charge of development at CharlesTown, and Charles Neal runs Lakewood Construction Company. The fourth child, Mary, manages Gaetano Realty Corporation, while the two youngest, Colleen and Gregory, are still students.

Vocal in expressing his views, enjoying a challenge and hard work, Charles Gaetano is a man with a mission—revitalizing and promoting Utica. The Tower of Hope, built by Gaetano Construction, is a fitting symbol for the city, the company, and the family. In the decades to come, the Gaetano family will continue to search for development opportunities in the area, with enthusiasm and faith in a bright future for Utica.

CAG Building, the former St. Luke's Hospital, is now the headquarters for Gaetano Associates.

GIBSON FUNERAL SERVICE

A death in the family brings not only sorrow, but considerable confusion. Few people know exactly what to do. For the past 25 years Gibson Funeral Service has provided guidance and dignified ceremonies for those in the greater Utica area who have suffered a loss.

Originally from South Carolina, Clyde Gibson attended the McAllister School of Embalming, located near the UN Building, and apprenticed in Harlem. Two years later an elderly gentleman suggested that Mr. Gibson look elsewhere for better opportunities, pointing out seven funeral homes within a few blocks.

After a fruitless search in Binghamton, Clyde Gibson discovered in Utica that the only funeral parlor serving blacks had failed. With the encouragement of the old man and help from a local lawyer, Mr. Gibson rented the first floor of 116 Washington Street, living in a tiny apartment in back of the funeral home. Mrs. Gibson remained in New York City, working to make ends meet.

Although the resident black population of Utica was largely established and growing, many of the early calls were charity work for migrant farmers. Since many in the labor camps came from Florida, it would often take up to nine months for Oneida County to collect and pay the Gibsons. Meanwhile, bills were due for the casket and vault companies and the cemetery. Struggling to survive financially, Mr.

Gibson Funeral Service was located at 116 Washington Street in May 1956. Note the flower car in the foreground.

Clyde and Geraldine Gibson, April 1951.

Gibson took a second job as a waiter at the Hotel Utica. He and his wife, Geraldine, scrimped and cut corners, often "robbing Peter to pay Paul."

Other calls were slow in coming, and the Gibsons were discouraged. However, noting that the calls included infant deaths, the old man again encouraged Clyde: "They trust you with their babies." The Gibsons managed to hang on, and in 1958 they moved to 415 Broad Street. There they remained 23 years, moving to their present address at 144 Eagle Street in 1981.

At the Eagle Street funeral parlor, as at all their locations, both Gibsons work

together, only hiring part-time employees the day of the funeral, mainly to drive. With just the two of them as the only full-time employees, Clyde and Geraldine have always worked very hard, cutting out things for themselves. Yet the Gibsons have always found time to help people, not only the bereaved, but also their "second family."

The Gibsons are proud of the many young people from Rome State School who have lived with them, one for almost 20 years. A number have finished college, some are married, and all have held jobs. In addition, several former residents of Marcy and Utica psychiatric centers live with the Gibsons, going to the day care center or the sheltered workshop on Arnold Avenue. Each person feels part of the Gibson family and brags about Geraldine's recipe for chicken. In addition to the funeral home and caring for this big "family," Geraldine Gibson has been active in school and regular elections and has worked on voter registration since 1958.

Most calls for the Gibson Funeral Service came from word-of-mouth recommendation, although calendars and paper fans advertising the firm are distributed to churches. Currently, a nephew is completing an internship on Long Island and plans to join the Gibson firm. He will find them still helping people and sharing their belief that while it isn't easy to make a business survive, it is possible. It takes energy and time and a lot of sacrifice, but it is worthwhile. Families who have lost a loved one and the residents who live in Clyde and Geraldine Gibson's home would agree.

HOLY TRINITY CHURCH OF UTICA

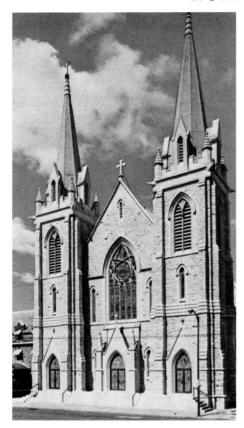

Holy Trinity's current church at 1206 Lincoln Avenue.

Its twin spires soar above the well-kept old houses behind Munson-Williams-Proctor Institute and command the attention of motorists on the North-South Arterial. The parish church of Holy Trinity is an impressive edifice. But the twin spires and high stone walls are merely physical evidence of an impressive history of sacrifice by, and service to, the Polish community of Utica and the entire Upper Mohawk region.

When the early Polish immigrants arrived around 1870 from the territory occupied by Prussia and Austria, they attended German services at St. Joseph's Church. They formed the Benevolent Society of St. Stanislaus in 1889 and brought Polish priests to Utica from time to time, particularly for Easter confessions. In 1896 the society purchased land for a church on Chenango (now Lincoln) Avenue and in 1897 Holy Trinity Church was incorporated.

The first pastor, Father Simon Pniak, offered Mass in a converted frame building and work started immediately on a permanent brick church. When dedicated in 1899, it was felt that this edifice would serve the parish for many years to come. But a new wave of immigration began in 1905 from the area of Poland dominated by Russia, so in that year plans were drawn for the present church. Construction required nearly five years and some $150,000 and was complicated by problems in securing the foundation next to the abandoned Chenango Canal. Two church bells were installed and blessed in 1910, one donated by the parish's own St. Michael's Society, the other by the Globe Mill, which employed many of the parishioners.

The parish school began in the basement of the old church in 1899 and expanded to occupy the whole building after the new church was completed. An addition was built in 1914. The present grammar school was completed in 1960 and serves some 350 pupils.

In the beginning Holy Trinity had no parish boundaries and served Poles, not only in Utica, but throughout Oneida and parts of adjoining counties. It is the mother church of four other Polish churches in the area, including St. Mary's in New York Mills, St. Stanislaus, Bishop & Martyr in East Utica, Transfiguration in Rome, St. Joseph's in Herkimer, and St. George's Lithuanian Church in Utica.

Holy Trinity was embroiled in a prolonged debate during the '50s and '60s over the original plans for the North-South Arterial, close to the rear of the church and school and cutting several streets that connected Lincoln Avenue with residential areas in West Utica. The parishioners' efforts to have the Arterial (renamed the General Casimir Pulaski Highway in 1981) sunk below grade were not successful, however, and the resultant intersections have proved hazardous and are objects of continuing debate.

Once almost exclusively Polish, the parish has become more cosmopolitan. For example, in 1975 construction began in the Holy Trinity Cemetery on the Resurrection Chapel Mausoleum, available to all area Catholics. But at the same time, Holy Trinity seeks both to promote an appreciation of its Polish heritage among newer parishioners and the community in general and to satisfy the spiritual needs of older Polish-speaking members and recent emigrants from Poland. Masses in Polish and in English and a broad range of parish activities and services all contribute to the continued success of Holy Trinity Church.

The church interior decorated for Christmas.

HEINTZ FUNERAL SERVICE, INC.

The Heintz Funeral Service, Inc., is the oldest funeral establishment in the greater Utica area operated solely by one family. Three generations of Heintzes have provided comfort and reassurance to thousands of families in times of personal loss.

Fred A. Heintz, Sr., who founded the firm in 1909, was born and raised in Utica. He began his career working for a casket company in Brooklyn, New York, and later attended Renonard's Training School for Embalmers in New York City. Upon completion of the four-week course, Mr. Heintz passed state examinations and was awarded his funeral director's license. Today a two-year associate degree in mortuary science is required for eligibility to take New York State licensing examinations.

Mr. Heintz returned to Utica and opened his first funeral home on Varick Street on April 1, 1909. The Utica *Herald-Dispatch* stated: "Mr. Heintz, after having several years' experience in New York and Brooklyn, opened his present undertaking parlor on April 1, 1909 . . . he is admirably equipped to assume all funeral ceremonies . . . and is always careful to save all his patrons unnecessary expense and carries out their instructions to the smallest detail." Three years later he married Theresa Lawless of Deansboro.

In 1928 the business was moved to 1517 Whitesboro Street, which remains today the firm's center of operations. Fred A. Heintz, Jr., joined his father in business in 1938 and became manager upon the death of his father in 1941. The senior Mrs. Heintz continued to take an active role in management. Two other brothers Edward C. Heintz (now president) and John W. Heintz, also joined the firm during World War II. John later retired to Arizona for health reasons.

The firm purchased the William Walsh Funeral Home on East Park Row in Clinton in 1946. The acquisition of this building, a landmark on the village square, marked the first major expansion of the Heintz Funeral Service. Others were soon to follow.

In the mid-1950s, the firm acquired property adjacent to its Whitesboro Street location and constructed an addition which more than doubled the funeral home's floor space, as well as substantially increasing on-the-premises parking. Further construction at this site provided additional chapels, the most modern preparation room facilities, and a complete casket and accessories showroom.

Other changes occurred over the years, too. The Heintzes' original horse-drawn hearse has given way to motorized vehicles. A funeral in one's own home is now a rarity, but the three Heintz Funeral homes provide the atmosphere of a private house, easing the burden on the family.

Fred A. Heintz, Sr. 1886-1941

The Heintz family incorporated the business in 1964, with Fred Heintz, Jr., as president. Upon Fred's death in 1981, Edward Heintz became the current president of the organization. A third generation of the family entered the firm when Fred A. Heintz III, Fred Jr.'s oldest son, joined in 1965. He was followed in 1970 by Edward's son, Richard P. Heintz, and in 1981 by Fred Jr.'s youngest son, Terrance K. Heintz.

Along with the addition of the younger Heintzes came further expansion of the firm's physical plant with the acquisition of the historic Weaver home on Herkimer Road in North Utica. Prior to its opening in 1979, the Heintz Funeral Service's third funeral home was enlarged and thoroughly restored to its 19th-century elegance. Bricks matching the original color were obtained and the restoration project earned the Heintzes a citation from the Landmarks Society of Greater Utica.

Although the Heintz Funeral Service, Inc., has experienced continued growth and physical expansion since its modest beginnings in a small funeral parlor on Varick Street some 73 years ago, the traditions of personal service and attention to detail established by its founder have remained the Heintz family hallmark.

1517 Whitesboro Street, circa 1937.

PETER A. KARL, INC.

What is an exporter doing in Utica? As the largest export management firm between New York City and Fort Wayne, Indiana, Peter A. Karl, Inc., often encounters this question. Since jet travel has replaced long boat trips and instant telex satellite communications are used instead of letters sent by steamer, Utica is an even more logical choice for the headquarters of an exporting firm than it was 60 years ago.

Peter A. Karl, the oldest of three children, was born in Utica of German parents. After attending local schools, he was graduated from Georgetown University in 1915. After service in World War I with the U.S. Marine Corps, Mr. Karl returned to his pre-war job in the export department of the W.R. Grace Steamship Company.

Peter A. Karl, who wanted to return to Utica, approached the Brunner Manufacturing Company with a view to organizing an export department for them. He was conscious of the overseas demand for American products and was interested in starting his own business. Also, he recognized that an export business did not have to be located in New York City or in a major port city because freight forwarders handle the loading of the merchandise on the ships.

While directing the export of Brunner air compressors, Mr. Karl began to sell companion products for garages and service stations, such as air-operated lubrication equipment and hoists. The unusual idea of representing several manufacturers of complementary products in order to reduce overseas sales costs allowed many manufacturers to enter these markets without the necessity of establishing their own export departments.

Despite his 12-week trips abroad, Peter Karl was very active in local civic affairs. He chaired many fund drives including the Community Chest and headed Utica's USO effort during World War II. Mr. Karl was also deeply involved in trade and export promotion organizations. He was a founder and served as president of the Overseas Automotive Club of New York City from 1927 to 1928.

John F. (Jack) Karl, the son of Peter Karl, is now president of Peter A. Karl, Inc. Mr. Karl is former chairman of the Utica Board of Water Supply and served two terms as the New York State Commissioner of Corrections. He was a founder of the Mohawk Valley State Bank and currently sits on the board of advisors of the successor institution, Bankers Trust Company of Albany, N.A.

A third generation of Karls is now with Peter A. Karl, Inc. Jack's son, Vincent P. Karl, joined the organization in 1977 after graduation from the American Graduate School of International Management.

Peter A. Karl, founder of Peter A. Karl, Inc.

A source of special pride to Peter A. Karl, Inc., is the President's "E" Award for Excellence in Exporting presented by the United States Secretary of Commerce. This award was made because Peter A. Karl, Inc., has competed effectively against stiff foreign competition and, in doing so, has contributed in great measure to the nation's export expansion program.

Initially the company operated solely on a commission basis. Today Peter A. Karl, Inc., takes title to the equipment it exports and assumes the risks of extending credit to overseas customers. To do this the management must keep abreast of rapidly changing economic and political conditions.

Yet, with all these changes, Utica remains an "ideal location for an export manager," explains Jack Karl. Although with modern communications, Peter A. Karl, Inc., could be located anywhere in the United States, the Karls consider Utica a great place to live and to raise a family. The company's foreign customers are consistently impressed with the quality of life in the Mohawk Valley and the beauty of the surrounding countryside. Peter A. Karl, Inc., recently moved from Utica to larger quarters in New York Mills. In managing export sales of automotive and industrial products for more than a dozen American manufacturers, Peter A. Karl, Inc., continues its founder's vision of providing American products to customers overseas.

LIBERTY PROTECTIVE LEATHERS, INC.

800 degrees Fahrenheit—too hot to handle! Yet Liberty Protective Leathers, Inc., makes some gloves which permit the user to handle objects up to 500 degrees Fahrenheit and others which will accommodate up to 800 degrees for five seconds. These gloves are made in Clark Mills by a firm founded by Dr. Louis J. Strobino, an orthopedic surgeon in Utica.

Born in Connecticut, Dr. Strobino worked in a tannery at the age of 15. As a chemistry major at Wesleyan, he became interested in leather chemistry and had developed a method of leather processing and reclamation of tanning liquors. He continued this interest through Harvard Medical School. In 1938, while interning in Boston, he became aware of a problem: a monthly fluoroscopic exam of patients required the use of a protective rubber glove which was stiff and lacked durability. Deciding that he could do better, Dr. Strobino formed a research group. The Liberty Dressing Company tried many types of tannages and impregnations. Finally, he felt the product was good enough to market, and the X-ray glove was born. In the fall of 1940 it was exhibited in Boston and 100 pairs were sold. At that time GE, Westinghouse, Picker, and Standard X-ray were among the firm's customers.

By 1952 Dr. Strobino had completed his military service and orthopedic residency, established a practice in Utica, and incorporated Liberty Protective Leathers. In

1961 he bought the stock of his partners. He erected the two current buildings in Clark Mills and was producing the X-ray glove, an X-ray apron, and a glove impregnated with refractory (heat-resistant) and insulating materials.

The raw material for these specialized gloves is capybara leather, which is imported from South America. The world's largest rodent, the capybara has skin so soft and porous that it impregnates easily. After tanning in Gloversville, the skins come to Clark Mills, where they are first split into layers by a machine almost 100 years old. They are impregnated in the drum room, cut by "clickers," annealed to preshrink, sewn, and hand-turned so that all seams are inside. The inner lining is sewn into the finger tips, avoiding separation of the plies when removing the glove from a perspiring hand.

The virtual disappearance of the raw material by 1977 resulted in the elimination of X-ray gloves, the apron having been discontinued also. Emphasis was placed on the heat-resistant glove which used less leather, placing it in strategic areas, and supplementing with Kevlar. Developed by Du Pont, Kevlar is heat-resistant and fire-retardant. The impregnated leather and

---

Raymond E. Martin (left), retiring manager, and David E. Strobino, new manager, beside an old hand-operated Sheridan Press (circa 1900-1910) used by Liberty when it first started in business.

Dr. Louis J. Strobino, founder and president of Liberty Protective Leathers, Inc.

Kevlar give Liberty gloves a dexterity, insulating power, and durability which cannot be achieved with asbestos. Sold primarily in the United States, they are often demonstrated at such conferences as the National Safety Congress and the International Tool Manufacturing meetings.

As well as maintaining a very active practice, Dr. Strobino served on the Clinton School Board, was president of the medical staff at St. Luke's Hospital, and is chairman of the Department of Surgery at St. Luke's and very involved in the design of a "central core" surgical unit.

All three of Dr. Strobino's sons have worked summers and vacations at the plant, and in 1980 David E., the youngest, joined the firm. Working closely with the original manager, Raymond E. Martin, who continues on a part-time basis, David is gradually assuming the role of manager. Today Liberty Protective Leathers employs 20 in the factory and works with over 100 safety-equipment dealers. These gloves are used by the chemical industry, foundries, manufacturers of rubber, glass, aluminum, titanium, and space metals (where the high-heat process can go through a pair of gloves in a single day).

In 1982, its 42nd fiscal year, Liberty Protective Leathers maintains an ongoing program of research and development. New cutting dies are designed and prototypes of new gloves are tested. In the years to come, this research and development may lead to new protective leathers as yet undreamed of, even by Dr. Strobino.

THE F.X. MATT BREWING COMPANY

Only a relatively few cities and towns across the country have a brewery.

For almost two-thirds of Utica's history there has been a brewery in the western section of the city. Called the West End Brewing Company since its founding in 1888, the name was recently changed to The F.X. Matt Brewing Company in tribute to its founder.

The firm is the only regional brewery in the country that has successfully marketed a premium beer, Matt's Premium, against its national competitors. The company produces—in addition to Matt's Premium—Utica Club beer, Utica Club Light, and Maximus Super, which has nearly 50 percent more alcohol than most beers. Just re-

cently the brewery introduced Matt's Light Premium beer. In addition to serving New York State these beverages are distributed in New England, Pennsylvania, and New Jersey.

The business was founded by F.X. Matt I (grandfather of the current president), who was born in the Black Forest region of West Germany. He learned the art of brewing at the Rothaus Brewery, once the private brewery of the Duke of Baden.

Immigrating to America around 1878, he went to work for Bierbauer's Columbia

------

The founder of the company, F.X. Matt I (1859-1958).

Brewery, then one of nine breweries located in Utica. After several years in Canajoharie with another Bierbauer brewery, where he learned the management, marketing, and shipping aspects of the brewing industry, Matt returned to Utica as manager of the Bierbauer brewery, and in 1888 reorganized it to form the West End Brewing Company. The name was changed in 1981 to The F.X. Matt Brewing Company because it was felt the old name was too provincial.

The business grew under F.X. Matt I, who for a time served as both brewmaster and star salesman. Then came Prohibition from 1919 to 1933. The brewery survived by making near beer (without alcohol), soft drink fruit beverages, malt syrup, and malt tonic. The soft drinks were continued until World War II.

After Prohibition when Matt was, as he would have said, "a young man yet" (of 74 years), he was joined by his two sons, Frank and Walter. Increased sales called for new buildings and machinery.

After World War II expansion was resumed. Matt was a truly remarkable man, remaining as chairman of the board until his death in 1958 at the age of 99. But he increasingly depended on his two sons, particularly Walter, who became president in 1950.

Walter Matt led the expansion program after the war. Working closely with his father, a new brewhouse was built, the first of many structures that would enhance the brewery's operation. High-speed, labor-saving equipment was installed. Since World War II more than $18 million has been spent on modernization and expansion.

Walter Matt saw the need for advertising. As the third generation of the family members joined the brewery, he worked with them. That collaboration produced some memorable advertising campaigns, the most famous of which was two talking beer steins, Schultz and Dooley, who talked and sang of the virtues of Utica Club and are still popular symbols of the company.

Walter Matt retired in 1980 and was succeeded by his son, F.X. Matt II, the current president. Other family members in the business are Robert Welch, son of F.X. Matt's daughter, Ella, and Frank S. Owens, Jr., son-in-law of Walter.

The F.X. Matt Brewing Company provides free tours of its brewery, which has been visited by people from all over the United States and from over 90 countries around the world. After the tour one returns via the famous Utica Club trolley to the reception area, which is furnished with authentic Victorian antiques. Then guests are invited to the brewery's "1888 Tavern" to sample the company's products.

CHARLES MILLAR SUPPLY INC.

A packet boat on the Erie Canal brought Charles Millar to Utica in 1838. Born in Greenwich, England, and educated as a master builder, Charles Millar erected some of Utica's most prominent older buildings, such as the old courthouse on John Street and several Utica schools.

Millar became superintendent of the Utica and Black River Railroad in 1861. That same year he purchased the tin-smithing, plumbing, and steam-fitting business that bears his name.

On his 21st birthday his son Henry was admitted to the partnership, forming Charles Millar & Son. As larger facilities were required, Charles Millar resigned from the railroad and remodeled the National Hotel, located at 127-129 Genesee Street. The company was then manufacturing cheese- and butter-making equipment, much of which was invented by Charles Millar. Such items were introduced to the area dairy industry.

By 1883 the firm had begun the manufacture of lead pipe and later organized the Utica Pipe Foundry Company, with the assistance of Nicholas E. Kernan and others. The firm manufactured cast-iron pipe, later adding soil pipe and steam fittings.

A fire destroyed the Genesee Street structure in 1890. Fortunately, the business was fully insured and continued operating at the Main Street warehouses. Farsighted management enabled Charles Millar & Son to weather several bank panics and depressions.

After struggling for years under adverse conditions, the Utica Pipe Foundry filed for bankruptcy in 1914. A suit was brought against the Millar company and the best lawyers of the day—including the Honorable Elihu Root—were retained; the suit was withdrawn before coming to court. Liquidation of the foundry enabled Millar to establish branches in Binghamton and Springfield, Massachusetts.

During 1907 the company's first truck was put into operation amidst criticism for being too "experimental." During World War I Charles Millar & Son offered to continue compensation and retain the position of employees who enlisted, and the company treasurer devoted almost full time to promoting Liberty Bonds.

Today Charles Millar Supply concentrates on piping, sheet metal, industrial supplies, and cutting tools, with branches in Binghamton and St. Johnsbury, Vermont. Four generations of Millars were involved in the company until 1969, when it was acquired by F. Eugene Romano. Henry W. Millar continued as president until 1980.

Romano's maternal grandparents arrived from Italy in 1888, exactly 50 years after Charles Millar. His father, Michael A. Romano, arrived in Utica at the age of 13 in 1913. Although an immigrant orphan, Michael A. Romano worked his way through school, graduating from Utica Free Academy in 1918. He received a bachelor's degree from New York University in 1925 and was a successful certified public accountant and real estate investor until his death in 1969.

F.E. Romano, present chairman of Charles Millar, graduated from Hamilton College in 1950, served in the Korean War, and founded Pacemaker Steel and Aluminum Company of Utica in 1956. His extensive experience in industrial distribution has proved useful in guiding the direction of the Millar organization during the turbulent decade of the 1970s.

Like the Millars before him, Romano continues the tradition of service to the community, especially in higher education, musical organizations, and medical facilities.

Some statistics indicate the average life of a business is seven years. Charles Millar's has passed the 100-year mark and is well into its second century of successful operation.

The first truck for Millar Company, a Packard, was purchased in 1907 after a prolonged debate among the directors as to whether the motor vehicle was here to stay, or just a passing novelty.

MUNSON-WILLIAMS-PROCTOR INSTITUTE

Named to honor families who contributed generously to the growth of Utica, Munson-Williams-Proctor Institute was created through an endowment established in 1919 by Mr. and Mrs. Thomas R. Proctor and Frederick T. Proctor. Since 1935 the Institute has prospered to become a diverse cultural resources center, admired widely for its architecturally significant Museum of Art, excellent collection of fine art, accredited School of Art, and highly respected programs in the performing arts.

The origin of Munson-Williams-Proctor Institute can be traced to Alfred Munson who distinguished himself in industry, banking, and philanthropy after arriving in Utica in 1823, and to his daughter, Helen, who married James Watson Williams, a former mayor of Utica and the son of Judge Nathan Williams who settled here in 1797. James and Helen commissioned the construction of Fountain Elms, their famous home where they lived with their daughters, Maria (Mrs. Thomas Redfield Proctor) and Rachel (Mrs. Frederick T. Proctor).

Chartered by the New York State Board of Regents, Munson-Williams-Proctor Institute serves all of Central New York and far beyond. It offers art exhibitions of national prominence, lectures, music, films, reference and lending libraries, art shop, sales and rental gallery, as well as professional training and avocational arts education for adults and young people.

Among works to be found in the Institute's collection of 19th- and 20th-

The Museum of Art, designed by Philip Johnson and cited by Architectural Forum *in 1962 as contributing to the developing art of architecture, opened in October 1960.*

century European and American art are Pollock's classic drip painting *No. 2* of 1949 and Cole's 1840 series, *The Voyage of Life.* Also in the collection are a work by Winstanley, one of the earliest landscapes painted in America, still lifes by the Peale family, early 20th-century American pictures by The Eight and the Stieglitz Circle, water-colors by Burchfield and contemporary works by Rothko, Kline, Gorky, Calder, Stella, and Morley, as well as examples of European modernism by Picasso, Kandinsky, Dali, Mondrian, Arp, Klee, Léger, and others.

The collection resides in a handsome building designed by the distinguished architect, Philip Johnson, and was opened to

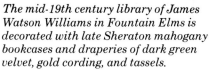

The mid-19th century library of James Watson Williams in Fountain Elms is decorated with late Sheraton mahogany bookcases and draperies of dark green velvet, gold cording, and tassels.

the public in 1960. It has been cited as an outstanding example of architecture by the Architectural League of New York (1961), the editors of *Architectural Forum* magazine (1962), and the New York Association of Architects, AIA (1981).

The School of Art has served thousands of adults and children for more than four decades, and recently entered a joint venture with three neighboring colleges to introduce a full-time, fine-art studio series for students seeking professional competence. The School of Art became an accredited member of the National Association of Schools of Art, Division III, in 1980.

The Institute presents concerts each year by artists of international stature, including such prominent figures as Isaac Stern, Artur Rubinstein, Edward Villella, Seiji Ozawa and the Boston Symphony Orchestra, the Philadelphia Orchestra, Zubin Mehta with the Israel Philharmonic, and Itzhak Perlman.

Over the years, the varied programs of Munson-Williams-Proctor Institute have elevated public taste in art while enriching the lives of hundreds of individuals. Whereas a half century ago, the creative arts remained almost exclusively the province of the elite classes of society, today, because of the Munson-Williams-Proctor Institute, they have become an important element in the everyday life of thousands of Uticans.

MURPHY EXCAVATING CORPORATION

A 1952 photograph of a three-quarter-yard Insley backhoe.

"Diversity" is the middle name of Murphy Excavating Corporation. Whether it be a 100-yard underground rifle testing range or a backyard swimming pool, the four Murphy brothers specialize in the unusual.

William and Margaret Murphy began a part-time business of snow and garden plowing and landscaping in 1946. They worked out of their home on Richardson Avenue, earning extra money for their children's education. In 1952 James W. Murphy, their oldest son, expanded the business to full time with a two-ton dump truck, Ford tractor loader, and three employees. Mrs. Murphy continued as secretary and bookkeeper until 1979.

James and his brother, Stuart, formed a partnership in 1956 and the two other brothers, Richard and Robert, joined the business in 1967. The addition of one of Stuart's sons means that three generations of the Murphy family have been involved. Now known as the Murphy Excavating Corporation, there are 13 on the payroll working in Central New York.

In addition to excavating and grading, the firm performs many specialized jobs such as erosion control, driveway bridges, pile driving, tennis courts, sheeting, mud work, and waste treatment. Hurricane Agnes meant extensive road and drainage work for Murphy crews, and in the blizzard of '66 they worked for four straight days, 24 hours a day, keeping open the Niagara Mohawk substations. When a large generating tube collapsed at a local power station, a backhoe was lowered 90 feet to the bottom of Trenton Gorge for repairs. On the Oswego Camden high-voltage job, more than one-million nuts and bolts were dis-

The one-yard Bucyrus-Erie backhoe, 1982.

assembled. One of the first gas-powered golf carts in the area was delivered by Murphy Excavating Corporation to Mr. Cottin, founder of Mosher & Cottin Advertising Company. More recently the firm moved a concrete statue of a zebra from Indian River, New York, to Munson-Williams-Proctor Institute for a folk art exhibit.

Murphy Excavating Corporation prides itself in staying in step with modern technology. It was one of the first in the area to use a laser beam to align sewer pipe. Always looking to increase productivity with the use of the latest equipment, the period of two days formerly required to excavate a cellar has been cut to five hours.

One of the oldest excavating firms operating in the greater Utica area, Murphy Excavating, by actively supporting and taking leadership roles in the many local community service programs, helps to maintain the area's excellent business climate. Wherever there is major construction in the area, Murphy equipment can be seen at work: Munson-Williams-

Proctor Institute, The Savings Bank of Utica, The F.X. Matt Brewing Company, Special Metals, and General Electric are just a few of the jobs the firm helped complete. Colgate, Hamilton, Utica College, Mohawk Valley Community College, and BOCES are some of the local educational institutions whose campus beauty reflect the Murphy touch. And in most of the surrounding villages and towns the company's specialized abilities are shown.

Thirty-six years after the beginning of a neighborhood business, Murphy Excavating Corporation now includes eight members of the family—with three of the brothers' wives managing the office—and one lifelong friend, Bernard Stephens, who has been working with them for 30 years. In this age of big corporations, the Murphys have been able to maintain the old tradition of a family business in Oneida County.

THE NEW CENTURY CLUB

The New Century Club was founded in 1893 to meet the needs of women in the Utica area. The wives and daughters of business and professional men needed a social center where they could offer cultural, educational, and vocational services to their members and to the community. Mrs. Frances A. Goodale, who had collected material on women authors of Oneida County for the Chicago World's Fair of 1893, urged the formation of a society similar to The New Century Club of Philadelphia (of which her sister was president). A small group met on November 11 in Library Hall in the Elizabeth Street building which later housed the Board of Education. They set up an executive board and various committees and at the third meeting Mrs. Goodale was elected president.

Membership soared to over 250 because the club offered many activities to its membership. For example, it sponsored a public lecture in 1894 by Susan B. Anthony whose call for woman suffrage encouraged local advocates. Outgrowing its rented rooms on Washington and then Court streets, the club decided to buy the home of Dr. H.C. Palmer on the corner of Genesee and Hopper streets. Despite the depression of the 1890s the members raised funds by buying bonds. In 1897 they erected the large auditorium in the rear of the house.

The New Century Club provided hundreds of women with a wide range of activities and spearheaded drives for civic improvements. Its auditorium hosted concerts, dramas, lectures, and dances. The dramatic department put on such ambitious productions as Shakespeare's *Twelfth Night, As You Like It,* and *The Merchant of Venice.* Miss Ida J. Butcher for decades taught a class in poetry. The

Critic, which Anna E. Jones edited for many years, published poems, essays, and stories written by members. In 1900 a committee wrote and published *An Outline History of Utica,* which remains a valuable guide. Members sponsored a kitchen garden in which youngsters were taught household skills. Luncheons and dinners were held in the dining room whose capacity of 100 was doubled after the fire of 1925.

The club often took the lead in urging city officials to provide additional services. After Mrs. George F. Ralph and her committee personally cleaned two blocks of Columbia Street, the aldermen set up a street cleaning department. The club urged the city to appoint a police matron and to introduce kindergartens in the schools. They actively supported the movement for public playgrounds and demanded the establishment of a children's

A production of Shakespeare's Twelfth Night, *circa 1906.*

court.

Each generation of officers and members has modified the club's program to meet changing needs. During the past quarter-century The New Century Club has raised money for scholarships for students from this region. Each Tuesday the members gather for their weekly meeting before and after a catered dinner. The officers have recently devoted much effort to renovating their property, especially the auditorium which they hope will once again become a meeting place for many activities.

Exterior of The New Century Club, circa 1940.

NIAGARA MOHAWK POWER CORPORATION

In 1927 Utica Gas and Electric's new headquarters at 258 Genesee Street was a classic landmark. The company no longer occupies this building.

A history of gas and electric service in the Utica area parallels the development of Utica itself. It is the story of the growth of small isolated energy enterprises that met the needs of a few customers, into one large, interconnected system that made available to all communities an almost unlimited supply of light, heat, and power for domestic and industrial use.

Two groups, the Utica Gas Light Company formed in 1857, and the Central New York Light and Power Company formed in 1882, merged in 1887, becoming the Utica Electric and Gas Company. In 1888 the Utica Electric Light Company came into being, and people began to see the tremendously important part that electric power would take in the development of Utica.

As Utica grew, so did the need for more electricity, and small steam-generating plants could not meet this growing demand. Hydroelectric energy was the answer.

Trenton Falls Electric Light and Power Company was formed in 1899 to begin the construction that would harness the waters of West Canada Creek north of Utica. The completion of the Trenton Falls operation in 1901 opened the way for the industrial and commercial development of the Utica area.

Meanwhile, it became increasingly evident that there was duplication of energy facilities, so the three enterprises supplying the city with power merged into one: the Utica Electric Light and Power Company.

The 1902 merging of that organization and another competitor, the Equitable Gas and Electric Company, formed the Utica Gas and Electric Company. Other mergers with small companies throughout the

Mohawk Valley took place, with surrounding communities also receiving power from the Utica-based firm.

Between 1922 and 1925 the Utica company made interconnections with the Adirondack Power and Light Company, the Northern New York Utilities, Inc., and the Niagara Power System. In 1926 a coal-fired, steam-generating station began operation at Harbor Point, and the following year a gas-manufacturing plant rose on a nearby site.

Utica became the center for the administration and distribution of power for the city and the adjoining villages. In 1927 the departments joined together in a new facility at Genesee and Court streets, from which the company served 38,000 gas and electric customers.

UG&E became part of a statewide system called the Mohawk Hudson Power System in 1926, and three years later joined with other companies in the northern and western parts of the state. Called the Niagara Hudson Power System, it formed the largest producer and distributor of electric power in the country at that time. All of the operating companies in the system consolidated into the present firm known as Niagara Mohawk Power Corporation in 1950.

Niagara Mohawk constructed a large service center on Campion Road in New Hartford, housing offices and the electric, gas, transportation, and service departments, in 1957. Two years later the utility built a new hydroelectric plant on West Canada Creek at Prospect. This station brought to 81 the number of hydro-generation plants in the Niagara Mohawk system.

Manufactured gas was furnished by local plants from 1848 until 1951, when Niagara Mohawk brought natural gas from southern states to supply the growing needs of Utica and the Mohawk Valley. Today Niagara Mohawk's operations in the Utica area cover 2,700 square miles and serve 120,000 electric and 75,000 gas customers.

An aerial view of the sprawling Harbor Point complex in the 1920s, when large manufactured gas holders were a common sight.

GEORGE A. NOLE AND SON, INC.

George A. Nole was a man who stressed craftsmanship in his work and a man who loved his native Utica. As an apprentice bricklayer for his uncle's firm, M.A. Fanelli Mason Contractors, he looked to the future of his city, wanting to be a part of it. In 1945 he took his first major step by forming his own business, George A. Nole Mason Contractors. Working out of his home at 215 Kossuth Avenue, and with only a couple of men to assist him, he began by contracting many small jobs, such as work on private homes.

There was no abundance of quality masons in postwar Utica, so Nole found it easy to rely on his reputation. By 1950 Nole's son Angelo was ready to join his father's growing business. The next year a two-acre parcel of land on Jefferson Avenue was procured and garages built on the site, chosen for its convenient location to projects on which they were working. Still operating offices out of their home but needing more space, the Noles moved to 721 Armory Drive. If the senior Nole truly wanted to leave his mark on his hometown, he certainly got his wish. His firm was hired by general contractors for virtually every major and many minor construction jobs in the Utica area from the early '50s until his retirement in 1968.

Angelo Nole succeeded his father as president in 1968; the firm had incorporated two years before. One of Angelo's first modifications was expansion into general contracting—no small undertaking indeed. Although this meant broadening the range of services offered, George A.

Angelo Nole, Jr. (far left), and his father, Angelo Nole (second from right), review plans in front of the Municipal Housing Authority project, a turnkey venture on which they did all the work.

George A. Nole, whose motto was, "never sacrifice quality for the sake of profit."

Nole and Son, Inc., remained masonry specialists. In 1971 Nole moved his offices to the Jefferson Avenue location because the volume of business was too large to continue headquartering at home.

Much of Nole's work during the '70s and early '80s was for either the state or city government. Projects have included the Terrace Park, the Sheraton Inn and Conference Center, the State Office Building, and the new post office. The modern George A. Nole and Son has also been awarded many restoration contracts, among them The F.X. Matt Brewing Company and Proctor High School. But perhaps the projects that have given the firm the most satisfaction are those on which it has done all the work, including Chicago Market Plaza East in Utica, Tehan's Inc., the Masonic Home Smith Wing Addition, the Church of the Holy Family in Vernon, and the Municipal Housing Authority project on Bleecker Street.

The corporation will continue to diversify in coming years, but government work should remain at its cornerstone. Angelo Nole hopes to be in the vanguard of "turnkey" projects, in which a general contractor is awarded an entire enterprise from conception and delivers a key to the buyer upon completion. Angelo Jr. is preparing at Bentley College in order to join his father on a full-time basis. He will become a part of a multimillion-dollar firm that employs 120 and is a highly respected name in Utica and all of Central New York; known by its slogan: "Building with the Integrity of a Proud Heritage."

ONEIDA HISTORICAL SOCIETY AT UTICA

The Oneida Historical Society at Utica was organized at the time of the national centennial in 1876 "to collect and commemorate whatever may pertain to the history of Central New York in general and the county of Oneida in particular." The Society's first president was former Governor Horatio Seymour. Its first project was the celebration of the 100th anniversary of the Battle of Oriskany in 1877 and it coordinated the construction of the Oriskany Battlefield Monument, dedicated in 1884. In 1882 it organized a celebration of Utica's semicentennial and placed a marker near the site of Old Fort Schuyler. The Society led the effort to preserve General Herkimer's home, and this dream came true in 1913 with its acquisition by the state of New York.

The Society was housed in the City Library on Elizabeth Street from 1878 until 1893. There it began to assemble an irreplaceable collection of books, documents, and artifacts. The Society occupied temporary quarters in the stable of its secretary, General Charles W. Darling, until 1896. Then it moved into its first real home, the Munson-Williams Memorial Building on Park Avenue at John and Elizabeth streets, a gift of Helen Elizabeth Munson Williams.

The Society flourished in the early 1900s under Thomas Proctor's patronage, but nearly ceased to function after his death in 1920. Revived from the late '20s through

The Munson-Williams Memorial Building, Park Avenue.

the '40s by William Pierrepont White, Dr. T. Wood Clarke, and others, it also began to receive support from the Munson-Williams-Proctor Institute. In the early '50s, president Glenn Thompson and curator Francis Cunningham began to organize usable local history collections out of the accumulation of nearly 80 years. In 1956 the Society abandoned the Park Avenue building for quarters provided by the Institute, first in the Brower house at the corner of Cottage Place and Genesee Street and since 1960 in Fountain Elms. The old building was later torn down, mourned by all except the staff who had worked in it.

Since 1960 the Society has continued to enlarge and improve its collections and to present interesting lectures and exhibitions. It operates a local history museum in the basement of Fountain Elms and a reference library rich in printed, manuscript, and graphic resources which are used by students from grade school to graduate school, history buffs, and genealogists. It has moved into such new fields as ethnic studies, oral history, school programs, and historic preservation.

The Oneida Historical Society celebrated the national bicentennial in 1976 with an exhibition of over 500 art, craft, and manufactured items "Made in Utica" and it sponsored the formation of The Drums & Fifes of Gansevoort's Third New York Regiment. This volunteer "living history" group has appeared throughout central New York, in New England, and as far away as the Henry Ford Museum in Michigan.

With each passing day, more people, things, and events can enter the record of human experience that is history. To prevent their being lost to history is the challenge faced by the Oneida Historical Society.

Society director Douglas Preston and president David Ellis examine an 18th-century ledger in the Society's archives.

ONEIDA LTD.

The Oneida Community attracted world attention in the mid-19th century as a social and religious experiment in family planning and communal living. Its founder, John Humphrey Noyes, and his followers adopted the ideal of "perfectionism" as their goal. Although George Bernard Shaw, H.G. Wells, and Karl Marx noted this Utopian experiment, the general public was more impressed with the excellence of its products, whether bear traps, canned goods, silk thread, or silverware. In 1881 the 200 or so members disbanded their community and voted to create a joint stock company to carry on the business activities. The name adopted was Oneida Community Ltd., later shortened in 1935 to Oneida Ltd.

The company perpetuated kinship and community ties plus the tradition of superior workmanship. At first the firm enjoyed only modest success and the Panic of 1893 threatened its existence. In 1895 a progressive faction gained control and placed Dr. Theodore Noyes in the president's chair and named Pierrepont B. Noyes, only 24 years old, as superintendent of the firm's three departments in Niagara Falls.

Miles Robertson, who succeeded Noyes as general manager in 1926, guided the firm through the Great Depression and the tumultuous war years. In world wars I and II and later the Korean Conflict, Oneida took on many defense contracts. Its skilled workmen produced ammunition clips, gas shells, bayonets, aircraft fuel

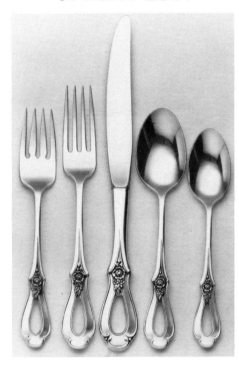

Oneida Silversmiths has stressed attractive designs, helping make the company the world's largest maker of stainless flatware.

tanks, and parachute quick-release devices.

When Japanese and Korean stainless steel flatware invaded the American markets in the early 1970s, Pierrepont T. Noyes, chairman of the board, president, and son of Pierrepont B. Noyes, decided to appeal to customers by offering them a more elegant stainless product well worth the extra cost. The Oneida Silversmiths Division has since become the largest maker of stainless flatware in the world with factories in Oneida, New York; Canada; Mexico; and Northern Ireland.

During the past decade Oneida Ltd. experienced revolutionary change as it became a diversified marketing and manufacturing company through the acquisition of several successful companies. The first was Leavens Manufacturing, maker of custom emblematic jewelry, acquired in 1973. Camden Wire of nearby Camden, New York, joined Oneida in 1977; it is one of the country's leading producers of copper conducting wire for industrial markets. And in 1978, Rena-Ware Distributors, one of the world's largest direct sellers of cookware, became part of Oneida Ltd. Further change occurred in 1981, when John L. Marcellus, Jr., was appointed chairman, the first chief executive from outside the founding Noyes family.

Although cookware has surpassed stainless flatware as Oneida's top-volume product, the tradition of quality set by the silversmiths still reigns.

The Mansion House, home of the original Oneida Community, is a large brick building which was erected in 1860 and remains an apartment house.

ONEIDA NATIONAL BANK

Born in a colorful period of bust and boom, robbed the night before its opening, Oneida National Bank, for the next century, has been both progressive and conservative, but always dedicated to the communities it serves.

Utica businessmen of Whig background petitioned the state legislature in 1836 for a bank charter, which was granted on May 13. So eager were citizens to invest in this bank that the stock offering was oversubscribed many times. To add to the excitement, robbers made off with $116,500 in cash and drafts on November 20 and escaped by canal boat. The bank, however, opened the doors for business and the directors chose Alfred H. Munson as president in December 1836, a post he held until 1854. Munson piloted the institution through the stormy days following the Panic of 1837 and placed the bank's resources behind the movement to construct textile factories in Utica.

In 1865 the directors secured a federal charter and the institution became Oneida National Bank. The bank continued to serve the community by lending money to business establishments, farmers, and homeowners. When the Great Depression struck, Oneida National Bank and Trust Company (the addition of "Trust" came in 1929) remained the most stable of local commercial banks.

After World War II Oneida National Bank management vigorously supported community efforts to attract manufacturing plants to replace the once-prosperous textile industry. As population, stores, and factories moved to suburban villages and towns, the bank opened offices to provide needed service. By 1980 the bank had 34 branches in seven upstate counties. Loans, a sensitive barometer of banking activity, rose from $170.1 million in 1969 to $437 million in 1980.

The bank expanded not only geographically but also enlarged its services to individuals and businesses. Making loans to farmers for buildings and equipment always has been a special concern of Oneida National. Its staff of agricultural representatives has become an important part of the New York farm community. Its branches in Old Forge and Sylvan Beach have helped revitalize those important resort areas. Urban communities have also played an important role in the bank's growth. Oneida National has worked with the Urban Housing Program and the Neighborhood Housing Service Program helping to revitalize U.S. cities. As a result, many low- and moderate-income families have achieved home ownership through its efforts. When downtown Utica needed funds for revitalization, Oneida National helped with financing for the new Sheraton Inn. Two major hospi-

The modern headquarters of Oneida National, Utica.

tals received loans to renovate their facilities and make additions. The bank has cooperated with local and federal housing authorities to construct and renovate quarters for older citizens. Local governments have come to rely upon Oneida National for loans for fire stations, health centers, garages, school buildings, water and sewage systems, and industrial parks.

Changes in the banking laws in the 1970s encouraged banks to acquire branches and

to affiliate with larger units. During this period, Oneida National merged banks in Little Falls, Central Square, Ogdensburg, and several other communities. In 1981 United Bank New York, headquartered in Albany, acquired Oneida National and, at the same time, took the new name of Norstar Bancorp, Inc. This new corporation has assets of $3.3 billion and 185 banking offices. However, Oneida National Bank retains its name and tradition of service while having access to greater capital resources, enabling its offices to serve their communities even better than before.

THE PAR GROUP

The PAR Group consists of three companies: PAR Technology Corporation (founded in 1968); Rome Research Corporation (1974); and PAR Microsystems Corporation (1977). All three are the creation of Dr. John W. Sammon II, a distinguished graduate of the U.S. Naval Academy, MIT, and Syracuse University.

In 1968, while employed at Rome Air Development Center, Dr. Sammon founded a consulting company to make his pioneering research in pattern recognition computer systems available to industry. This venture was Pattern Analysis and Recognition (PAR), the nucleus from which the PAR Group would grow. In 1969 he left the government to devote his time to PAR. His staff included his former administrative assistant, Charles A. Constantino, who became executive vice-president of the

PAR Group, and Dr. Jon Sanders, chief scientist at PAR Technology. PAR's first office was at 310 East Chestnut Street, Rome; here the corporation set out to obtain government research and development contracts.

PAR's projects developed through the early '70s, resulting in the construction of large computer systems for the Air Force and various special agencies of the United States. The Chestnut Street quarters soon became cramped, so the corporation moved in 1971 to 128 East Dominick Street in downtown Rome. After a temporary move caused by Rome's urban renewal, PAR moved into 228 Liberty Plaza in 1974. By

———————

Dr. John W. Sammon II, president of The PAR Group.

1981 PAR had leased space in four downtown Rome locations.

In addition, PAR opened offices in Los Angeles, California, and in Colorado Springs, Colorado (both in 1978), in order to better serve its government and aerospace customers.

As an outgrowth of PAR's early work, Rome Research Corporation (RRC) was founded in 1974 to pursue specialized work in electronic countermeasures. As of 1982, most of RRC's staff was located at Air Force test sites around the Mohawk Valley.

During the mid-1970s, the corporation decided to diversify by developing a commercial product. A point-of-sales (POS) terminal was designed for the fast-food industry, specifically for the McDonald's Corporation. A small manufacturing unit at 811 Broad Street was established in Utica in 1977, and PAR Microsystems was founded as a wholly owned subsidiary of PAR. As the company grew, it moved to 109 North Genesee Street, also in Utica. Again in 1980, Microsystems expanded and moved to Seneca Plaza, New Hartford.

Early in 1982 the PAR Group consolidated all of its local corporate activities into a completely refurbished 108,000-square-foot facility in Seneca Plaza, New Hartford. Since its inception, the PAR Group has achieved an average annual growth rate of 58 percent. By 1981 it had achieved sales of $21 million and employed 430 persons with an annual payroll of $7.2 million.

In 1982 several point-of-sales and related computerized hardware/software products were under development for application in the restaurant industry. Also, PAR had begun marketing its point-of-sales equipment internationally, having shipped and installed its products in Canada, England, Ireland, Australia, and Singapore. With these activities, PAR had established its goal to become the dominate computer manufacturer for the world's restaurant industry. In parallel, PAR initiated several advanced research projects in two newly emerging markets: robotics and computer security. Other products under development in 1982 involved large software systems which used advanced sensor sub-systems to gather and present intelligence information.

PAR's future is based upon an aggressive growth plan which stresses the development, manufacture, and sales of new and advanced computer products for both commercial and military sectors. Other plans include expansion geographically by establishing both research and development offices to serve government contract work, and sales offices for computer-based restaurant equipment.

PLYMOUTH BETHESDA UNITED CHURCH OF CHRIST

Plymouth Bethesda Church is the oldest religious institution in Utica. On New Year's Day, 1802, 14 Welsh people formed the Welsh Congregational Church. Two years later its wooden chapel on the corner of Whitesboro and Washington streets became the first church structure in Utica. Its first permanent pastor, Dr. Robert Everett, served for nine years after 1823. Everett moved to Steuben where he founded and edited *Y Cenhadwr Ameri-can-aidd,* the journal of the Welsh Congregationalists.

In 1834 the congregation voted to replace its frame structure with a brick building that could accommodate over 500 people. The Reverend R. Gwesyn Jones, pastor for most of the period between 1867 and 1901, healed a church split and led the drive for a new church on upper Washington Street. The people adopted the name "Bethesda" in his honor because he had come to Utica from Bethesda, Wales.

Meanwhile, on June 25, 1883, a group of 47 persons who had been meeting together near Oneida Square decided to form Plymouth Congregational Church. Many were young people of Welsh ancestry who preferred to worship in English, but transplanted New Englanders also joined the congregation. The congregation, which purchased the property on the corner of Plant and State streets and erected a small chapel, enjoyed one of the best locations in Utica and grew in numbers. During the

The Plymouth Bethesda United Church of Christ as it looks today.

pastorate of Alfred V. Bliss it erected by 1906 the present stone church designed by Frederick Gouge.

Increasing activities led Plymouth to start a campaign for funds to erect a church house on Plant Street. The members pledged $126,000 for this building, which included kitchen facilities, a gymnasium, church offices, and Sunday School rooms.

When urban renewal took Bethesda's building in 1963, it merged with Plymouth—cementing long years of association. In 1971 South Congregational Church disbanded but most of its members joined Plymouth Bethesda. South Congregational, formed in 1920 on the corner of Genesee Street and Beverly Place, suffered severely from the Depression and a small membership. When the United Church of Christ was formed in 1959, Plymouth naturally became part of this denomination.

Plymouth Bethesda has attempted to serve the needs not only of its own members but also the community. The Oneida Square Teen Center, usually open two evenings a week, has provided a wholesome place of recreation for young people of the neighborhood. Hundreds of needy citizens have received help from the food bank, which operates from the church house. Plymouth sponsored one of the first senior clubs in Utica before the government took action in this field. The church has provided quarters for a nursery school and the New School, a private agency.

Plymouth Bethesda United Church of

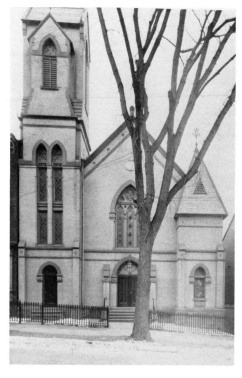

The Bethesda Congregational Church on Washington Street.

Christ has always adhered to its basic function: to witness for Jesus Christ and to deepen the spiritual growth of its members. Even the children in the Sunday School realize this goal when they contribute their nickels and dimes to buy heifers for mission stations.

POWER LINE CONSTRUCTORS, INC.

The same year, 1963, that Betty Friedan in *The Feminine Mystique* called on women to find fulfillment in outside work as well as in the home, Delores Y. Critelli helped found Power Line Constructors, Inc. She and her partner, Elmer Wahl, entered the business of constructing and maintaining high-voltage electrical systems. At first the company had only four employees at its office on Main Street in Utica, but it grew rapidly. The Power Authority of the State of New York and private utility companies were steadily enlarging their operations in an effort to meet the demands of corporations, government agencies, and residents for more power. Power Line Constructors was a necessary link in bringing surplus energy from the Power Grid of the gigantic Quebec Hydroelectric Facilities in Canada to customers in the New York State and Vermont area.

Officials and businessmen found that the company performed high-quality work and met time schedules. Villages, cities, counties, state, and federal agencies throughout the upstate region awarded it contracts for street lighting and for traffic systems. For example, Power Line Constructors was awarded the contract to provide lighting for Route 81 south of Syracuse. When the Power Authority of the State of New York built the 765-KV (kilovolt) transmission lines, Power Line Constructors was responsible for all of the steel erection work on the 765-KV substation in Massena, New

Delores Y. Critelli, president of Power Line Constructors, Inc.

York. Power Line Constructors joined with two giants in the field in bidding successfully for the $32-million contract calling for 81 miles of transmission line from Massena south to Marcy. Many local corporations such as General Electric, Special Metals, CharlesTown, and Niagara Mohawk have come to rely upon Power Line Constructors. It has also provided many services at Griffiss Air Force Base, including overhead electric distribution, underground cable, and street lighting.

Business increased by 1972 to the point that the firm needed more space for offices, storage, a repair shop, and a yard for equipment. As a result, it constructed a

new building on Robinson Road in Clinton; from there work teams fanned out across the upstate region. Some built overhead lines, erected poles, and constructed substations and towers. Other teams with excavating equipment prepared the way for underground installations—conduit duct systems, wiring, concrete encasements, vaults, and foundations. Less dramatic but equally important has been the maintenance of transformers and grounding systems as well as responding to emergency calls, always a problem in Utica's rigorous winters. Power Line Constructors frequently assists local governments in improving and renewing their traffic signals. The number of employees, which varies with the seasons, has ranged from 20 to 40.

When Wahl retired in 1976, the company became a family concern with Mrs. Critelli as president and son David, vice-president in charge of technical and field work. Mrs. Critelli is equally proud of son Steven, a corporation lawyer, and daughter Jane Ostrowski, a music teacher and songwriter. This young company tries to keep up with the slogan above her desk: "Keep pedaling—the only direction you can coast is downhill." Mrs. Critelli has served on several important committees such as Congressman Donald Mitchell's task force on economic revitalization. She presently serves on the Business Council of New York State's Construction Industry Council, which was formed at the request of the governor of the state of New York, and is on the boards of the Mohawk Valley Workshop for the Handicapped and of the Children's Hospital and Rehabilitation Center of Utica.

Steel towers erected for 765 KV substation at Massena, New York, for Power Authority of the State of New York (PASNY).

REMET CORPORATION

Once the payroll office for a bleachery in Chadwicks, the handsome brick building is now headquarters for Remet Corporation, a technical sales and manufacturing organization which serves the precision investment casting (PIC), ceramic, chemical, and allied industries. A broad line of expendables is supplied to their customers throughout the world. The products are principally chemical, refractory, and metal—hence the name, Re(fractory) Met(al).

Founded in 1970 by James R. Pyne as a West Coast distributor, Remet became an expert in all facets of precision investment casting, filling a gap between manufacturers of the raw materials and the end users. Because of this commitment to technical service, Remet was urged by its suppliers to represent them on a nationwide basis. A native of Utica, Mr. Pyne considered the city a good place in which to relocate. The base of operations was moved to Utica in 1972 and from here Remet serves its customers worldwide.

While the PIC industry is Remet's primary market, it also serves the general foundry, specialty steel, ceramic, and refractory industries, supplying products made to its own rigid specifications. Nationwide sales offices and a staff of 60 serve over 500 customers on an international basis, with sales in excess of $20 million. Included in the broad list of products are refractory materials (ceramics), binders, expendable pattern material, crucibles, abrasives, specialty waxes, mold releases, and metal. Stock is stored in seven warehouses coast-to-coast, assuring fast product availability and Remet's own fleet of cross-country trucks ensures on-time deliveries.

Early in 1976, Remet Chemical Corporation was formed to manufacture proprietary chemicals for the PIC industry. Sophisticated production equipment and stringent quality control assure maximum product consistency. Among the products are silica binders (the "glue" that holds refractories together) and specialty coating compounds for corrosion-resistant paints for ships, bridges, and chemical plants, as well as fuel additives.

All sales offices are staffed by technically trained personnel backed by a technical service department. A Remet sales engineer works the problem at the customer's, his own, or the principal supplier's facilities. This specialized expertise has aided many customers in solving some of their most difficult process problems.

By 1974 Remet Corporation found itself beyond "the state of the art" in certain areas, particularly in the realm of product application. This necessitated the establishment of the firm's own applied research facilities in mid-1975 at Pompano

The Remet headquarters building.

Beach, Florida. Research and quality-control laboratories in Utica will continue to develop new products and processes and provide technical advice to their customers.

A growing area of interest is fuel additives, and in 1982 metals were added to the line. As more products and processes are developed by Remet, Mr. Pyne looks to the ongoing expansion of Remet Chemical facilities in Utica and a continuation of Remet Corporation's commitment to meeting customer needs with customized products and technical expertise.

The main chemical reactor and processing room at Remet Corporation.

RICH PLAN OF UTICA, INC.

Bob Evans (left) and Bruce Evans (right) of the Rich Plan of Utica, Inc.

In May 1953 three men organized Rich Plan of Utica. Harold Averill had been involved in store appliances, such as meat cases and grinders; Fran Charboneau was in air conditioning; Robert A. Evans constructed walk-in freezers and coolers and operated locker plants where farmers or other customers could rent lockers on a monthly basis. Beef was cut, wrapped, and stored in the lockers as freezer space in home refrigerators was small and not at zero degrees.

Meanwhile, at the end of World War II, wartime manufacturers had converted to making home freezers. An appliance dealer in Mar Vista, California, John Rich, was unable to sell this new product, so he created a need: he offered homemade pies bought in quantity at a discount. Soon customers wanted other items, so he added meats and vegetables. Business grew rapidly and John Rich was able to sell all the freezers that Amana was manufacturing, about 3,000 a month. The next step was to franchise new areas with his concept of a "Better Way of Living." Averill, Charboneau, and Evans obtained the franchise to better serve the Utica area.

Rich Plan of Utica is the second oldest franchise in the United States. Its first year 12 people were employed, with an average wage of $1.25 an hour. Today 120 are employed in Utica alone. The current building was constructed on Commercial Drive in 1955, at that time situated in the middle of a bean field. Since then there have been many additions to keep up with the growing business. In 1961 Rich Plan of Utica went from a 12-foot by 16-foot cooler to one measuring 15 feet by 60 feet, which could hold 60 head of beef and was refilled about every 10 days from Midwest packing plants.

The founders started another Rich Plan franchise in Syracuse in 1958. A processing and delivery plant employing nine people was located in Lake Clear, near Saranac Lake, in 1969. The following year Robert A. Evans became the sole owner of Rich Plan of Utica, buying out Harold Averill, the retiring former president. Fran Charboneau had previously sold out to Averill and Evans. With a keen financial sense, and by "not selling for more than you have to," "Bob" Evans made the Utica and Syracuse franchises the largest Rich Plan dealers in the United States. A new plant was built in 1979, near Geneva, New York, and the Rich Plan of Vestal (employing 50) was purchased the following year.

Behind Rich Plan of Utica's building is Arctic Cold Storage, the warehouse and supplier for other Rich Plan dealers in the United States. It is also the national headquarters for food and freezer distribution for the Rich Plan Corporation. Robert A. Evans is current chairman of the board and past president of Rich Plan Corporation and has been the key motivator of the firm since it was purchased from Carrier Corporation in 1964.

That same year, R. Bruce Evans, son of Robert A. Evans, came into the business. After working in all phases, he is now chief executive officer, responsible for the day-to-day operation for all plants. Evans feels that the increased number of two career families, the severe local winter driving conditions, and the convenience, quality, and service of Rich Plan of Utica combine to make this the franchise with the highest food volume in the country.

The Rich Plan of Utica building, 1956, was located in a bean field which is now a highly commercialized area.

RIVERSIDE MATERIALS, INC.

A

B

C

D

The story of Riverside Materials began at the nadir of the Great Depression when Louis P. Balio and Philip Ruggiero formed a trucking partnership, hauling coal out of Frankfort, New York. B&R Trucking was their first success story, providing their livelihood for 23 years.

The two men saw a new opportunity in the growing city of Utica of the late 1950s. They sold B&R Trucking and began planning a roofing and housing materials company. They selected a plot of land on the then-underdeveloped River Road, centrally located between Utica and Rome, and began construction of their original 3,200-square-foot building in November 1958. In less than a month Riverside Building Supply Company was open for business, with Ruggiero's son Anthony assisting his father in selling, delivering, and warehousing; Balio and a secretary handled planning and paperwork.

Founders of Riverside Materials, Inc. (left to right), Philip Ruggiero (A) and Louis P. Balio (B); sons John L. Balio (C) and Anthony J. Ruggiero (D), president/vice-president and secretary/treasurer, respectively, since 1977.

Roofing materials have always been their principal line, in the beginning supplemented only by insulation and wallboard. Their first customer was a Mr. Tamulonis, whose five-dollar bill is proudly displayed in the company's office. Paramount Home Improvements of Utica was the first charge customer, in March 1959.

The '60s saw change and constant growth accompany the firm's excellent reputation. Its building was expanded for the first time in 1962 to make way for new lines of siding and paint. John L. Balio, who had remained with B&R Trucking

after his father left, joined in 1965. He too started as a general warehouseman and deliveryman in a firm that was by then dealing heavily with contractors as well as featuring lumber, hardware, and carpeting.

On October 8, 1970, the company became a corporation, Riverside Materials, Inc. To complement this move, a stock building was erected behind the main structure. Philip Ruggiero passed away in 1974 and Louis P. Balio retired in 1977, leaving the corporation in the hands of two succeeding generations. The firm now has 16 employees (including six family members) and 28,000 square feet of space. A branch was also opened in Watertown in 1980, adding three employees. Today Riverside Materials deals with large and small builders and is involved as a supplier on about one-third of the Utica area's major construction projects.

ST. JOHN'S ROMAN CATHOLIC CHURCH

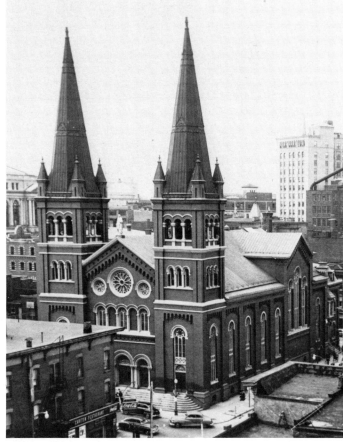

St. John's first church, completed in 1821.

St. John's third and present church, first used on Christmas Day, 1869.

One of the most historic churches, not only in Utica, but in all of upstate New York, St. John's was incorporated in 1819 under the descriptive title "The First Catholic Church in the Western district of New York." At that time the nearest Catholic church was in Albany and, in addition to John and Nicholas Devereux of Utica, the original trustees included men from as far away as Johnstown and Rochester. St. John's first pastor was Father John Farnan of Albany who had visited Utica as a missionary, usually saying Mass at one of the Devereux homes. St. John's first church was completed in 1821 on the same site as the present church at Bleecker and John streets. In the early days the parish priests served not only Uticans, but workers all along the Erie Canal and Catholics as far from the Mohawk Valley as Cooperstown.

St. John's shared in Utica's rapid growth and the congregation expanded from 16 families in 1825 to some 600 people only three years later. In 1836 the second church was constructed, again on the same site as the present church.

As Utica and upstate New York grew, new parishes were established with St. John's as their "mother church." But even as its former territory was reduced, St. John's continued to grow, in membership and in service to the community. Under its auspices, the Sisters of Charity came to Utica in 1834 and established an orphanage and school for girls, the forerunner of Utica Catholic Academy. Assumption Academy for boys was opened in 1854 and in 1862 part of the building became an orphanage for boys.

St. John's outgrew its second church and so it gave way to the present church, first used on Christmas Day, 1869. The towers and spires were completed in 1893.

The 20th century brought continued change and challenge. In an era when many downtown churches have been forced to close their doors, St. John's has survived by offering a multifaceted program ministering to a variety of people with a variety of needs. At its sesquicentennial in 1971, St. John's described itself as four parishes. The "traditional parish" serves Catholics within the parish boundaries (Mohawk Street, South Street, Broadway, and the Conrail tracks) as well as other families who maintain ties with the church of their ancestors; names such as Devereux and Kernan are still prominent in the parish. The "downtown parish" serves downtown workers and others who find St. John's a convenient place to attend weekday Mass, fulfill Holy Day obligations, or simply enjoy private prayer.

The "inner-city parish" started in the 1950s, when St. John's began ministering to the spiritual and temporal needs of the city's growing Hispanic community. More recently, with the advent of "deinstitutionalization" and the concentration of former mental patients in downtown Utica, St. John's has sought to meet their special needs. Finally, the "housing development parish" ministers to the predominantly black population of Washington Courts and the other "projects" adjacent to downtown.

St. John's historic physical plant has been expanded and renovated in recent years. A former store on John Street was converted into a parish center in 1969 and is used for religious education, social events, and service programs. Major restoration of the church and rectory have been in progress since 1979.

With historic but updated facilities, a willingness to respond to changing needs, and a staff as dedicated to service as the pioneers who founded the parish 163 years ago, St. John's looks forward to many more years of service.

ST. JOSEPH - ST. PATRICK ROMAN CATHOLIC CHURCH

St. Joseph-St. Patrick Church, at Columbia and Varick streets in West Utica, was formed in 1966 by a merger of two historic congregations. Among Utica's Roman Catholic parishes, St. Joseph's was second in age only to St. John's and it traced its roots back to 1835 and the organization by several German Catholics of a "Bethaus" or "house of prayer." A society to aid the sick, named in honor of St. Joseph, was formed in 1839 and the following year the parish began. A "national" parish without boundaries, it served German-speaking Catholics throughout the area. The former First Methodist Episcopal Church on Lafayette Street behind the present church was purchased. The parish school began in 1851 and a new wooden church was built the following year. In 1859 the church hierarchy, citing abuses of power by the parish's lay trustees, placed it under the care of the Franciscan Friars of the Conventual Order. In 1873 St. Joseph's dedicated its third and present church. This brick edifice, one of the most elaborate in

the city, was placed on the National Register of Historic Places in 1977.

One of the early parishioners of St. Joseph's Church is now on the way to official sainthood. Barbara Koob (Cope) born in Germany in 1838 and raised on Schuyler Street, joined the Sisters of St. Francis in 1862. Working with Father Damien among the lepers in Hawaii, she was called Mother Marianne of Molokai. Her order is currently researching and advocating her "cause."

Meanwhile, St. Patrick's Church was organized in 1850 to serve the Irish and other English-speaking Catholics of West Utica and in 1851 its first edifice was built on the corner of Columbia and Huntington streets. Unfortunately, dissent and dwindling support caused this church to close in 1887 and it burned down two years later. But the parish was revived and a new church was dedicated on the same site in

Mother Marianne of Molokai (1838-1918).

The main altar of St. Joseph-St. Patrick Roman Catholic Church, erected in 1889.

1895. A school and a convent were built in 1918. The church was extensively redecorated in 1947.

The passage of years and shifts in population were hard on both parishes. In 1870 St. Mary's of the Immaculate Conception was started on South Street to serve the Germans of East Utica, and in 1897 the German-speaking Poles who had attended St. Joseph's formed their own church, Holy Trinity. St. Patrick's, a "territorial" parish, was reduced by the formation of the parishes of Our Lady of Lourdes (1918) and Sacred Heart (1926). Finally, in 1966, with the language barrier long gone and with many residences in the area demolished for urban renewal, the Bishop of Syracuse ordered St. Patrick's closed and merged with its historic neighbor. St. Patrick's was razed in 1968.

The German heritage of St. Joseph's and St. Patrick's is evident in the names on its countless memorials and in the annual bazaar which is called a German Picnic, reigned over by a "Miss Edelweiss." But to the right of the main altar, robed in bright green, stands a statue of St. Patrick brought from across the street. And each March, sons and daughters of Erin gather here to sing Irish songs, to attend a special Mass, and then to adjourn to Varick Street for the first, the coldest, and one of the liveliest of many parades held each year in Utica.

But St. Joseph-St. Patrick Church looks to the future as well. It serves some 600 families of diverse backgrounds and has 168 children enrolled in its grammar school. With its dual heritage of faith, it symbolizes the variety of traditions which enrich Utica and the nation.

SCHEIDELMAN INC.

Scheidelman Inc. has been distributing food in the Utica area for over 80 years. It services independent supermarkets as well as "Mom and Pop" corner grocery stores.

Philip F. Scheidelman founded his business in 1898, when he utilized horses and wagons to distribute his products. He launched his career by selling 70 pounds of cheese from his wagon. Soon he added butter and eggs to his stock. The business prospered and during World War II his firm moved to a large warehouse located on Stark Street, then in 1963 constructed a new 90,000-square-foot warehouse on Thorn Street in West Utica. Scheidelman has become the only major locally based distributor of food products in the Utica area. The firm's 15 tractor-trailers serve customers throughout New York State. Approximately 1,000 businesses are served by Scheidelman Inc. and P.F. Scheidelman and Sons (beer distributor).

The organization employs about 70 people. Some drivers load up each night for early-morning deliveries. Located on a railroad spur, Scheidelman enjoys low-cost handling of goods. Within the warehouse merchandise is loaded and unloaded on pallets and carts towed by electric tuggers.

Although the firm has adopted computers for inventory control, billing, and other operations, the executives seek to maintain personal contact with their customers. In 1964 Scheidelman sponsored the Foodland Market chain, providing them with most of their food products. This chain has since enjoyed a steady growth.

The company maintains good relations with its employees, who belong to a union. They receive many benefits and annual bonuses. The managers call frequent meetings with employees, informing them of business conditions and asking for suggestions. The drivers are called "Knights of

Scheidelman Inc., as it looked some 80 years ago.

the Highways" because of their skill and consideration of motorists. In the past few years the firm has added an entire line of frozen foods in its cash-and-carry division. Scheidelman stocks and delivers over 7,000 items, including candy, tobacco, health and beauty aids, dairy products, frozen foods, as well as dry grocery items.

America has developed a most efficient system of distribution of goods from farm to store shelves. In the local area Scheidelman Inc. is an essential link in this chain of distribution. Dean Willis, president, states, "We intend to continue and provide a service to the people of upstate New York. After all, food is rather important." As you might suspect, the firm still sells a lot of cheese.

THE SAVINGS BANK OF UTICA

The Savings Bank of Utica, "The Bank with the Gold Dome," is a Utica landmark. It stands out because of both its impressive gold dome and close affiliation with the history and growth of Utica and the Mohawk Valley. The bank is nearly as old as the city. Its origin extends back to the days before the Erie Canal, when Utica was merely a village.

The history of The Savings Bank of Utica begins with John C. Devereux, who left Ireland just before the Rebellion of 1798. After arriving in the just-named village of Utica in 1802, he opened a general store. His younger brother, Nicholas Devereux, joined him in 1806. At that time Utica was at the center of Mohawk River trade and an important transportation point for pioneers moving westward. As such, it became an early hub of commerce within the state.

The Devereuxs built a new brick store on the west side of Bagg's Square in 1814. It was comparatively fireproof and its strongbox (on display in the bank today) was safe against ordinary theft. Uticans respected the honesty of the brothers and a few of them began to entrust their excess cash to the Devereuxs. It is not known whether the Devereuxs first offered this service as a neighborly convenience or as a response to requests from their customers. However it began, the Devereuxs were soon accepting cash, not only for temporary safekeeping, but long-term savings.

The Devereux brothers and Stalham Williams, their clerk, began investing their depositors' savings and paying them divi-

Nicholas Devereux (d. 1855), cofounder of the bank, merchant, and philanthropist.

dends. This informal beginning of The Savings Bank of Utica occurred two years before the formal opening of the country's first savings bank. Thus, The Savings Bank of Utica may be said to be among the first savings banks in the United States.

The first section of the Erie Canal from Utica to Rome opened in 1819. Trade flourished and as it did the task of providing safekeeping for workers' savings, which the Devereuxs had undertaken five years earlier, became a great responsibility. They considered it wise to establish a formal bank and accordingly applied for a charter, which the state granted in 1821.

This charter was for a bank owned by the depositors and managed by a board of trustees, members of which would have no financial interest in the bank and serve without pay. The trustees would safely in-

vest all money deposited. The income earned would, after proper deductions for expenses and a surplus held to protect the safety of the institution, be paid to the depositors as dividends. Although this first charter was not put into effect, officers were elected, including John C. Devereux, president.

In 1837 the first of the great financial panics swept the country. Many people, particularly land speculators, suffered large losses. Probably as a reaction to the panic, the Devereuxs experienced a large increase in the number of depositors. No doubt influenced by the increase in the volume of business, the Devereuxs applied for a second charter, and, on April 26, 1839, The Savings Bank of Utica was formally chartered. John C. Devereux became the bank's first president, Thomas Walker

has become known as "The Bank with the Gold Dome."

Twice since the building was constructed, it has undergone major renovations. In 1929 a 30-foot wing was added to the north side and a 10-foot addition to the rear. In 1964 a mezzanine floor was added, new front and parking lot entrances opened, the ceiling under the inside of the dome lowered, and a 65-foot teller counter installed.

The bank has continued to grow, both in the number of services offered and in deposits. As part of its growth, it opened its first branch office in the New Hartford Shopping Center in 1961. By the mid-1970s, additional branches had been opened in Whitestown, Herkimer, and the Riverside Mall in Utica. In late 1977 the bank began construction of a new 50,000-square-foot annex contiguous to the main office. This building opened in January 1979 and provides an attractive, modern work environment for many of the bank's approximately 200 employees, as well as several tenants.

The Savings Bank of Utica is a leader, as symbolized by its landmark main office building, in providing financial services to the residents of the Mohawk Valley. In terms of deposits, it is one of the 70 largest savings banks in the country. "The Bank with the Gold Dome" can look back proudly at its history as one of the pioneers in the industry.

These two photos contrast the lobby of the bank as it was in 1914 (above), to what it became after the 1964 remodeling (left). Frederick Marshall's murals, which can be seen in each photo, were installed from 1900 to 1904.

1900. The most striking feature of the building is a large gold dome with an outside diameter of 52 feet and an inside height above the lobby floor of about 50 feet. The dome has always been covered with real 23-karat gold leaf and the bank

The Savings Bank of Utica as it appears today. Note the addition of 1929 to the left of the last column, and the new building which opened in 1979.

became vice-president, and Stalham Williams became secretary and treasurer. The bank was located in the offices of Nicholas Devereux on Bleecker Street.

About 1852 the bank moved to 167 Genesee Street, just south of Bleecker Street. Deposits increased greatly during the Civil War years, from $565,433 at the end of 1861 to $1,254,750 at the end of 1865. This growth made larger quarters necessary and the trustees directed the construction of a new building on the southwest corner of Genesee and Lafayette streets. This building, completed in early 1870, had an iron facade painted to resemble marble. The bank was promptly nicknamed "The Iron Bank," an informal title which stuck until the present building was constructed.

By the end of the 19th century, the bank again needed more space. It purchased the former home of Alexander Bryan Johnson and began construction of a new building in July 1898. The new Italian Renaissance edifice, designed by R.W. Gibson of New York City, opened for business in February

D. B. SMITH AND CO., INC.

Founded in Utica in 1888 by Dewayne B. Smith, D.B. Smith & Co. is now the oldest of only four manufacturers of agricultural sprayers in the United States. Dewayne B. Smith was born May 6, 1847, on a farm in Deerfield, New York. He was educated in Deerfield and Utica and it is believed that Smith Hill in Deerfield is named after his family. In 1879 Smith joined the Utica firm of J.M. Childs & Co., dealers in agricultural equipment. During his nine years at Childs, he expanded his natural mechanical and engineering abilities by redesigning and improving many of their products. In 1888 he moved out on his own, forming D.B. Smith & Co. with Charles H. Poole. Mr. Smith had 25 patents approved in his lifetime. Among them were the "Smithmobile," which was displayed at Madison Square Garden one year before Henry Ford began mass producing the earliest Fords, and a bicycle pump which rewarded him the then unheard of sum of $15,000.

D.B. Smith & Co., which was originally located at 48 Liberty Street, was the result of Dewayne's insight into the problems of farmers in the 1800s. He recognized a need for an efficient and effective means of pest control. After spending several years developing a hand-held sprayer, Smith had 300 dozen manufactured to his specifications. For a year he traveled the countryside demonstrating to the local farmers the value of his product. He sold his original 3,600 units and made the sprayer an indispensable farm implement. In 1907 the increasing demand for labor-saving devices necessitated the move to a new facility at 414 Main Street.

After Dewayne's retirement his sons—first Myron, then Alfred—took over the leadership of the company and expanded its marketing area to the Midwest, the South, Canada, and Central and South America. The Smiths also continued their father's pioneer spirit and developed the first knapsack sprayer which was used by U.S. armed forces in World War I.

In 1921 Alfred answered a great worldwide need for portable fire-fighting equipment with the development of the "Indian" fire pump. Still manufactured and marketed by D.B. Smith & Co., it has become standard equipment with rural and city fire departments as well as with foresters in the United States and abroad.

During the reigns of Dewayne and his sons, D.B. Smith & Co. designed and developed a wide range of multipurpose sprayers. It wasn't until the advent of the company's present owner, F. Eugene Romano, a native Utican, that D.B. Smith & Co. actually began manufacturing its own products. Mr. Romano, who acquired the business from Dewayne's grandsons in 1972, also added a new line of "Space Age" polyethylene sprayers. The 1976 establishment of a new manufacturing operation in Chadwicks, New York, the 1974 acquisition and relocation of Parco Products from Pennsylvania, and the 1978 acquisition and relocation of the Fire Equipment Development Corp. (FEDCO) from California have enabled D.B. Smith & Co. to continue its history of quality, innovation, and growth.

Fighting a fire with the "Indian," circa 1925.

Fighting a fire with the "Indian," circa 1980.

SMITH'S LAUNDRY & DRY CLEANERS, INC.

Frank Smith purchased People's Laundry on Lansing Street in Utica in 1928 and renamed it Smith's Laundry. Today Smith's Laundry & Dry Cleaners, Inc., as it was later renamed, employs 45 people and is a leader in laundry, dry cleaning, and health care services. The plant is at the same location, 622 Lansing Street, and is run by Smith's two grandsons, Wayne, who joined the company in 1954, and Dale, who joined in 1960.

The founder, Frank Smith, was in the lumber industry in Bleecker, New York, for many years where he manufactured broom handles until 1926. At age 49 he sold the business, moved to Utica, and purchased the laundry with a partner whom he bought out two years later. In 1932 his son, Howard J. Smith, came into the business and served as president of Smith's Laundry & Dry Cleaners until his death in 1971. It was Howard who was principally responsible for the direction and growth of the firm in the difficult '30s and '40s.

After attending the Utica School of Commerce, Howard graduated in the second class from the American Institute of Laundering in Joliet, Illinois. His experience and perseverance were needed, for Smith's had to struggle against stiff competition from 11 other family laundries in Utica. It took long, hard hours, but by the end of World War II, Howard Smith could look with pride at the success of Smith's Laundry & Dry Cleaners and its many satisfied customers.

As in many other industries, the changes that have occurred in the laundry business during the past 50 years are vast. At first Smith's Laundry washed and heavily

Frank Smith (left), founder of the company established in 1928, and Howard J. Smith (right), president until 1971.

starched separate collars, did wet washes (which customers took home to dry), and in the 1960s, ironed from 8,000 to 9,000 shirts weekly. In those days when a man received a pay raise, he would say to his wife, "Now you may send the shirts out to the laundry," thereby saving her hours of ironing.

The addition of dry cleaning facilities in 1939 meant that Smith's could provide more complete service. In 1961 Smith's purchased special equipment to block draperies after cleaning, and became the only company in Central New York that could guarantee drapery length and even hemlines. All along, the firm has changed methods, equipment, and services to meet the demands of new fabrics and new lifestyles.

Smith's has continued to expand, acquiring White Laundry in Rome and branches in Syracuse and Herkimer. In 1971 Smith's made a major diversification to provide laundry and linen supply service to the health care industry. The variety of services and special custom programs to completely handle each institution's total laundry and dry cleaning needs has made possible Smith's continuing growth and excellent reputation in that industry.

In order to provide the best service at the most affordable price, Smith's uses a computer to pinpoint costs, control inventories, and monitor water, supplies, and energy. Using the computer is only one way Smith's Laundry & Dry Cleaners maintains its reputation of high-quality service. The community knows that the third generation of Smiths will continue to run a complete laundry and dry cleaning company, changing methods to meet changing needs, from families to institutions.

These 1934 Ford delivery trucks were part of Smith's fleet.

SPECIAL METALS CORPORATION

Special Metals' "Number One" vacuum induction melting furnace was the means by which an entire high-technology industry was established in Oneida County, New York.

"... No machine would have been in space had not some person dreamed of going there. Machines do. Men dream. From these dreams we build the American adventure...."

Those words ended NBC correspondent Lloyd Dobyns' documentary on rocket pilots. But the adventure he described for a network audience also took place before the jet aircraft, rockets, and space vehicles were actually assembled. The technological adventure occurred when a group of 20 or so metallurgical engineers and workers gathered in an ancient mill in Clayville in the summer of 1952.

It was there that commercial vacuum induction melting started. It was there that the experiments of two engineers in a government facility in Cleveland were put to practical use. The experiments were successfully completed in a test laboratory established by a respected tool manufacturer, Utica Drop Forge, and headed by a young, Turkish-born, Harvard-educated engineer named Falih Darmara.

Darmara and his colleagues were determined to find answers to the urgent need for higher stress and temperature levels in metals used in jet turbine engines. The Darmara team built and successfully tested the original commercial vacuum induction furnace, "Number One," today an international landmark of the American Society for Metals located outside the company headquarters on Middle Settlement Road in New Hartford. The six-pounder provided the first metal for jet turbine blades to withstand temperatures of 1,500 degrees Fahrenheit.

The buckets began another American adventure ... Special Metals. In less time than it takes many companies to create a market and become established, Special Metals became a major producer in metallurgical technology meeting a worldwide demand. It developed and patented well-known alloys such as Udimet 500, 520, 700,

and 720.

In the 1950s and 1960s, Special Metals was a major contributing factor in creating the modern air transport. Said Allegheny International, the parent company, in its publication *Allegheny Illustrated:* "Special Metals opened the way for a whole new generation of alloys that would operate at higher stresses and temperatures than traditional ones. Alloys that would allow for thrust-to-weight ratios of 10-to-1 instead of 1-to-1 or 1-to-2. In short, alloys which gave birth to not only an industry, but to an era. ... " Its superalloys billets have helped develop jet engines that can operate reliably for thousands of hours instead of hundreds.

But the corporation didn't stop its exploration of technology when it had perfected billet production. From its early days, research and development were given priority—and still are. Special Metals has earned a reputation within its industry for maintaining one of the most extensive laboratories of any firm involved in metallurgical research.

Its Udimet Powder Division, which was organized in the mid-1970s, provides the gas turbine industry with high-performance, cost-effective powdered metals and powdered metal rotating hardware. Engine manufacturers who require high-performance hardware as well as high-purity protective metal coating materials rely on Special Metals' products.

The famous F-15 U.S. fighter plane, an aircraft considered vital to the defense of a number of countries, is powered by Pratt and Whitney engines which used Udimet forged powder billets.

Military use of powder is only part of the story, however. When the Columbia shuttle mission was catapulted into space in April 1981, Special Metals' alloys were utilized in the reusable ship's three main rocket engines. The pioneering experiments in the manufacture of NARloy Z, used in the fabrication of the engine components, were conducted by the reliable old "Number One" furnace.

Special Metals developed a new, low-expansion alloy—Udimet LX—which has attracted manufacturers of gas turbines in

Presenting a plaque designating Special Metals' "Number One" vacuum induction melting furnace a historical landmark (in 1979) is (left) Elihu F. Bradley, president of the American Society for Metals. Accepting the plaque are Dr. F.N. Darmara (center), founder of Special Metals Inc.; and R.D. Halverstadt (right), its past president.

North America. The alloy provides the potential for greater fuel efficiency in gas turbine engines—an important consideration today and tomorrow.

And the New Hartford corporation has entered the health care field, too. Special Metals has developed cast alloys that are used by dentists for crown and bridge work. The company's dental experimentation laboratory has produced an internationally marketed corrosion-resistant amalgam which has the potential to last throughout the patient's lifetime. The firm is producing metals that have utilitarian as well as aesthetically pleasing properties to replace the use of more costly substances such as gold.

Product and process development is a continuing effort, says past president R.D. Halverstadt, who succeeded Dr. Darmara. "We are proud of our people who established SMC's reputation and who are constantly working with forward-thinking companies on tomorrow's alloys. Our Udimet trademark is an everyday name to all users of metallurgical products who place high store in product excellence, reliability, and integrity."

As an example of process development, president J.W. Pridgeon stated that the new VADER melting process in development at Special Metals may lead to the most important development in processing of superalloys in recent history.

From the six-pound "Number One" furnace have come successive generations of larger furnaces. The one shown here is Special Metals' "Number Nine" furnace with a capacity of 30,000 pounds.

STATE UNIVERSITY OF NEW YORK COLLEGE OF TECHNOLOGY AT UTICA / ROME

Acting upon a need that was perceived by the late 1950s, the Oneida County Legislature commissioned Dr. Michael Brick of Columbia University in 1964 to assess the need for a new institution of higher education in the Mohawk Valley. Passing a resolution based on Brick's suggestions, the state university board of trustees agreed, in 1966, to establish an upper-division college (junior and senior years) in the Herkimer-Rome-Utica area with curricular emphasis on applied science and technology to serve the needs of students as well as those of local employers.

During the following three years progress on the new "Upper Division College," as it was then known, was steady. A college council headed by Rome attorney George B. Grow was appointed by the governor in 1968. The search for a permanent future site for the campus was completed a year later with the selection of an 800-acre parcel in Marcy, two miles northwest of Utica's Busy Corner. That same year the first classes were held at West Frankfort Elementary School.

The new college quickly outgrew its first temporary location, and in May 1971 transferred operations to the old Globe Mill building on Court Street. The mill, a major manufacturing center in Utica until the early 1950s, was gradually remodeled and rehabilitated with classrooms, offices, and libraries. Dr. Robert MacVittie became the college's first president in the autumn of 1971. However, when hoped-for levels of funding were not forthcoming in the state's 1972 budget, MacVittie resigned and

As president of the college from 1973 to 1982, Dr. William R. Kunsela steered the school through its most perilous decade.

returned to a previous academic position.

Not until February 1973 did the university appoint a new president, Dr. William R. Kunsela, then president of the State University Agricultural and Technical Col-

Over 100,000 square feet in this 1870s woolen mill at 811 Court Street were put to use by the early 1980s.

lege at Delhi. That year, under Kunsela's leadership, the college cleared an important hurdle—it was granted authority to offer its first baccalaureate degrees—and it passed a significant milestone—it welcomed its first 47 full-time undergraduates.

Once firmly established, the college grew and expanded rapidly. The amount of space leased at the old Globe Mill increased tenfold. Three additional buildings were leased to accommodate growing upper-division academic programs in behavioral science, business/distributive education, business/public management, computer/information science, criminal justice, electrical technology, general studies, health services management, human services, industrial technology, mechanical technology, medical records administration, natural sciences, nursing, social science, and vocational-technical teacher education. The college's name was officially changed to the State University College of Technology at Utica/Rome in 1977 and the first bachelor of technology degrees were awarded in 1979. Enrollment had climbed to around 3,600 full-time and part-time students by 1981-82.

Groundbreaking ceremonies were held on October 30, 1981, for the construction of the new $50-million campus on the Marcy site. When completed in the summer of 1985, the complex will feature a technology lab, a library/classroom/administrative building, an apartment housing facility, a health/physical education/student center, and a service building.

TRI - STATE INDUSTRIAL LAUNDRIES, INC.

A delivery service of one horse and one wagon was established. The brothers later added a small truck to the "delivery fleet." They operated the washing machines and fired the boiler on Monday, Tuesday, and Wednesday, and delivered the overalls to Utica factories and homes on Thursday, Friday, and Saturday. The company continued to expand and in 1937 moved to larger quarters on Lincoln Avenue. Although all of the work is still processed at the Lincoln Avenue plant, after World War II the firm set up distribution centers in Albany and Batavia, New York; Hartford, Connecticut; and Wilkes-Barre, Pennsylvania.

In 1975 Tri-State began a new service, the decontamination of protective clothing used by employees of nuclear power plants. More recently, the company constructed a Clean Room for processing specialized clothing required by employees in high-technology facilities, where cleanliness is so important that the slightest micron of dirt or dust can cause a problem.

The firm has a subsidiary which sells uniforms to industrial, institutional, and other special customers such as police, sheriff, and fire departments. This enterprise is Nuber and Nuber, Inc., also located at the Lincoln Avenue complex.

Over the years, three sons of Arthur J. Cobb have joined Tri-State, which remains a family-operated business. Arthur D. Cobb serves as executive vice-president; Richard F. Cobb as vice-president of transport, safety, and security; and James P. Cobb as secretary-treasurer.

An explosion and fire blew out two walls of the laundry and caused many thousands of dollars of damage in 1952. The Utica Fire Department responded and did a fine job in controlling the blaze. As a result, that Christmas—and every Christmas since—Tri-State has furnished a complete Christmas dinner for all members of the Utica Fire Department who are on duty Christmas Day. The company also provides summer camperships for children of its employees, and it has a scholarship fund for children of its employees who want to attend college.

Today about 98 percent of the garments that are laundered or dry cleaned by Tri-State are owned by the firm and furnished to its customers on a rental basis. In addition to pants and shirts, the company rents jackets, coveralls, laboratory coats, Clean Room garments, and other specialized clothing. The company also rents industrial wiping cloths, dust mops, and a wide variety of floor mats.

Executive vice-president Arthur D. Cobb is "confident that Tri-State will continue to grow and add strength to the Utica community."

Who would imagine that two brothers, both recent arrivals in the Utica area from Scotland, could establish an industrial laundry service serving not only New York, but also Massachusetts, Vermont, and more recently, Connecticut, Pennsylvania, New Jersey, and Maryland? With hard work, good planning, and the help of their wives and later their sons, the Cobb brothers did just that.

Tri-State Industrial Laundries became a Cobb family enterprise in June 1920, when Arthur D. Cobb and his brother James L. bought tiny Mechanics' Overall Laundry, located at the corner of Nichols and Rutger

Tri-State's time and temperature sign along the North-South Arterial has become a local landmark.

streets. Prior to that time Arthur was a meat cutter and James was employed by the New York Central Railroad.

Their small wooden plant was located next to the duplex in which the Cobb brothers and their families lived. The plant was so small that when the business moved away from that location in 1937, the plant was replaced by a two-stall garage. The company started out with eight employees; today it has a payroll of 240.

THE UNION FORK AND HOE COMPANY

In 1907 America's farmers and gardeners began buying hand farm and garden tools from a new firm, The Union Fork and Hoe Company of Frankfort, New York, and Columbus, Ohio. This year the firm celebrates its 75th anniversary, still owned by the same family at the same locations.

Through the efforts of George B. Durell, an innovative pioneer in the steel goods industry, The Continental Tool Company of Frankfort and The United States Hoe and Tool Company of Columbus were merged to become Union Fork and Hoe. A leased locomotive repair shop in Frankfort on a two-acre plot was remodeled and expanded to house manufacturing operations. Over the years, an original 35,000 square feet of floor space has grown to 350,000 while Union Fork and Hoe has grown to be 75 years old—still at the same site.

After 31 years as a tenant, Union bought the Frankfort land and building, and has repeatedly improved and expanded its facilities. It has also acquired the acreage and facilities of several neighboring plants, including the Pratt Fork and Hoe Corporation. The holdings now include 40 contiguous acres between the old "West Shore" railroad tracks and East Main Street.

Union Fork and Hoe has always been a family-owned and -operated business. George B. Durell was responsible for the merger that created the original company. His son, Edward Durell, joined the firm in 1919 and became its president in 1934. George Britton Durell II assumed the firm's presidency in 1968, succeeding his father (Edward), who became chairman of the board. At various times the firm has operated other plants in New York including sawmills at Margaretville and North Creek, and handle plants at Arkville and Portville, the latter still operating. The skills and loyalty of Union's employees, more than half of whom have been with the company 10 years or more, and the fact that the firm has never been absorbed into a conglomerate of diversified operations, are credited as major factors in its prosperity.

At Frankfort, George B. Durell developed a new method of making tool handles that improved drying, reduced the size of inventory, and produced straighter handles. Formerly, wood had been sawed and stacked for drying in handle-length squares which tended to split and warp, and were hard to stack. The improved method involved drying wood in a parallel dowel shape that could be used to turn any needed handle shape. The entire industry soon adopted Union's method of drying "in the dowel."

Another major innovation first introduced at Union's Frankfort plant was the shovel design called RAZOR-BACK™. Developed by Edward Durell while he was company president, it was cut from specially rolled steel so as to be thicker in the center than on its side edges. This design was strong and lightweight, and retained its shape even with heavy use. It became the standard lightweight shovel of the nation.

With the skilled labor force available in the valley, and management's determination to stay where the business climate is favorable, the Frankfort plant will continue growing and undoubtedly will originate other industry improvements.

A locomotive repair shop, abandoned by the New York Central Railroad, was converted by The Union Fork and Hoe Company in 1907 for manufacturing its farm and garden tools.

UTICA DUXBAK CORPORATION

Utica Duxbak Corporation's factory, 1916.

The Utica Duxbak Corporation was founded in 1904 as a partnership known as Bird, Jones and Kenyon. The partners had backgrounds in production, accounting, and selling and established the venture for the purpose of manufacturing work pants, shirts, and overalls.

An article in the *Utica Observer* of that year reported that "the new firm will begin operations in the Williams Building at 3-9 Blandina Street. About 100 hands are to be employed and electric power will be used."

In 1906 the development of the Cravenette water repellent process changed the course of the company to the manufacture of hunting and camping clothing. This process allowed closely woven fabrics to shed water and remain breathable and eliminated the discomfort of wearing oil-skins or rubberized clothing in order to stay dry in foul weather. It is reputed that Bird's barber coined the phrase, "Sheds Water Like a Duck's Back," from which came the name "Duxbak." Both the name and the slogan were trademarked and became the identification for the company's hunting clothing. The name "Kamp-It" identified the firm's camping products.

The demand for this new type of clothing caused rapid corporate growth and in 1908, having outgrown its original location, the plant was moved to its present manufacturing facility at 14 Hickory Street—now known as Noyes Street. Through the use of the finest materials and the excellence of its workmanship, Duxbak soon established itself as one of the leading manufacturers of hunting, camping, and fishing attire. It soon became necessary to devote all of the

production to these new items and the manufacture of work clothing was discontinued.

With the financial assistance of Quentin McAdam, president of the Utica Knitting Company, in 1916 Albert G. Jones and his sons—Ralph, Carleton, and Wardwell—purchased the interests of the other

partners and the business was incorporated as the Utica Duxbak Corporation. The foresight of management in recognizing the value of national advertising and utilizing the principle of selling directly to retail stores resulted in expanded sales; soon the sales force was covering the entire country. Since that time there have been two additions to the original factory; in 1967 a building of equal size was purchased on Gray Avenue for stock and warehouse space and in 1978 a factory outlet store was built on Sunset Avenue. The firm currently employs 100 people, and the fourth generation is involved in management.

Since its early years Duxbak has expanded its product line to include shirts, insulated outerwear and underwear, socks, hats and caps, and gloves and mittens. The company's basic philosophy of providing the best possible value through excellent fabrics, superior workmanship, and well-designed clothing remains as strong today as 78 years ago. As Duxbak continues to broaden its market in the area of sportswear and general outerwear, its officers believe there will always be a need and a demand for fine-quality clothing; they look forward to continued growth and a prosperous future in the Utica area.

A Utica Duxbak ad from 1906.

UTICA NATIONAL INSURANCE GROUP

The enactment of the Workmen's Compensation Law in New York State during the legislative sessions of 1913 and 1914 authorized the establishment of mutual insurance companies, specializing in such compensation, with the power to return dividends to policyholders. Oneida County's representative in the state legislature for the years directly preceding the passage of this law was Merwin K. Hart, a man convinced that such a company could be founded in Utica. The law was to take effect on July 1, 1914, giving Hart only a short time to make his conviction a reality. Early in that year he persuaded 12 prominent business leaders to join him as incorporators, and on February 13 Utica Mutual Compensation Insurance Corporation came into existence.

In March 1914 John L. Train resigned his position with the New York State Insurance Department to become general manager of the new organization. The first election of officers took place on April 4, when D.D. Smyth was named president; Hart, vice-president and general counsel; and Train, secretary. In the months that followed, Train was busy addressing groups of businessmen throughout the state promoting the venture. Employers were eager to learn about the compensation law. While they were compelled to secure payment of compensation to their employees, there remained the options of becoming self-insured, insuring with a stock company, or insuring with the new mutual companies.

During these initial months of solicitation the firm had its offices in what was known as the Second National Bank Building, at 73-75 Genesee Street. When it began business officially that summer the firm boasted 131 policyholders representing over 24,000 employees. Early records tell us that the first policy, dated July 1, 1914, was issued to the Adirondack Maple Company of Lowville. The first claim was made by Helen Barry, an employee of the Clayville Knitting Company, while the first compensation payment was made on August 21 to John Bennis of Utica. In the fall of that year operations were moved to the City National Bank Building at 110 Genesee Street, soon to be known as the Insurance Building. There were no substantial losses in the first year and the company closed its books with assets of $110,000 and a surplus of $14,073.

The first branch office was opened in Troy on April 1, 1916. In August a second branch was established in Buffalo. In 1917 additional branches were opened in Rochester and Watertown, and by the end of the year Utica Mutual had become the largest mutual casualty insurance company in the state. The legislature deemed the firm solvent enough to write private and commercial automobile insurance,

and with these expanded powers its name was shortened to Utica Mutual Insurance Company. Business volume necessitated home office relocation in the Mayro Building. Within a few years the company had a branch in New York City and was servicing policyholders as far away as Milwaukee and Richmond. In 1926 the home office was again moved, this time to the First National Bank Building at the corner of Genesee and Elizabeth streets.

Under the leadership of Hart and Train the firm prospered during the '20s and bested the Depression years. Branches were established in Richmond and Philadelphia during 1936, and in Atlanta in 1938. A second building, at 20-26 Devereux Street, was purchased to accommodate a larger work force and land was leased in the suburb of New Hartford for future construction. This added space was put to use as Utica Mutual's growth was again complemented by changes in the state insurance law, from 1947 to 1951, allowing it to write virtually all types of property and casualty insurance.

In 1950 the board of directors endorsed plans to erect a new home office building on the New Hartford site. Construction commenced in the spring of 1951, with all the major contractors being policyholders

The first office of the Utica Mutual Compensation Corporation in 1914.

in the company. One of the largest moving operations in the history of Utica occurred the weekend of April 17, 1953, as Utica Mutual moved from its downtown locations to the new 173,000-square-foot building. On Monday, April 20, 600 employees reported for work at the 180 Genesee Street address. The firm continued to expand its operations and experience substantial growth for the rest of the decade.

The next milestone in the Utica Mutual story was reached in 1964. The company celebrated its 50th anniversary with assets of approximately $100 million and a new president, Victor T. Ehre. Ehre brought with him vitality, fresh ideas, and a firm sense of direction. With a solid grasp of the industry, Ehre steered the business toward the breaking of new ground. In 1967 Utica Mutual entered a pooling agreement with Graphic Arts Mutual, a pacesetter in insurance for the printing industry. Along with Utica Mutual's accelerated horizontal and vertical service expansion came the need for additional office space. To meet this need, a six-story, 63,000-square-foot tower was added at the New Hartford location in 1971.

Ehre was elected chairman of the board in 1970; Jack B. Riffle, who joined the company in 1965, became president in 1974 and president and chief executive officer in 1979. The organization became truly diversified and national in scope under the direction of these men, and the name

"Utica National Insurance Group" was adopted in the mid-1970s to reflect this. Today the group includes Utica Mutual, Graphic Arts Mutual, and seven ancillary companies, among them, UNI-Service Excess Facilities, UNI-Service Risk Management Corporation, and Utica National Life Insurance Company. Utica National is a full multiple-line insurance organization, and while still respected in the line of workers' compensation, also specializes in insurance for the printing industries and in errors and omissions insurance for insurance agents. Approximately 750 are employed in New Hartford, out of a total of 1,450 nationwide.

The group has its home office and

The current home office under construction in 1952.

eastern regional office at the New Hartford complex and has 18 additional regional and district claims offices located across the country. Major facilities are centered in Boston, New York City, Richmond, Atlanta, Dallas, and Los Angeles. Assets for year-end 1981 reached nearly $540 million and sales nearly $300 million—a far cry from the early days. Under the able guidance of Ehre and Riffle, Utica National spreads the name of its home community throughout all 50 states and Canada while still remaining an active and integral part of that community.

Victor T. Ehre (right) and Jack B. Riffle (far right) have remained community-oriented men while leading Utica National to a prominent position in the industry.

UTICA RADIATOR CORPORATION

Energy conservation is a hot topic at Utica Radiator Corporation—"the heat makers"—and has been since its founding. Incorporated in 1928, Utica Radiator began business in the spring of 1929. The company was formed by Earle C. Reed, formerly head of Dunkirk Radiator, Lewis N. Murray and William C. Murray, both of whom were also involved in the heating business. In 1982 James F. Benson completed his 45th year with Utica Radiator, now serving as president. Robert E. Reed, former president and current chairman of the board, and Earle C. Reed, vice-president of sales, bring second and third generations to the corporation.

The first office and plant was at their current location, 2201 Dwyer Avenue, formerly the Lincoln Radiator Company. There Utica Radiator Corporation manufactured cast-iron radiators for installation in residences, commercial buildings, and churches. An early brochure is illustrated with many Utica landmarks whose architects specified Utica radiators.

During World War II Utica Radiator played an important role, but it was a story that could not be told until the War Department lifted the veil of secrecy. In February 1943 Utica Radiator converted 100 percent into the manufacture of hundreds of light, tough magnesium alloy castings of parts for B-29s, the Superfortresses flown against Japan. This required a major investment in new equipment and the removal of virtually all machinery used in iron castings in order to fabricate the magnesium tail turrets and gasoline tank vents for the heavy bombers. After the war Utica Radiator converted

Oil and gas boilers, products of Utica Radiator Corporation.

back to the cast-iron operation, but retained its magnesium and aluminum facilities, looking forward to postwar production of magnesium castings such as baseball catcher's masks.

The introduction of a new cast-iron baseboard radiator was a highlight of 1953. This completely redesigned and highly efficient radiator generated great interest in the heating trade.

Today Utica Radiator Corporation oper-

The Utica Radiator plant as it appeared in 1948.

ates solely out of the original Dwyer Avenue plant. Cast-iron radiators have given way to energy-efficient oil and gas boilers with an emphasis on fuel conservation. Utica boiler castings are produced in their own foundry under rigid quality controls, providing a complete range of cast-iron boilers for residential, commercial, and industrial hydronic heating. The 20-year limited warranty which accompanies each boiler reflects the confidence they have in their product.

Just as Utica Radiator Corporation emphasizes ruggedness in their boilers, so, too, do they encourage it in Utica residents; to celebrate their 50th anniversary in 1978 the company sponsored the Boilermaker Race, an AAU-sanctioned event. Now every year in July, runners from several states cover the 15-kilometer distance from Utica Radiator to The F.X. Matt Brewing Company.

The Utica "boilermakers" are determined to run ahead of the pack in the '80s by developing a complete line of highly efficient oil- and natural gas-fired heating equipment which will meet modern energy needs and will enable their customers to achieve substantial fuel savings. This commitment to product improvement assures that Utica Radiator Corporation will remain the quality name in hydronic heating.

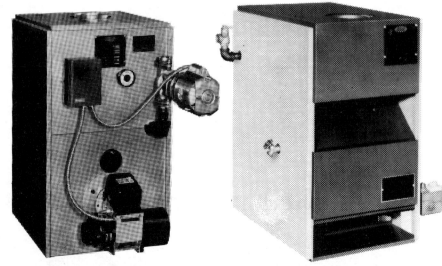

SERIES POB OIL FIRED
Hot Water Boiler

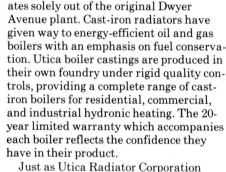

SERIES AGB GAS FIRED
Hot Water Boiler

WOLFE NEWS SERVICE, INC.

The vitality of every community depends on its sources of information and communication. For 80 years Wolfe News Service, Inc., has provided reading material to inform, amuse, and entertain.

Founded by Sam J. Wolfe in 1900, Wolfe News remains the only wholesale distributor of newspapers, paperback books, and magazines in Central New York. It proudly claims to be the oldest family-owned and -operated news business in the United States.

Before the turn of the century, Sam Wolfe was selling papers on street corners. According to family recollection, he became known as the "News King." After picking up his papers every morning at 3:00 a.m. at the local railroad station, he would drive his horse and wagon making deliveries to local newsstands and soliciting new customers. He persuaded sweet shops, ice cream parlors, and drug stores to become his first retail outlets. In 1903 Wolfe opened a stand at Bagg's Square and hired a team of newsboys. To accommodate parishioners, the youngsters sold papers outside of local churches on Sunday mornings. Stimulated by Sam's energy and ambition, and with population growth, expanding education, and rising living standards, the news business grew.

Before long, forerunners of the publishing and distribution industries began to accommodate special interests. For example, women, eager to see the latest fashions, bought *Vogue* and other magazines catering to their tastes. When men and women followed sports on their crystal, and later

A current photograph of Wolfe News Service headquarters and trucks.

television, sets, Wolfe News provided magazines chronicling the achievements of early heroes of the gridiron, diamond, golf course, and hockey rink. The golden age of Hollywood led to a keen interest in stars whose private lives were covered in another group of magazines. And, of course, children and many adults loved comic books.

With his fast-growing number and volume of publications, in 1920 Sam moved his operations to larger quarters on the Busy Corner, where he could sell to the thousands of people going to stores, offices, and factories. Eight years later he moved to the corner of John and Bleecker streets, and two years later to an even larger building on Elizabeth Street. Weaned on newspapers and magazines, Sam's children, Myron, Ray, and Betty, were becoming increasingly active in the business.

Myron Wolfe, with the same dedication and a modern approach, made numerous innovations, improving service to the area with an eye to reaching the growing

population in the suburbs. He expanded wholesaling operations to outlying communities in Rome, Oneida, Little Falls, and as far as 100 miles into the Adirondacks. In 1949 the volume of rail deliveries made it necessary for the company to move closer to Union Station.

In 1967 the officers constructed a modern facility on Stark Street, adjacent to the North-South Arterial. The firm now has 20,000 square feet for storage and distribution with a fleet of 15 trucks fanning out in all directions. The entire operation is computerized. The business handles over 2,000 magazine titles, over 5,000 paperback book titles, and many major out-of-town newspapers.

The family concern is now directed by Myron's son, Harry J. Wolfe, a member of the third generation. He became president in 1971 and continues to stress the word "service" in his company's name.

Wolfe News Service employees and vehicles posed for this photograph in 1932.

PATRONS

The following individuals, companies, and organizations have made a valuable commitment to the quality of this publication. Windsor Publications and the Oneida Historical Society gratefully acknowledge their participation in *The Upper Mohawk Country: An Illustrated History of Greater Utica.*

Automobile Club of Utica and Central New York*
Bank of Utica
Blue Cross and Blue Shield of Utica*
H.J. Brandeles Corporation*
Mr. & Mrs. Jim G. Brock
Richard M. Buck Construction Corporation*
Miss Martha G. Butler
Casatelli Electric, Inc.*
Central New York Coach Lines, Inc.*
Chicago Pneumatic Tool Company*
Adeline E. Coriale
Benita J. Denemark
Ferraro Landscape Co., Inc.*
Firsching Knitting Mills
    J.A. Firsching & Son, Inc.*
Florentine Pastry Shop*
Gaetano Associates*
Gibson Funeral Service*
Edward F. Goggin Insurance and Real Estate
Alice B. Griffith
Hapanowicz Bros.
Heintz Funeral Service, Inc.*
Herkimer County Historical Society

Holy Trinity Church of Utica*
Peter A. Karl, Inc.*
Liberty Protective Leathers, Inc.*
March Central Labs
The F.X. Matt Brewing Company*
Mid-York Library
Charles Millar Supply Inc.*
Munson-Williams-Proctor Institute*
Murnane Associates Inc.
Murphy Excavating Corporation*
The New Century Club*
Niagara Mohawk Power Corporation*
George A. Nole and Son, Inc.*
Oneida Historical Society at Utica*
Oneida Ltd.*
Oneida National Bank*
The PAR Group*
Plymouth Bethesda United Church of Christ*
Power Line Constructors, Inc.*
Remet Corporation*
Remsen-Steuben Historical Society
Rich Plan of Utica, Inc.*
Riverside Materials, Inc.*
Mr. & Mrs. P.A. Romanelli
St. John's Roman Catholic Church*

St. Joseph-St. Patrick Roman Catholic Church*
The Savings Bank of Utica*
Scheidelman Inc.*
D.B. Smith and Co., Inc.*
Smith's Laundry & Dry Cleaners, Inc.*
Special Metals Corporation*
State University of New York College of Technology at Utica/Rome*
Tri-State Industrial Laundries, Inc.*
U.S. Materials Handling Corp.
The Union Fork and Hoe Company*
Utica Duxbak Corporation*
Utica National Insurance Group*
Utica Radiator Corporation*
Wolfe News Service, Inc.*

* Partners in Progress of *The Upper Mohawk Country: An Illustrated History of Greater Utica.* The histories of these companies and organizations appear in Chapter 11, beginning on page 160.

CHRONOLOGY

1734 Cosby Manor granted by governor and council of colony of New York

1758 Fort Stanwix (Rome) and Fort Schuyler (Utica) constructed

1768 Treaty of Fort Stanwix established line of property between colonies and Six Nations of the Iroquois

1773 Earliest settlement in Deerfield

1777 Battle of Oriskany

1784 First permanent white settlement at Whitestown

1791 First Religious Society of Whitestown organized; in 1802 it became the First Presbyterian Church of New Hartford

1798 Old Fort Schuyler became Utica and a village

Oneida County set apart from Herkimer County

1802 First Congregational Church (Welsh)

1812 Bank of Utica, first local bank

1817 Utica received charter as town separate from Whitestown

1817-1825 Erie Canal under construction

1821 St. John's Roman Catholic Church consecrated

1832 Utica chartered as a city

1835 Utica and Schenectady Railroad began

1836 Chenango Canal opened

1840 Charter amended to provide for election of mayor; John C. Devereux elected

1843 New York State Lunatic Asylum opened

1847 •Utica Steam Cotton Mills incorporated

1863 Draft in Civil War

Horatio Seymour, governor

1868 Horatio Seymour, Democratic candidate for President

1870 City of Rome chartered

Village of New Hartford incorporated

1874 Paid fire department established

1875 Faxton Hospital founded

1876 Oneida Historical Society founded

1881 Utica *Saturday Globe* founded

1883-1884 Construction of the West Shore Railroad

1892 Dedication of the Masonic Home

1899 Movement of Utica Free Academy to new building on Kemble Street

1900 Savings Bank of Utica opened building with "gold dome"

1904 Utica City National Bank erected skyscraper

1907 Completion of moving Mohawk River channel to the north

Thomas R. Proctor presented park system to city

1911 Parkway opened to Mohawk Street

1914 Union Station opened

Utica Mutual Insurance Company founded

1916 YWCA acquired building on Cornelia Street

North Utica annexed from town of Deerfield

1917 American Knit Goods Association set up headquarters

1918 Barge Canal completed

1921 Community Chest (United Way) begun

New York State Hospital at Marcy opened

Annexation of most of the land from Prospect Street to Sauquoit Creek

1922 Frank Gannett acquired Utica *Observer-Dispatch*

1925 Station WIBX opened

1928 Stanley Theatre opened

1929 New post office on Broad Street

1931 Merger of three banks into First Citizens Bank and Trust Company

1935 Estate of Mrs. Thomas R. Proctor left to Munson-Williams-Proctor Institute

Utica Daily Press became part of Gannett chain

1936 Thomas R. Proctor High School opened

1937 Utica acquired property of Consolidated Water Company

1942 Opening of Rome Air Depot, later Griffiss Air Force Base

1945-1954 Mayor Boyd Golder and civic leaders spurred revitalization

1946 Utica College opened at Oneida Square

NYS Institute of Applied Arts and Sciences (later MVCC) opened

1949 WKTV on air

1951 Construction of General Electric French Road plant for military-electronic equipment

1953 Utica Mutual Insurance moved headquarters to New Hartford

1954   First Bank and Trust absorbed by Marine Midland

1955   New York State Thruway opened

1957   New Hartford Shopping Center opened

1958   Mohawk Airlines established headquarters at Oneida County Airport

        "Sin City" scandals publicized

1960   Opening of new Museum of Art

        Utica Memorial Auditorium opened

1961   New campus of Mohawk Valley Community College dedicated

        Burrstone Road campus of Utica College opened

1966   Upper Division College (later College of Technology) opened

1967   New City Hall dedicated

1968   Old City Hall demolished

1970   WUTR-TV on air

        Oneida County Office Building opened

        State Office Building opened

1974   Stanley Performing Art Center took form

        Riverside Mall opened

1979   Sheraton Inn opened in downtown Utica

1980   Sangertown Square opened in New Hartford

1981   Oneida National Bank absorbed by United Bank New Nork, later Norstar Bancorp

        Selection of site of SUNY College of Technology in Marcy

1982   Utica celebrates sesquicentennial of incorporation as a city

Above
This composite of portraits of Utica's mayors 1832-1932 (and of the presidents of the Village of Utica 1798-1832) was assembled in honor of the city's 100th birthday. Charles S. Donnelley served as mayor in 1932-1933. (OHS)

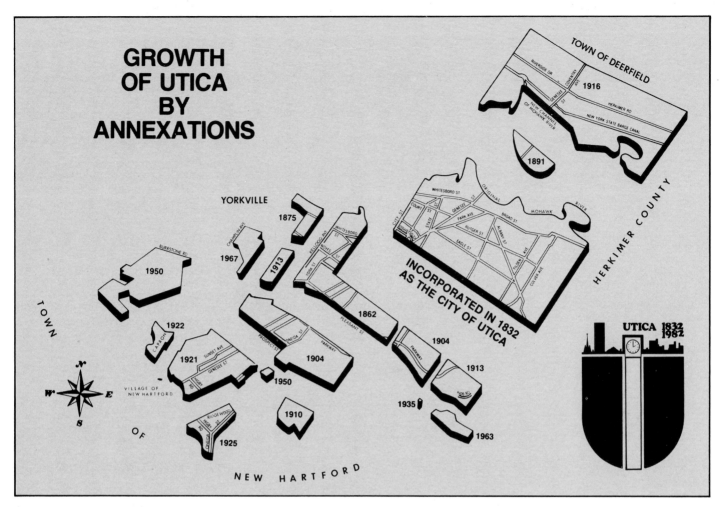

GROWTH
OF UTICA
BY
ANNEXATIONS

TOWN OF DEERFIELD

1916

HERKIMER COUNTY

YORKVILLE

1875

1967

1950

1913

1891

INCORPORATED IN 1832 AS THE CITY OF UTICA

1922

1921

1862

1904

1904

1913

1950

1935

1910

1963

1925

VILLAGE OF NEW HARTFORD

TOWN OF

NEW HARTFORD

UTICA 1832 1982

Above
GROWTH OF UTICA BY ANNEXATIONS
The territory of Utica has grown by bits and pieces since it was incorporated as a city in 1832. At that time its boundaries were the Mohawk River (north), the Herkimer County line (east), a line just south of Oswego Street (south), and the line of present City Street (west). The city first expanded in 1862, south to Pleasant Street and west beyond the State Lunatic Asylum to Kellogg Avenue, with another westward extension toward Yorkville in 1875. A crescent north of the Mohawk River was transferred from the Town of Deerfield in 1891 in anticipation of the straightening of the river. The years 1904-1913 saw the city line moved south to take in the growing residential areas to Prospect Street, together with Forest Hill and New Forest cemeteries and the park lands given by Thomas R. Proctor. Another large piece of Deerfield was annexed in 1916, later known as North Utica. Most of the area between Prospect Street and the Village of New Hartford—known as "no man's land" after World War I—was taken over in 1921, followed in 1922 by the area called Capron around Richardson Avenue and Lomond Place, and the eastern portion of Ridgewood around Oneida Street and Higby Road in 1925. A small area near the bend of the Parkway was added 10 years later. Two more pieces were carved from the Town of New Hartford in 1950, the peninsular Rhoads Hospital site on the southwest for the General Electric French Road plant and a tract on Oneida Street, the site of Hillcrest Manor Apartments. In 1963, an area just south of Nob Road was added. The city reached its present limits in 1967 with the addition of a major portion of Utica College's

Burrstone Road campus west to Champlin Avenue. Adapted from Utica: A City Worth Saving.

Above
A composite of Utica's 10 mayors since Mayor Donnelley was assembled for inclusion in a Sesquicentennial exhibition presented by the Utica Public Library. (OHS)

UTICA SESQUICENTENNIAL
MAYORS 1934-82

SAMUEL SLOAN
1934-1935

VINCENT R. CORROU
1936-1945

J. BRADBURY GERMAN
1944-1945

BOYD E. GOLDER
1946-1955

JOHN T. McKENNAN
1956-1959

FRANK M. DULAN
1960-1967

DOMINICK ASSARO
1968-1971

MICHAEL R. CARUSO
1972-1973

EDWARD A. HANNA
1974-1977

STEPHEN J. PAWLINGA
1978-

Top right
The official logo of Utica's Sesquicentennial celebration was designed by graphic artist Mark Ciola, and selected in a contest run by the Utica newspapers. It incorporates the block letter "U," the new City Hall clock tower with the clock from the old City Hall, and the skyline of downtown Utica with its variety of historic and modern churches and commercial and public buildings. Courtesy, Utica Sesquicentennial Commission.

BIBLIOGRAPHY

Government documents and reports contain a great deal of valuable information dealing with Utica, Oneida County, and the Utica-Rome Standard Metropolitan Statistical Area. The latter unit covers Oneida and Herkimer counties. I have used both the state and federal censuses to discover the national composition of immigrants to the Upper Mohawk Country. In addition I have consulted the bulletins, reports, and special studies made by the New York State Departments of Commerce, Labor, and Education. After Oneida County set up its Planning Board in 1963, it generated many reports on transportation, soil, land use, higher education, water supplies, and industrial development. The various City Directories are a mine of information about business activities, craftsmen, and products made in Utica. The first volumes came out intermittently: 1817, 1828, 1829, 1832, 1834, and 1837. Thereafter they appeared annually.

Bagg, Moses M. *Memorial History of Utica, from Its Settlement to the Present Times.* Syracuse, 1892.

———. *The Pioneers of Utica From the Earliest Settlement to the Year 1825.* Utica, 1877. Excellent source.

Bartholemew, Harland. *A Preliminary Report on Major Streets, Utica, New York,* 1921.

Benton, Nathaniel S. *History of Herkimer County, Including the Upper Mohawk Valley.* Albany, 1856. A better than average county history.

Berkhofer, Robert Frederick, Jr. *The Industrial History of Oneida County, New York, to 1850.* M.A. Thesis, Cornell University, 1955.

Clarke, T. Wood. *Utica: For a Century and a Half.* Utica, 1952. Dr. Clarke, a fine research scholar, is particularly good on military history, health institutions, and events from 1900 to 1950.

Cookingham, Henry J. *History of Oneida County.* 2 vols., Chicago, 1912.

Coventry, Alexander. *Memoirs of an Emigrant: The Journal of Alexander Coventry, M.D.,* 2 vols. Albany, 1978.

Crisafulli, Virgil C. *An Economic Analysis of the Utica-Rome Area.* Utica, 1960.

———. "Economic Development Efforts in the Utica-Rome, New York Area," in *Community Economic Development Efforts, Five Case Studies.* New York, 1964.

Donato, John A. *History of the Utica Police to the 20th Century.* M.A. Thesis. SUNY, Utica, n.d.

Durant, Samuel. *History of Oneida County, New York, 1667-1878.* Philadelphia, 1878.

Ellis, David Maldwyn. "The Assimilation of the Welsh in Central New York," *New York History,* 53 (July 1972) pp. 299-333.

———. *Landlords and Farmers in the Hudson-Mohawk Region, 1790-1850.* Ithaca, 1946.

———. "The Welsh in Utica." Unpublished paper, 1980.

Fowler, Philemon H. *Historical Sketch of Presbyterianism Within the Bounds of the Synod of Central New York.* Utica, 1877.

Frost, John; Gillet, Moses; and Cole, Noah. *A Narrative of the Revival of Religion Particularly in the Bounds of the Presbytery of Oneida in the Year 1826.* Utica, 1826.

Galpin, W. Freeman. *Central New York, An Inland Empire.* 3 vols., New York, 1941.

Gurley, Robert G. *Here Comes the Trolley!* New York, 1964. Excellent pictures.

Holy Trinity Church. *Holy Trinity Church, Utica, New York: Diamond Jubilee, 1896-1971.* Utica, 1971.

Interfaith Religious Census. *Religious Preferences in the Utica Area.* Utica, c. 1963.

Jackson, Harry F. *Scholar in the Wilderness: Francis Adrian Van der Kemp.* Syracuse, 1963.

Jackson, Harry F., and O'Donnell, Thomas F. *Back Home in Oneida: Hermon Clarke and His Letters.* Syracuse, 1965.

Jones, Pomroy. *Annals and Recollections of Oneida County.* Rome, 1851. The standard early account of city, town, and county with much colorful detail.

Kay, Marshall. "Geology of the Utica Quadrangle, New York," in *New York State Museum Bulletin,* no. 347. July 1953.

Kelly, Virginia B.; O'Connell, Merrilyn R.; Olney, Stephen S.; and Reig, Johanna R. *Wood and Stone: Landmarks of the Upper Mohawk Region.* Utica, 1972. Excellent photographs and informed commentary.

Kohn, S. Joshua. *The Jewish Community of Utica, New York, 1847-1948.* New York, 1959.

Macfarlane, Sidley K. "Utica," in John H. Thompson, ed., *The Geography of New York State.* Syracuse, 1966.

Miller, Blandina Dudley. *A Sketch of Old Utica.* Utica, 1895.

Mitchell, Stewart. *Horatio Seymour of New York.* Cambridge, 1938.

Morrison, Howard Alexander. "Gentlemen of Proper Understanding: A Closer Look at Utica's Anti-Abolitionist Mob," *New York History,* 62 (January 1981) pp. 61-82. Scholarly analysis.

———. "The Finney Takeover of the Second Great Awakening during the Oneida Revivals of 1825-1826," *New York History,* 59 (January 1978) pp. 27-54. A revisionist account.

Moses, John. *From Mt. Lebanon to the Mohawk Valley.* Utica, 1981. Story of Lebanese migration to the area.

Museum of Art, Munson-Williams-Proctor Institute and Oneida Historical Society. *Made in Utica.* Utica, 1976. Lavishly illustrated. Much detail on crafts of Utica.

Nassar, Eugene. *East Utica: Selections from a Prose Poem,* designed, and with original woodcuts by Robert Cimbalo. Utica, 1971.

Nassar, Fred. *What Utica Needs: A Program for Action.* Utica, 1965.

New York State Department of Commerce. *New York State Means Business in the Mohawk Valley Area.* Albany, 1946.

Nichols, Roy E., and Martin, C. Irene. *Social Studies Program—Utica and Oneida County.* This booklet of the New York State Education Department (1942) is an excellent summary.

O'Donnell, Thomas F., and Franchere, Hoyt C. *Harold Frederic.* New York, 1961.

Oneida County. *The History of Oneida County.* Utica, 1977. Several fine articles and town histories. Some detailed bibliographies.

Oneida County Division of Research and Department of Planning. *Oneida County Government.* Utica, 1970. Short pamphlet.

Oneida Historical Society. *Transactions.* Utica, 1881-1898.

Pilkington, Walter, ed. *The Journal of Samuel Kirkland: 18th Century Missionary to the Iroquois, Government Agent, Father of Hamilton College.* Clinton, 1980.

Porter, Bruce. "I'll Do Things My Way, Mayor Edward Hanna," *New York Times Magazine,* September 19, 1976.

Preston, Douglas, ed. *Centennial History of the Utica Fire Department.* Utica, 1974. Authoritative.

Przybycien, Frank E. *Utica: A City Worth Saving.* Photos by P.A. Romanelli. Utica, 1976. Scores of photographs of ordinary structures as well as important buildings.

Richards, Leonard L. *"Gentlemen of Property and Standing": Anti-Abolition Mobs in Jacksonian America.* New York, 1970. Good analysis of 1835 riot in Utica.

Rohman, D. Gordon. *Here's Whitesboro.* New York, 1949.

Rubin, Harold. "Revitalization of an Area," *New York State Commerce Review,* 13 (October and November, 1959).

Ryan, Mary P. *Cradle of the Middle Class: The Family in Oneida County, New York, 1790-1865.* New York, 1981. A scholarly study utilizing quantification.

Saint John's Church, 1820-1970. New York. South Hackensack, New Jersey, 1970.

Savings Bank of Utica. *Utica and Its Savings Bank, 1839-1939.* Utica, 1939.

Schiro, George. *Americans by Choice: History of the Italians of Utica.* Utica, 1940.

Shaw, Ronald A. *Erie Water West: A History of the Erie Canal, 1792-1854.* Lexington, Ky., 1966.

Sheehan, Robert. "Take Utica, For Instance . . ." *Fortune,* 40 (December 1949) pp. 126-130.

Stevens, Frank W. *The Beginnings of the New York Central Railroad: A History.* New York, 1926.

Todd, Charles L., and Sonkin, Robert. *Alexander Bryan Johnson Philosophical Banker.* Syracuse, 1977. This biography contains much information about the economic, social, and political life of Utica.

Todd, Charles L., and Blackwood, Russell T. *Language and Value.* New York, 1969. This book contains the proceedings of the centennial conference on the life and works of A.B. Johnson.

Upson, George. "Utica's Art and Artists," *The Way to Wealth.* Utica, 1939.

Utica Community Renewal Program. *Final Report.* Utica, 1971.

Utica Gas & Electric Company. *The Upper Mohawk Valley.* Utica, 1923.

Utica Memorial Auditorium. *A City Reborn: A Story of Achievement.* Utica, 1960.

Utica Public Library, compiler. *A Bibliography of the History and Life of Utica: A Centennial Contribution.* Utica, 1932. Old but valuable as a guide.

Wager, Daniel E. *Our County and Its People.* Boston, 1896.

Walsh, John J. *From Frontier Outpost to Modern City: A History of Utica, 1784-1920.* Utica, 1978. Typescript.

———. *The Theater and Entertainment in Utica, from Early Times to the Opening of the Stanley Theater.* Utica, 1976. Typescript.

———. *Vignettes of Old Utica.* Utica, 1982. Judge Walsh has been an indefatigable researcher in the city's history.

Williams, John Camp. *An Oneida County Printer.* New York, 1906. This biography deals with William Williams.

Williams, Paul B. *Industrial Changes in Utica Since 1940.* Utica, 1959. The author, editor of the *Utica Press,* was a close observer of events.

Witt, Stuart K. *The Democratic Party in Utica.* Syracuse, 1963.

"Wide-open Town." *Newsweek,* 51 February 24 1958.

ILLUSTRATIVE ACKNOWLEDGMENTS

As noted in the credit lines, the Oneida Historical Society was the most important single source of pictures for this volume. Thanks are due to the countless individuals who have donated photographic prints and negatives, as well as documents and artifacts, to the society over the past 106 years. It should go without saying that the society welcomes more such donations.

The principal sources of recent black and white photos (and of valuable reference information) were the files of the Utica newspapers. The newspapers also encouraged area residents to submit pictures for their Sesquicentennial edition and these were also considered for this book. Thanks are due to Sal DeVivo, publisher, for permission to reproduce pictures and to staff members Jim Armstrong, Barbara Charzuk, Joe Kelly, and Frank Tomaino for many acts of assistance. Unfortunately, the original negatives of Dante O. Tranquille and many other fine photojournalists remain unavailable at this time. They should be preserved for posterity in an accessible archive.

The Utica Public Library provided a number of rare pictures and documents as well as much information. Thanks go to Dr. Eugene Nassar, president, and Helen Dirtadian, library director.

Retired judge, now city historian, John J. Walsh provided invaluable assistance through his numerous historical articles and his splendid book, *Vignettes of Old Utica.* Judge Walsh also shared freely from his research files and his personal knowledge of the city's history.

Joseph Skane, Jr., proprietor of Russell T. Rhoades & Company, graciously allowed the use of valuable negatives, mostly from the 1940s. Joe and his staff, particularly Rich Brennan, also contended with many problems to provide clear reproductions of several stained and faded engravings, maps, and documents.

Special thanks are due to Edward Michael of Ryder's Camera Center for all of his prompt and courteous black and white photo processing, and especially for making prints from several large and fragile glass-plate negatives.

Pat Romanelli displayed patience and skill and travelled to a variety of locations to fill my requests for original color photographs. His work speaks more eloquently than I can.

John Caruso shared generously from his collection of color slides of Utica.

In addition to the above sources of multiple images, pictures no less valuable were drawn in ones and twos from private collections and public archives from coast to coast. All are cited with their pictures.

I thank Dr. David Ellis for his patience and for recommending pictures, proofreading captions, and attempting to convert my writing to the active voice.

I thank my already-overworked secretary, Diane Mathews, for work "above and beyond the call of duty" on this project and especially for "holding the fort" at the Oneida Historical Society during my numerous book-related absences.

I thank my wife and son for their forbearance during the many odd hours devoted to this project.

Finally, as director of the Oneida Historical Society, I thank Windsor Publications for the opportunity to have a pictorial history of Utica published for the city's Sesquicentennial. And I especially thank the following Windsor staff members: Sales Representatives Tim Emmons and Anne England, Designer John Fish, Partners in Progress Editor Karen Story and Picture Editor Jana Wernor, with whom I have worked so closely this past year.

Douglas M. Preston

INDEX

Numbers in italics indicate illustrations

THIS BOOK WAS SET IN CAMBRIDGE AND TYPO ROMAN TYPES, PRINTED ON ACID FREE 70 LB. WARRENFLO AND BOUND BY WALSWORTH PUBLISHING COMPANY HALFTONE REPRODUCTION BY ROBERTSON GRAPHICS

About the Author

David M. Ellis, a native of Utica, graduated from Hamilton College in 1938 and earned his doctorate at Cornell University. When his thesis was published in 1946, entitled *Landlords and Farmers in the Hudson-Mohawk Region, 1790-1850,* the American Historical Association awarded it the John H. Dunning Prize as the outstanding monograph in U.S. history.

After teaching two years at the University of Vermont and spending a year at the University of Michigan on a postdoctoral fellowship, Dr. Ellis joined the faculty of Hamilton College in 1946. He became a professor in 1957, chairman of the history department in 1968, and P.V. Rogers Professor of American History—a title he has retained since his retirement. During his career Dr. Ellis has taught summer-school classes at Cornell and Syracuse universities and at several branches of the State University of New York. In 1981 he was visiting professor at SUNY, Albany.

Dr. Ellis is the author of many books on New York history, including five published by the Cornell University Press. He is the major author of *New York: The Empire State,* which has appeared in five editions. He has also contributed numerous articles to journals and reference works such as the Encyclopaedia Britannica, Encyclopedia Americana, and Collier's Encyclopedia.

Honored for his research and writings in New York history, Dr. Ellis was named a fellow of the New York State Historical Association. He has served on the executive board of the Agricultural History Society and the American Studies Association, and has been president of both the New York State American Studies Association and the New York Conference of Teachers of New York History. Since 1972 he has been a member of the editorial board of *New York History,* and more recently he has been contributing editor of *NAHO,* a journal of the New York State Museum.

A lifelong resident of the Upper Mohawk Valley, David M. Ellis lives in Clinton.

Douglas M. Preston, the director of the Oneida Historical Society in Utica, is the ideal person to do the picture research for an illustrated history of the Greater Utica region. Born in Cooperstown, he received his B.A. in history from Syracuse University and an M.A. from the Cooperstown Graduate Program in History Museum Training. He served as an assistant curator at the Fort Pitt Museum in Pittsburgh before accepting his present position.

Mr. Preston has extensively researched the history of the Upper Mohawk region for such publications as his *Centennial History of the Utica Fire Department* (1974) and the popular Landmarks Calendars (1978-1980), as well as essays in the exhibit catalog, *Made in Utica* ("Manufactured Products") and *The History of Oneida County* ("The Ethnic Dimension," with David M. Ellis). He is a member of the American Association of Museums, the Landmarks Society of Greater Utica, the National Railway Historical Society, and the Society for the Preservation and Appreciation of Antique Motor Fire Apparatus in America. He takes special interest in collecting memorabilia about fire engines and trains. Married, he has one son.

Anne P. (Happy) Marsh, a graduate of Vassar College, has been a resident of the Utica area for the past 14 years. She is a free-lance writer who has contributed articles to a number of publications and is an amateur watercolorist. Formerly a teacher of history and English and a director of Canadian and American junior leagues, she is a mother of three, is interested in personal financial management, and enjoys sailing and cross-country and downhill skiing.